ART MEETS LAW IN EDUCATION

Yearbook of the European Association for Education Law and Policy

Volume 4

The titles published in this series are listed at the end of this volume.

Art meets Law in Education

Yearbook of the European Association for Education Law and Policy

Edited by

Jan De Groof,
Chantal De Smet

and

Hilde Penneman

This publication is sponsored by

S.A. PHILIP MORRIS BELGIUM N.V.

This book is published with the support of the Flemish Ministry of Education and the Spanish Ministry of Education of Aragon

KLUWER LAW INTERNATIONAL
THE HAGUE / LONDON / BOSTON

A C.I.P. Catalogue record for this book is available from the Library of Congress.

ISSN 1387-2664
ISBN 90-411-1537-4

Published by Kluwer Law International,
P.O. Box 85889, 2508 CN The Hague, The Netherlands.

Sold and distributed in North, Central and South America
by Kluwer Law International,
101 Philip Drive, Norwell, MA 02061, U.S.A.

In all other countries, sold and distributed
by Kluwer Law International, Distribution Centre,
P.O. Box 322, 3300 AH Dordrecht, The Netherlands.

Printed on acid-free paper

Printed and bound in Great Britain by Antony Rowe Limited.

Table of Contents

JAN DE GROOF

Preface

From time immemorial, culture, education and training have been assigned an essential role in preserving and developing common values that tie the international community together. Distinguished documents of international conferences and in various treaty texts and protocols show how cultural policy is the pre-eminent driving force for improvement of the immaterial quality of individual and social life. Culture and education make an incommensurable contribution to the integration of a person in society and of the European society as such. Also from time immemorial, the principles of freedom and equality find their application in cultural and educational policy. Both support the rights to social multiformity and to protection of minorities; both also remind us that certain human values transgress every 'local' culture.

'Culture is about having a future.'

But is this basic principle reflected in the newly drafted European codex of human rights? The *Draft Charter on Fundamental Rights of the European Union* does include the well-known passages, such as: 'The Union contributes to the development of these common values while respecting the diversity of the cultures and traditions of the peoples of Europe as well as the national identities of the Member States [...].' The Draft Charter, however, does not otherwise contain a single positive right with regard to cultural perception, nor any more than indirectly in exercising educational rights.

This is regrettable as education and culture shall continue to be the cement, by preference of the Union of the fifteen and, in the future, perhaps at some point the Europe with three times as many members.

During the 1998 congress in Salzburg, the Board of the *European Education Law and Policy Association (ELA)* proposed studying more closely the mutual interrelationship between education and culture. A rather uncommon topic for education lawyers and policy-makers: *Arts in Education and Education in the Arts.* The steering committee finally opted for the overall title: '*Arts meets Law in Education*'.

Is the right to culture rooted in national education legislation? In the educational policy that the cultural heritage is meant to foster within the multifaceted

Jan De Groof, Chantal De Smet and Hilde Penneman (eds.), Art meets Law in Education, ix–xi.

school context and by means of para-scholastic activities? How relevant, how vital, are the arts for education? And are artists of any significance with respect to initiatives that are aimed at cultural education (and who, for that matter, is the artist)? Which reforms on art practice, on educational practice, are needed?

This book does not only consider in detail the recent trends in the organisation and structure of Art in Education, but also the interplay between the two within standard education, the application of the principle of freedom of movement and *Mobility of Teachers and Students*, the equivalence of diplomas, and so forth. The *Questionnaire* this time also included the correct resource means for analysing policy and regulations as a comparative tool. The reader will find a broad range of surprising findings in the chapter that includes the country reports and in each of the contributions that are included in this volume.

The topic was suggested in part by the Spanish branch of the *ELA* and its prestigious chairmanship led by colleague Embid Irujo. The Spanish government counted the reform of art education as one of its priorities and insisted that a reflection on the European level regarding the legal specification of '*Art in Education*' should take place in Spain. The efficient team under the leadership of Fernando Cassamayor would assume the actual preparation of the 1999 congress. This was at the same time a sign of appreciation of the very dynamic work that has characterised the Spanish 'Education Law and Policy Association' since its inception not that long ago.

It was obvious that such a meeting would take place in one of the most prestigious cultural locations of Spain, namely Granada. Its renowned university, the Government of Andalusia and the Municipal Government provided their practical cooperation.

The intellectual cooperation with *ELIA* (*European League of Institute of the Arts*) and in particular its chairman, Chantal De Smet, in a certain sense make this book a joint publication. Michael Scheck, former director of the renowned Conservatory of Antwerp and member of the steering committee, also had an undeniable influence on and input to the success of the congress.

With this topic, the *ELA* concludes the series of more traditional topics that were discussed in detail in the previous books, respectively published by ACCO (Leuven, Belgium) and Kluwer Law International (The Netherlands) and helped determine the agenda of the national and international education debate: *Subsidiarity (1993), The Legal Position of the Teacher and Mobility (1994), Minorities in Education (1995), The Legal Status of Pupils (1996), Education Law and Urban Policy (1997), Autonomy (1998).*

It seems to be a subject that will have an impact beyond the end of the twentieth century, faster than one would think. It also seems to be a topic that forms an excellent introduction to the congress of 2000 that will take place in Paris about: '*Responsibility (and Liability) in Education*'.

After all, education challenges each individual to take on *his or her* responsibility. Culture and art must continually take on *their* task: revealing, discovering, modernising and creating a climate of responsibility.

Eventually every teacher, administration, organising authority of a school, university or polytechnic must be able to show how art and culture are integrated in education that is reinforced in concrete terms. This generation of young people, and the next generation, possess the *moral right* to force the governments into giving answers – preferably answers that will open up new horizons.

MARIA LUISA ALEJOS-PITA RÍO

Introduction 'Art meets Law in Education'

It was a great honour for the Spanish organisation for Education Law and Policy, founded in the Community of Aragon, to be able to organise and support the seventh 'Art meets Law in Education' Conference together with the European Organisation for Education Law and Policy and the European League of Institutes of the Arts (ELIA). The Spanish Association was set up with the purpose of conducting academic research into education law and policy in Spain at both higher and non-higher levels of education.

I would like to extend my special thanks to Professor Embid Irujo of the University of Zaragoza for the efforts he has made so far for the developments of the education law in our Community of Aragon and in all of Spain. It was barely a year ago that under his leadership, the Spanish Association was created for the study of the Education Law and Policy. This association with research objectives is a non-profit incorporated society. The Board of Directors is made up of professors at Universities, legal advisers and officials from various education administrations.

The first seminar focusing on 'Legal aspects of University adminstration' which took place at the University of Zaragoza in 1998 was of very high quality due to the efforts of many. Evidence of this is the extensive publication: '*Ill seminario sobre aspectos jurídicos de la gestión universitaria*'. During this seminar, a collaboration agreement was concluded between the Spanish Association and the European Organisation for Education Law and Policy with Professor Dr. Jan De Groof as Chairman. This organisation forms a network of academics, high-level officials and policy-makers from all the European Member States. The European comparative Education Law was established and further developed by this organisation with the aim of harmonising European education legislation and policy.

The special topic of the seventh European Conference was 'Art meets Law in Education'. It is in the field of legislation and policy with regard to art education that law, art and education form an indivisible whole. The aim was to study the relations within this whole, to detect its problems and to offer solutions within the broad range of socio-political and art-educative alternatives that our small but rich

Jan De Groof, Chantal De Smet and Hilde Penneman (eds.), Art meets Law in Education, 1–2.

European continent has to offer. The topic was examined from a concrete artistic, pedagogical and juridical reality.

The legislation of Art Education was particularly important for the Government of Aragon. During this term the government undertook to arrange and to extend this regulation taking into account the competence of the Community of Aragon in the field of education.

The efforts made during this conference which resulted in the formulation of recommendations directed at European institutions and national governments, will constitute an important contribution for further creation of a 'European Education Space'.

This publication consists of two parts. On the one hand, the contribution written for the plenary sessions and the work groups organised during the Conference and on the other hand, the country reports submitted by experts in answer to a questionnaire, which was drawn up and distributed beforehand, with regard to education law and art education.

I am certain that this book, partly due to its various angles of approach, will have a considerable influence on the general cultural education and on higher art education, not only within our national borders but also throughout all of Europe. The book gives us a conceptual framework for the promotion of the interaction between art, education and law at various levels. It provides a broad interdisciplinary overview of the ideas and perspectives that are alive in the world of jurists, pedagogues, teachers, artists and philosophers. It is an initial impetus to the development of a European model for general art education. It can contribute to the harmonisation of the art education programmes in the various European Member States, taking into account the importance of cultural diversity in each Member State. It is the reader who will decide if this publication meets his or her expectations.

MANUEL PEZZI CERETTO

Annual Conference of the European Association for Education Law and Policy: 'Arts Education in Europe' and 'The Cultural Mission of Universities and Schools'

I should like to thank the Spanish Association for Education Law and Policy for their kind invitation to participate with you all here today in the opening of these sessions devoted to the study of 'Arts Education in Europe' and 'the Cultural Mission of Universities and Schools'.

It is true to say that the question of arts education, its legal framework, regulation and inclusion within the educational system, poses problems that are peculiar to itself, and more complex than other dimensions of education, whose status and situation within the legal and functional structure of the system are well established and defined. So much so, that any potential reforms barely touch it – so to speak – or its position within the elements that make up a country's educational system.

Certainly in Spain, this type of education has traditionally formed a network apart from what we might consider general education. The problem lies not so much in the differences as in the danger of disconnection, or separation, from the central educational body.

Arts education has taken on many forms over time and it has developed at different points in time, depending, on occasions, on the pressure of social demand; this has resulted in wide diversification internally, in addition to the danger of disconnection I have already referred to.

It would certainly be very interesting and enlightening to trace, from historical, philosophical and legal perspectives, the influence of the various concepts and interpretations of art and its social function with respect to the equally diverse educational ideals that have arisen over the course of time. Perhaps guidelines could be established to explain this phenomenon that is both intermittent and somewhat set apart from the regular framework of the educational system.

But, let us leave this question, which calls for wide knowledge and solid documentation, to the speakers and experts gathered here.

Jan De Groof, Chantal De Smet and Hilde Penneman (eds.), Art meets Law in Education, 3–5.

What is true is that when dealing with educational reform in Spain, as included in the General Education Development Act, which we are still in the process of applying, the question of coordinating arts education with the other branches of education was of prime concern, because we wanted to ensure that the identity and content of this type of education would not mean separation or marginalisation with regard to the educational system as a whole.

For this reason, the holding of this Conference on arts education is so important and relevant, because without doubt, the work of the experts can open up new perspectives, especially when projecting the way art is managed by education on to the European horizon.

Thus, based on the fact that arts education forms a heterogeneous whole which includes knowledge, arts, abilities and skills of a widely diverse nature, and with an equally diverse scope, given that the establishments responsible for teaching these subjects traditionally have their own particular form, and their students come from different age groups and have different expectations, the reform of this type of education was directed towards achieving a series of fundamental objectives, which we have been developing over the last few years.

Firstly, artistic training needs to be an important factor within the general educational system syllabus, and therefore, a subject to be studied by all students. Thus, arts education has been incorporated, as basic artistic training, into Compulsory Primary and Secondary Education levels, with the aim of providing all students with knowledge of their artistic sensitivity as an indispensable part of an integrated training. This basic preparation also provides access to the arts Baccalaureate, and subsequently to Higher Education in the various artistic fields.

In addition, arts education is promoted in activities provided by cultural organisations, directed at the general public. In this case, the effectiveness of education is linked to the use of leisure time, recreation and relaxation, following hobbies, etc.

This is an important aspect which should not be neglected, in that it reaches the whole of society, and in this respect, the education authorities have encouraged centres in which the arts are taught as a profession to open up to the artistic-cultural life around them. The ideal scenario would be for each centre to maintain regular channels of communication and exchange with these artistic and cultural bodies.

Similarly, these centres carry out joint activities in collaboration with local authorities, which, within the municipal programme, consist of events, courses, performances, exhibitions, etc., aimed at the fostering of the enjoyment of the visual arts, music, drama and so on.

Finally, as a relevant objective of our Educational Reform, we should emphasise the stimulus given to arts education as a path to a specific qualification, with fundamentally professional perspectives. In this field, we have specific educational establishments and institutions: Conservatoires, Schools of Applied Arts, Dance Schools, and so on, all included within the framework of Special System Education.

Arts education incorporates the principles that have inspired Educational Reform as a whole, and a major effort has been made to bring the syllabus, structure and methodology up to date, with a notable advance in teacher training.

All efforts concentrated in the planning of arts education in its various dimensions are mirrored in what this Conference has termed as 'The Cultural Mission of Educational Institutions'. I am referring to the huge demand for knowledge and enjoyment of our historical-artistic heritage, through visits to major exhibitions, museums, monuments, archaeological sites, and so on. Awareness of our cultural heritage, and how we use and enjoy these assets, has begun to be part of the life and cultural habits of the men and women of our century.

But, in order to form close contact with art, one has to know something about it, otherwise the potential visitor might see his expectations dashed. For this reason, arts education is particularly relevant.

All through the nineteenth century, international and national bodies alike were involved in developing a regulatory system, in which firstly the concept of a historical and artistic heritage was defined, and secondly, as a development of this, the concept of a cultural asset, which would confer a new dimension on works of art in general, with a view to their protection and safekeeping, and their conservation and transmission to future generations.

Thus, a whole series of documents or 'charters' were approved in various countries, proceeding from vastly different institutions, all directed at the conservation and growth of mankind's cultural heritage. These documents pressed for an ever-broadening concept of cultural assets, while at the same time emphasising the need for education to contribute decisively to the appreciation and conservation of these cultural assets, so that arts education also acquired this important dimension of contributing to the conservation of the cultural heritage.

The major role to be played by education in the conservation of this heritage is now formulated in the 1931 Athens Charter. After the Athens Charter, all documents were to include, to a greater or lesser extent, the need to foster knowledge of the common heritage by means of education.

We have gradually reached the conviction that the conservation of our cultural heritage can only be achieved with the participation of everyone, and therefore this awareness-raising needs to be begun in schools.

Although this link with our heritage is not the only cultural function of educational institutions, it does today constitute a field which is particularly fit for exploring the potential of teaching and learning in artistic areas from an operational perspective, more committed to social requirements.

I imagine that some of the questions outlined in my address, and many others regarding arts education, will be brought up in the talks, round tables and discussions over the next few days.

Art meets Law in Education: Recommendations

In December 1999 the European Association for Education Law and Policy organised a conference in Granada with the theme of 'Art meets Law in Education'. This conference received the backing of the European Commission and the Flemish government. A number of highly placed experts and scientists from the fields of art and education took part in the 2-day conference.

On the basis of the legal and scientific supporting speeches, and the constructive discussions that followed, a number of recommendations were put forward aimed at serving the best interests of cultural and artistic education in our schools and universities.

Below you will find the summary of the recommendations for (a) primary and secondary education and (b) higher education as the result.

We are convinced that at the start of the new millennium every official organisation that plays a direct part in educational decisions should bear these recommendations in mind, and ensure that the minimum requirements are met as quickly as possible.

'Art meets Law in Education'

A. Arts and Education

'The child has the right to leisure, play and participation in cultural and artistic activities.'

Children's rights as of the United Nations Children's Fund.

Preamble

- Our societies are based on economics, politics, culture and individual developments. It is a duty for the relevant authorities to pay attention to all these aspects within education.

Aims for general education

- Consciousness of aesthetic aspects of life and society.
- Initiation in cultural development.

Jan De Groof, Chantal De Smet and Hilde Penneman (eds.), Art meets Law in Education, 7–9.

- Cultural participation and integration.
- Stimulation or personal cultural development.

Recommendations

Relevant local, national and European authorities accept responsibilities for:

- Stimulating cooperation between those responsible for arts, culture and education at all political, administrative and operational levels.
- Considering every restructuring of education in an international context.
- Giving to arts and culture a full part in the educational process.
- Developing new areas of study, with flexible curricula, and new methods of assessment.
- Drawing up new forms of teacher training.
- Creating open relationships between schools and cultural institutions. All cultural institutions have the duty to develop educational activities, as well as all educational institutions have the duty to develop cultural activities.

B. Higher education in the arts

Preamble

- Higher education in the arts means professional training at university level.
- Higher education in the arts embraces diversity of approach.
- Higher education in the arts contains institutional, emotional and practical skills.

Aims for higher education in the arts

- Higher education in the arts needs to be internationally orientated.
- The higher arts education systems need to be transparent and internationally comparable.
- The Bologna declaration is a welcome instrument. The specificity of arts education, however, needs to be considered within the framework of the European educational agenda.
- The institutions of higher arts education have the right to build up their training programmes, based on specific artistic needs and insights.

Recommendations

Relevant regional, national and European authorities accept responsibilities for:

- Considering every restructuring of higher arts education in an international context.
- Recognising professional arts education in all countries as a part of higher education.

- Accepting autonomy in creating curricula.
- Creating an efficient and transparent system of diploma recognition.
- Enabling arts institutions to respond to the growing social needs for the evolving role of the artist as a cultural facilitator. This implies a closer collaboration with local and regional communities.
- Facilitating transparency by an agreed system of quality assessment characterised by:
  - Self-assessment by the institutions delivering the programme.
  - Development of a system of international peer review.
- Creating transparent and less bureaucratic legal and administrative procedures fostering mobility of teachers as well as of undergraduate and postgraduate students.

General Framework

CHANTAL DE SMET

Art & Education–Education & Art

The relation between arts on the one hand and education on the other can be considered from different – at least two – points of view. For all those involved in the worlds of arts and education this is obvious, but for many others it is not. Therefore I want to make these different points of view as clear as possible to avoid any misunderstandings further on.

Our subject deals with two main themes: Education in the arts (what is known as arts education) and arts and/in education.

ARTS EDUCATION

In this kind of education we generally see, depending on the country, three major forms: education on a higher educational level, that is, in institutions of higher education, polytechnics and universities. This form exists in almost all European countries, except for small countries like Luxembourg, Liechtenstein, Monaco or Andorra, that do not organise higher education. In some countries – France for instance – those schools, mostly rather small ones,[1] are independent entities. In other countries these schools are part of universities or polytechnics. Sometimes – in Austria, for instance – they are independent art universities. In yet other countries there exists a combined system – for example the United Kingdom, The Netherlands, Germany – where you have both independent art institutions and schools being part of multisectorial higher educational institutions: universities in the UK, polytechnics in The Netherlands and both in Germany.

This all means that in Europe there is no such thing as one identical structure for higher arts education.[2]

1 On the European scale 'small' means under 500 students.

2 Therefore ELIA (the European League of Institutes of the Arts) undertakes a comparative study on the educational structures of higher arts education in the countries of the European Union.

Jan De Groof, Chantal De Smet and Hilde Penneman (eds.), Art meets Law in Education, 13–19.

Is there an identical structure for a second form, namely education in the arts within compulsory education, i.e. mostly on a secondary level?[3] No, there is not. Education in the arts in compulsory education is nevertheless a well-spread form of education, although less present in the different European countries than higher arts education structures.

When I speak of education in the arts on the secondary level, I do not refer to artistic subjects within the 'normal' curricula, but of a secondary education structure dealing with, on the one hand, general subjects, and, on the other hand, artistic subjects, and mostly in a proportion of 1 to 3 to 1 to 1. This kind of education is to be compared with technical education or vocational training on the secondary level and often – although not always – prepares the pupils for higher arts education. This is, nevertheless, always the case in the countries where education in the arts on the secondary level exists, specifically for education in music and dance, since these disciplines demand a training starting at a young, sometimes even a very young age.

The structure of arts education on the secondary level is very dependent on the structure of secondary education as a whole and therefore varies from country to country. In some countries secondary arts education is linked to prestigious art institutions – for example, the Ecole de l'Opéra de Paris – or to institutions of higher education as academies or conservatories. In other countries, however, secondary arts education is independent. Moreover, it can be organised as a specific curriculum within a large institution of secondary education. Therefore, it is not possible to speak of one structure, or even, I guess, of one common aim of arts education within compulsory education.

A third form is additional arts education or part-time arts education in a parallel educational circuit, given in classes in the evening or at weekends. In this sector we have without any doubt the largest possible disparity in Europe, as in certain countries it is a full and integrated form of education and in other countries only organised on a local and private initiative.

Even where it is integrated in education, it can have different structures referring to, for instance, different kinds of public. In some countries, extra structures for talented youngsters are foreseen within education, whereas for adults who want professional training there is part-time education within the higher education structures.

Adults or children wanting to skill themselves in an interesting and fascinating free-time occupation but who do not intend to realise a profession in the field of the arts, are then orientated towards projects organised within the framework of the broad cultural field. This is in structures separate from the educational structures, very often under cultural services or the ministry of culture.

In some countries – and I must say in mine (the Flemish community in Belgium), although it is, as far as I know, rather exceptional – there is a complete

3 As it is clear that some art disciplines cannot be taught at primary level i.e. fine arts, audiovisual arts (or media), applied arts, design or architecture. They need a certain maturity before they can be introduced.

parallel circuit of arts education in evening classes from 6 years until 99 or older. There you will find young people being prepared for higher arts education, adults wanting to have a professional training, as well as people who just want to be introduced to the broad world of the arts. I nevertheless must say that although this is a full and complete educational structure in Flanders, it does not lead to recognised qualifications and this, of course, weakens its position.

Thus, additional arts education is situated at the fringes of the educational world. It is generally the history of an educational system that decides the place of that kind of education within the educational systems of a given country. Even where lifelong learning is considered as a priority, additional arts education is very seldom considered as being part of the lifelong-learning circuit.

One could say that these three structures in fact refer to one fundamental given field: that of education and training *in* the arts.

In order to situate these structures, we need to go back in time. I will take as an example the history of arts education in my own country, not because it is exemplary, but because I know it best. Moreover, I will take the example of institutions dealing with fine arts, not only because I myself have always been much more involved with the fine arts but also because these institutions are the oldest in the field of arts education and can therefore be seen as a kind of *pars pro toto* for the others.[4,5] The first academy of fine arts was founded in 1563 in Florence, whereupon more academies of fine arts were founded in different European countries. The oldest of the Belgian academies was founded in 1663. It is the Royal Academy of Fine Arts in Antwerp.

The founding of academies in the lowlands can be seen as a reaction against the suffocating power of the guild as well as in a more economic and local perspective, namely the training of artists and artisans for the local needs: artists and their work were needed (for instance, painters and architects) and instead of being forced to look for them in other cities or abroad, they wanted to have their 'own' people for the jobs available. Soon enough this had as a consequence that factors other than just artistic value or competence started playing a part in the enrolment of members of staff, as appointments were evidently economically based and mostly local people were selected. Moreover, the training was part-time and mainly dedicated – that is until 1961 as far as Belgium is concerned – to a mixed public: artists as well as pupils, journeymen as well as amateurs.

In the early nineteenth century a schism occurred when fine arts were separated from more applied arts and architecture. In my country technical schools or polytechnics took over a part of the tasks and duties from the academies, and the academies from then on specially dealt with 'art'.

4 De Wilde G.A., *Geschiedenis onzer Academieën van Beeldende Kunsten* (Leuven, Davidsfonds, 1941).

5 Knolle P., 'Tekenacademies in de Noordelijke Nederlanden: de 17° en de 18° eeuw', in: *De Lucaskrater* (Groningen, AMP, 1984).

Later on this movement underwent a change and this change, initiated by two major movements, brought fundamental new artistic-philosophical concepts in our academies: on the one hand the influence of the Arts and Crafts Movements and of the Art Nouveau abolished the schism between fine arts and applied arts, so that schools merged or fine arts schools dealt with applied arts, and vice versa. On the other hand academicism was conceived as the highest art form.

The last concept is particularly important, as it introduces the fundamental idea of the correlation between master and pupil and implicitly states the elaboration of rules and examples – and the necessity of them – within the teaching of the fine arts.

The latest, at least in the teaching of the visual arts, have been abolished in the meanwhile, but the correlation between master and pupil is still considered as an essential aspect, as well as the training of solo artists. In that way our academies still reflect the nineteenth-century model today, a model that moreover was a rather elitist one.

Parallel to the restructuring in education, arts education underwent drastic changes in the 1950s and 1960s and so secondary arts schools were no longer part of or a preparation for higher education, but became autonomous entities in themselves. Schools that never obtained a higher level continued to exist but organised weekend courses or evening classes for youngsters and/or adults. Thus the threefold structure I referred to was set up.

Arts Education, that is education in the arts, is very often regarded as a whole, without any distinction between education at the higher level, the compulsory level or additional education. In the beginning of its history, it was – as I mentioned earlier – meant for artists, pupils, journeymen and amateurs, but, as time went by, distinctions were made:

higher education for the formation of artists;
compulsory and more generally secondary education as a preparation for higher education; and
part-time education as a form of meaningful pastime.

But, of course, such divisions do not always match with reality: youngsters who want to dance, for instance, need to start very early in life, and musicians cannot start their training in higher education. Moreover, the fine artist does not always have a degree in the arts: many of them do not have a degree at all, neither in the arts nor in any other form of higher education.

And then there is still the fact that higher education pretends to train artists, by which I mean the solo artist, although only a minority of their graduates will ever be artists who generate their income out of purely artistic activities. In itself, the curriculum is indeed a nineteenth-century curriculum, where no attention is given to all the other forms of artistic activity, including the activities in the margin of the solo practice.[6] It is for this reason therefore that ELIA is deeply involved in

[6] Staines J., 'Survival skills: equipping students for work', in: *European Journal of Arts Education*, 2(1), November 1998.

a project called 'employability skills for young artists', where a plea for a new curriculum is developed.

Finally, all of this is a problem that art education, art educators and artists themselves need to consider: what they will define, of course, will need to fit within given educational structures, but the aim, the task and the mission of education in the arts must certainly be subject of discussions of artists and all who are involved in the world of the arts. Therefore I would like to quote the so-called Groningen Statement, issued at the conference celebrating the 200th anniversary of the Minerva Academy (Groningen) that clearly states in its first recommendation:

> Until these days various obsolete ideologies about art and the artist dominate in art education and as a consequence of this about the nature of art education itself. It is a necessity that these ideologies can be changed to meet the demands and conception of another era. It is therefore an obligation of the art educators to formulate the current position and role of art and herewith the place of the artist in society. From this statement the tasks and nature of art education will follow.[7]

ARTS IN/OUT OF EDUCATION

In addition to this we have arts *and* education, and arts *in* education.

Here too a large disparity exists in Europe, although, to be sincere, the intention to dedicate attention to this aspect of education is growing more and more. The grounds for this are multiple, but before focusing on them I need to say that as far as I am concerned, when I speak about arts in/and education, I do not speak of one art discipline. Introducing arts in/and education is not introducing youngsters to music and teaching them music, nor is it introducing dance and teaching them dance, nor is it introducing painting and teaching them painting, and so on. When I speak of art in/and education, I speak of all disciplines, or at least an introduction to all art disciplines, a stimulation of hunger for all art disciplines, an awakening of interest for all art disciplines and for all cultural manifestations. Little by little youngsters will be more seduced by one discipline or another, or will want to learn more about it, or even want to apply for a job in the field of the arts. Training them is the task of the arts education; the task of primary and secondary education is to stimulate all youngsters to participate and be active in the broad cultural field.

I said that there are multiple grounds for the increasing interest in arts in/and education. I will now give you some of these grounds, although there are without any doubt a dozen others: First of all, there is the growing consciousness that art and culture are an essential part of our lives. Next to economics and politics, culture is one of the three main areas our lives are focused around. Gerard Mortier, the

[7] 'The Groningen Statement, The Art Academy of the 21st century' (Groningen, Minerva 200, 1998).

actual intendant of the Salzburger Festspiele, defined it in his speech at the founding conference of ELIA in 1990 as such:[8] the political system is the system that directs the relations between human being and the institutions they created; the economical system is the system that regulates production and exchanges of products; the cultural system introduces the human being and offers him the opportunity to use all his talents within society. All of those systems are as important and it is only by relating those systems to each other that the human utopia of the dream come true is possible.

Second, in education for too long (and still) everything has been focused on facts and figures, not on attitudes and the unreachable and unattainable things such as those on which culture is determined, for instance. This makes our youngsters trained just to know these facts and figures, the politics and economics as Gerard Mortier would say, but nothing about quality of life, about interhuman relations and so on. It is not by accident that more and more demands are put on education and that education cannot respond to these demands. Life cannot be caught in facts and figures only.

All this results in a third aspect: arts and culture have always been destined for the happy few. When representatives of the poor in my country, the so-called fourth world, in collaboration with the 'Boudewijn Foundation'[9] wrote a report on their situation in society they stressed their strong resentment of their exclusion from art and culture as being the most striking one. Being a part of society to them also meant taking part in the artistic and cultural life.

It is the task of education to break through this isolation, since it is a human right for all and must be offered to all. Research proves that participation in cultural life has in fact less to do with one's educational level than with the examples one sees in one's environment, in one's milieu. Therefore, it is essential that all children from all layers of society should participate in the cultural field. It is an element that hinders exclusion, and that ensures participation in society. Moreover, it ensures an awareness of the link between the past, the present and the future. Naturally this is an aspect that most people will find difficult to believe. Therefore, I would like to give you the example of South Africa, a society that is trying to build a new nation, the so-called Rainbow nation. For them the cultural dimension, introduced on all levels of education, is an essential key to realise this democratic Rainbow nation. They know that teaching facts and figures only is not enough, and that the extra dimension can only be introduced through teaching of the arts and by emphasising participation in the artistic and cultural life.

And there is more, although even I am a bit reluctant about that 'more'. It is said that people who have been trained through the arts are more flexible and even more critical. This is in itself, of course, a wonderful thing to know, but it is also

8 Report on ELIA's founding conference, Amsterdam, 1991.

9 'Algemeen verslag over de armoede', Koning Boudewijnstichting i.,s.m. ATD Vierde Wereld België en Vereniging van Belgische Steden en Gemeenten, 20.12.1994.

exactly this aspect that has been emphasised over the last years by industry and their captains: they are not so much interested in the arts as a given human manifestation, as they are very interested in young employees who are flexible and who will easily learn and take up new duties and new jobs. Whether we like it or not, it is clear that this is the world our young people will be living and working in. The arts and an introduction to the arts throughout the curriculum of compulsory education will without any doubt emphasise the flexibility of generations to come.

THE CORRELATION BETWEEN ARTS EDUCATION AND ART IN/AND EDUCATION

The above-mentioned grounds for the increasing interest for arts in/and education all treat art and education separately, but also study how they relate to each other and in what direction this relationship goes, because at some point the two meet.

The most exciting thing that has happened over the last years is the growing interest for and the importance of arts within education for young people. This is, of course, not a self-evident process. A strengthening of arts education is possible because of this process and, even more, feasible. On the other hand, this process will also be dependent on the strength of arts education today and how it sees and conceives its mission in the future. Do we only train young artists or do we also train young men and women who will be the young artists of tomorrow? We can ask ourselves who will monitor the process of arts in education. Teachers trained to work in kindergartens and compulsory education having had no special training for art disciplines during their teacher training course or teachers who have been trained by professional artists and have been taught the multidisciplinary approach? I hope the latter, but then under the condition that this monitoring and the monitoring within the teacher training courses becomes an integrated part of this training. This monitoring is not integrated yet, just as the students are not trained to find a job in the broad field of the cultural industries. These cultural industries are, as you may or may not know, the only exponential sector in the European labour market.[10]

Much still has to be done, not only in the structures, as the Bologna declaration will urge the higher education to do, but also in the minds and attitudes. Any discussion is therefore welcome, but especially a discussion with eminent specialists in educational law.

[10] cf. J. Delors' so-called 'White Paper'.

JAN DE GROOF AND ANNICK SCHRAMME

Culture and Education – A Few Basic Principles

1. CULTURE, CULTURAL EDUCATION AND EDUCATION – THEIR MULTIFACETED AND INTERNATIONAL NATURE

1. Definitions of culture are very numerous. It is therefore a concept in more than one sense.

The noun 'culture' comes from the Latin 'cultura', which itself is derived from the verb 'colere' which in the first place means cultivating and developing land. The noun is also used in a metaphorical sense, namely culture as 'the practice of' or 'a certain manner of dealing with'.

The myriad of definitions can usually be reduced to two basic interpretations. The first is of a more *general nature*. All that people make, think, know or perceive to know, the manner in which they become conscious of their feelings and give shape to their actions, all of that is part of culture. In contrast to the concept of civilisation, culture is dynamic. It is not only about the prosperity amassed in the past, but it also has bearing on the present and on the future.

The second interpretation relates to culture in the more restrictive meaning of the *fine arts*. Since the Enlightenment (modern society), the concept of culture refers to the practice and the acquisition of intellectual goods: literature, visual arts, music, philosophy and so forth.

This brings us to the relationship between culture and education, or the desire for *cultural education*. Until recently, *cultural education* was thought of in terms of the '*Bildungsideal*', educating to be a better person through culture. Beauty and goodness were thereby equated with one another. Cultural education then means primarily a cultural transfer from a defined whole of cultural goods that are associated with 'higher culture'. The earlier classical humanities departed from this viewpoint.

Through the democratisation of education and of culture in general, the approach to the concept of culture has been considerably broadened. It is no longer just about the fine arts, having refined manners or being well-read, but also about skills and attitudes; in short, everything a person learns and masters as a member

Jan De Groof, Chantal De Smet and Hilde Penneman (eds.), Art meets Law in Education, 21–40.

of a society. In this sense, cultural education also relates to the cultivation of a 'cultural attitude', in other words a cultural sensitivity, awareness, an openness with respect to social changes. Culture is in that case something that is continually in motion, man's search for forms of society, for answers to scientific and philosophical questions. In that way, it becomes the goal of cultural education to make young people sceptical of all the answers that are too simple. This interpretation of culture leaves more room for modesty and for a call for critical confrontation and cooperation. In this sense, cultural education is not the exclusive domain of subjects such as art education, expressive and musical training, or aesthetics, but rather each subject carries within it a cultural component. Education is increasingly moving toward a similar ideal of cultural education.

2. Culture is by definition altruistic, dynamic and social, it is geared to fellow man and to the community. It fosters its own heritage yet at the same time is indispensable for the future of the individual and of people within an international and especially the European perspective. A dynamic cultural concept for that reason has a certain contradiction, aptly described by the Dutch cultural philosopher Ton Lemaire: culture distinguishes itself from others through its own identity and yet it strives to allow others to share in its culture and thereby removes that very distinction.

Many essays have already been written about the description and the task of cultures.[1] According to Public Law 209 of the 89th US Congress, setting up the National Foundation for the Arts and Humanities, the term 'the arts' includes music (instrumental and vocal), dance, drama, mime, puppetry, folk art, creative writing, architecture and allied fields, painting, sculpture, photography, graphic and craft

1 Belgian legislation has always found it difficult to define the concept. In the Law of 21 July 1971 concerning the powers and the operation of the cultural councils for the Dutch-speaking cultural community and the French-speaking cultural community, and later, by extension, in the Special Law of 8 August 1980 on institutional reform (amended by the Special law of 8 August 1988), cultural matters were described as follows: 1° Protection of the language and its splendour; 2° Encouraging the education of researchers; 3° The fine arts; 4° Cultural heritage, museums, and other scientific and cultural institutions (with the exception of monuments and landscapes); 5° Libraries, record libraries, and similar services; 6° Radio and television broadcasting, with the exception of announcements of the federal government; 6° bis Support to the written press; 7° Youth policy; 8° Permanent education and cultural activities; 9° Physical education, sports, and outdoor activities; 10° Leisure activities and tourism; 11° Pre-school education in kindergartens; 12° Post- and extracurricular education; 13° Artistic education; 14° Intellectual, moral, and social education; 15° Social promotion; 16° Vocational retraining and further vocational training, with a few explicitly stated exceptions. By conferring the authority on 'cultural matters' in international cooperation to the cultural communities, the third constitutional revision of Belgium (1968–1971) recognised an evident fact: cultural autonomy implies a foreign policy. This responsibility for culture does indeed presuppose significantly more than the other powers of the language communities, namely 'international co-operation, including the concluding of treaties', according to the current Article 177, § 1, 3° of the Constitution.

arts, industrial design, costume and fashion design, motion pictures, television, radio, tape and sound recording, the arts related to the presentation, performance, execution and exhibition of such major art forms, and the study and application of the arts to the human environment.

However, 'culture' cannot be placed into this enumeration. The Court of Arbitration in Belgium (the quasi-Constitutional Court) determined in its decree no. 70 of 14 December 1988 that the term 'cultural life' should be interpreted in a much broader sense. In this respect, the tendency to make cultural authorities come under different policy departments should be restructured: after all, further fragmentation further undermines a coherent policy. *Cultural education* offers a superior response to that.

Nor does culture allow itself to be restricted by national boundaries. A minister for culture should likewise apply himself as a minister of 'international affairs'. The present context of increasing European and international cooperation forms a challenge for various cultures. It does not have to lead to a culture clash as Samuel Huntington predicted in a doom-laden scenario. On the contrary, cultures have something to offer one another if they enter into mutual dialogue. Within the European Union, cultural regions can be the driving force of a Europe in which cultural diversity is fully appreciated (the *Europe of cultures*).

2. Right to culture in the European context

(a) *Basic principles*

3. The fact that the right to culture is a fundamental right was endorsed as early as 1948 by the United Nations in Article 23 of the Treaty on Human Rights. The international consensus regarding the close link between culture and education in a democratic society was further developed by UNESCO during the October 1970 conference in Venice.

With the implementation of the Maastricht Treaty on 1 November 1993, culture was for the first time also recognised as an explicit area of authority of the European Union, according to Article 128: 'The Community contributes to the development of the cultures of the Member States with respect for the national and regional diversity of those cultures, but at the same time also placing emphasis on the common cultural heritage'. Nevertheless, the development of this article was coupled with a great deal of tumult. The smaller countries especially feared that European interference in matters of culture would lead to cultural uniformity, where there would be no room for the smaller cultures. Hence, not only was cultural diversity recognised in the treaty, but also the principle of *subsidiarity*.[2] The European Union

2 See De Groof, J. (ed.), *Subsidiarity and education. Aspects of comparative educational law* (Acco, Leuven, 1994), 449.

will only be able to undertake action when doing so means added value in addition to what the Member States are already doing on an individual basis.

The treaty distinctly aimed to bring the European Union closer to the citizens through culture and to increase the democratic standard of the Union. Jean-Marie Domenach wrote in his book, *Europe: Le défi culturel*: 'any pronouncement that does not represent an educational theory for Europe must be treated with suspicion'. As not only an economic but also a political Europe comes into being, however, the importance of cultural diversity will come to the fore even more.

A flood of publications has already appeared about the singularity of European culture. Often, that identity is sought in the joint history that is characterised by democracy, tolerance and other European values. It has already been conclusively demonstrated that the European values are nonetheless no historic achievements, but rather principles upon whose basis we laboriously try to build a more humane society. 'Europe still has everything to prove.' The most common, but at the same time also vague definition of European cultural identity, is the reference to 'unity in diversity'.

European policy wants to promote, in addition to cultural diversity, which is characteristic of European identity, respect for the cultural identity of the separate Member States and regions. This duality is also reflected in education policy, and particularly in cultural education. On the one hand, a great deal of importance is attached to *intercultural understanding and tolerance* with respect to other cultures. As early as 1988, the European Council accepted a resolution on the importance of the European dimension in education.[3] On the other hand, one wants to emphasise and even strengthen one's *own national cultural identity*.[4]

This dialectic between national cultural identity and a transnational European identity is found, amongst others, in the *Melina Project* from Greece (1995). With this project, Greece wants to upgrade the aesthetic training in schools and make students familiar with their cultural heritage and their historical background: 'Children should be offered the opportunity to choose from the widest possible variety of approaches to national culture. United Europe projects and seeks mutuality

3 In addition to the many intergovernmental agreements on this subject, it remains a point of attention for the future too, cf. the 1999–2000 annual report of the Council of Europe. In the European Year of Education and Lifelong Learning (1996), among other things, the importance of the development of the European dimension in primary and permanent education was emphasised. (*Report of the Commission to the Council, the European Parliament, the Economic and Social Committee and the Committee of the Regions on the implementation, results and overall assessment of the European Year of Education and Lifelong Learning (1996)*, in accordance with Article 8 of Parliament and Council Decision No. 2493/95/EC (COM (1999) 447 – C5-0205/1999 – 1999/2163 (COS)), 14 July 2000.

4 In Norway, for instance, it is explicitly stated that Norwegian culture is based on Christian religion and the Christian tradition. Ken Robinson, *Culture, Creativity and the Young. Arts education in Europe: A Survey* (Council of Europe, 1997) 23, 111.

through difference. This is a precondition for the harmonious and creative coexistence of European peoples.'[5] The Melina Project considers in-depth understanding of one's own culture to be the best guarantee for later interest in other cultures. This vision is based on the sufficiently well-known principle that only self-respect and one's own value perception supports pluralism.[6]

For that matter, individual cultural identity can be supported in various ways. For example, a great deal is being done in the field of language, such as the Lingua exchange programmes between schools or the efforts being made to translate literary works.[7] History, religion or other subjects can also be considered as part of the cultural identity and be involved in the process of outlining a policy of cultural education.

(b) *Value of culture versus the concrete importance of cultural education in providing education?*

4. Just about every European country formally emphasises the importance of the cultural dimension in education and claims to encourage the artistic skills of young people. In practice, however, the subject does not receive such a high priority. The concrete policy in the Member States uses a rather narrow definition of the term culture and does not get much further than scheduling a few isolated hours of art and music into the education programme. In the Northern European countries, there *is* a broader interpretation of cultural education. They pay attention to a balance between artistic and physical development. The cultural activities at school are also further addressed extracurricularly by a network of cultural institutions.

There are also considerable differences between each of the countries with regard to curricula.[8] Some countries have strict regulations governing content and criteria for evaluation, while in other countries, such as the Netherlands and Flanders, thanks to the final attainment levels (core objectives), there is much more freedom for schools to fill in the curriculum. In most European nations, cultural education is required in primary education and the first years of secondary education, after that (from ages 14–16 onward) it is organised on an optional basis.[9]

5 'Education and Culture: The Melina Project' (Ministry of National Education and Religious Affairs, Ministry of Culture, General Secretariat of Popular Culture, Athens, 1995).

6 De Groof J., *Pluralisme: kind van de democratie?* (Leuven, Davidsfonds, 1983) 142.

7 See also European Parliament and Council Decision No. 2085/97/EC of 6 October 1997 establishing a programme of support in the field of books and reading (Ariane), which includes translation.

8 Ken Robinson, *Culture, Creativity and the Young. Arts education in Europe: A Survey*, n. 4 above.

9 Several studies are already shaped in that respect. Among others, the 1996 report of the *European Task Force on Culture and Development*: 'In one form or another, the arts are

5. Art, however, usually has a lower status than mathematics and the sciences. Under pressure from the economic world, the importance of cultural education appears to be reduced even further. Various European countries, such as Finland, Norway and also the Netherlands and Flanders, reformed their education systems in the 1990s. They were especially tailored to the wishes of the labour market.

---

included in the compulsory curricula of most European countries. Usually there is an emphasis on the visual arts and music. Drama and dance are seldom included as separate subjects. Where it is taught, dance is often included within physical education or gymnastics. Drama is increasingly seen as an important medium for teaching a wide range of other subjects. Literature is usually associated with the teaching of the national language. There are significant national variations in conceptions of the arts in schools. In many countries, fine art teaching is strongly based on drawing. Sometimes it is linked to the crafts; elsewhere, art includes both fine art and design and, on occasion, design is linked with technology. In Germany, art education in some Länder includes media, advertising, architecture and film as well as design. Finland incorporates media education, craft skills, drama and children's circus. In Norway, there is no concept which is directly synonymous with the English idea of art. […] In most countries the arts are part of the curriculum for children up to the age of 12, but there are examples of more generous provision. In France, art and music are compulsory to 15 and become optional for the baccalaureat. In Sweden, pupils have compulsory lessons across the discipline at first level, develop their work in one discipline at the second level and organise specialist and vocational options at the third. The Dutch include two arts subjects in a compulsory curriculum of fifteen areas, but they are optional in secondary schools. The United Kingdom's new curriculum incorporates art and music, but, although once compulsory, they (together with dance) are now optional after the age of fourteen.'

Conclusion: Arts influence European education: they are an integral – although often not very highly esteemed – *element in primary and secondary school curricula education.* They have their own institutions of lower and secondary professional training and, in higher education, arts universities and institutes maintain an important role in undergraduate training and, in the humanities departments of so-called 'science-based' universities.

But there is a *paradox* indeed, further sharply analysed by Ken Robinson, Professor of Arts Education (University of Warwick), in his brilliant report on '*Culture, Creativity and Young People*' n. 4 above. Even if there is explicit commitment to the arts in schools, *in practice they are accorded a low priority* (excluding special schools), *with the result that they are often given few resources and little time in the teaching schedules.* The tendency to decentralise curriculum planning seems not to guarantee a strong position of these arts subjects, and to let teachers decide how important they really consider arts subjects to be. And a further reason for the relative ineffectiveness of arts education is that the interests and talents of students vary greatly and those with artistic talent can, and often do, take up voluntary artistic activities outside the regular curriculum and school hours (in some countries, as in Finland, the providers of the extra-curricular art education receive public subsidies). May I refer also to the quite unique *Belgian part-time art education system.*

A recent French study on arts education argues that although considerable progress has been made in recent years in promoting arts education in schools, the education system remains strongly resistant to arts, according to the previously mentioned *Council of Europe report*, n. 3 above. 'Reason and logic are given priority over creativity and sensitivity.'

Utilitarian thinking prevails. This criticism is not new, but the economically-geared emphasis of education is what remains surprising. At the European Top in Lisbon on 23 and 24 March 2000, it was decided that the European education and training systems must be adapted to the needs of the information society and the necessity of more and better employment opportunities. Recently, on 22 June 2000, another motion by the European Parliament and the Council regarding European cooperation in the matter of quality evaluation in school education was passed. This motion does not define cultural education as a criterion for quality evaluation, but it states that 'quality education is of fundamental importance for labour market policy and the free movement of workers within the European Union.' Already in the White Paper on growth, competitiveness and employment, the White Paper '*Teaching and Learning*', which is based on the concept of the information society and the concept 'lifelong learning', as well as in the Green Paper on 'Innovation', it has been emphatically pointed out that the quality of education and professional training is one of the 'key elements of competitiveness'.[10]

In secondary education, the humanities notion has come under pressure. In education, this is expressed in the prestige associated with certain disciplines. Likewise, there is less and less a matter of a *universitas* notion at the *universities.*

Notwithstanding these developments, the European Commission in April 1994 called upon the ministers of education and culture to cooperate.[11] Since then, France and the Netherlands have been working intensively developing close cooperation between the Department of Culture and the Department of Education. In Flanders, the so-called culture unit, *Canon*, has been in operation in the Department

[10] In the early 1990s, the Commission recognised the importance of the quality of school education. Also, Article 126, paragraph 1, of the European Union Treaty already stated that the development of high-quality education was one of the objectives of the Union. Even earlier than that, it was already called the key competence. (De Groof, J., and Friess, B., 'Opportunities and limitations for a European Education policy', in *European Journal for Education Law and Policy* (Dordrecht, 1997) 9–17.) Seeing that the quality of education in academic institutions is of crucial importance, the Education Council decided, in November 1991, to set up a community action plan for quality assurance, which started with the university sector and was subsequently expanded to secondary and primary education. This process was supported by the launch of a model project, for which the decision was already taken in 1997 by the Education Council and which took place in 1997 and 1998. More than a hundred schools, in Member States as well as in three EER countries (Iceland, Liechtenstein, and Norway), took part in this project.

[11] The personality-building value of cultural education as a compensation for a one-sided technological education was also emphasised. After all, cultural and artistic education amount to 'a search for pleasure through learning, a pedagogical approach founded on the exploitation of the natural curiosity of children and also an effort to improve communication at all levels'. (Ken Robinson, *Culture, Creativity and the Young. Arts education in Europe: A Survey*, n. 4 above.) In other words, it stimulates children's eagerness to learn, because it enables them to explore the world in a playful way.

of Education since 1995, but one cannot yet really speak of any intense collaboration between the world of education and the cultural sector (see further below).

Both the world of education and the cultural sector benefit from intensive cooperation. An active cultural practice at school encourages pupils and furthers the school environment,[12] and cultural establishments have a chance to introduce themselves to their future audience. The importance of culture for education and vice versa will be covered in more detail later.

3. The importance of education for culture: the concern for broad participation

6. The concern for broad participation of the population is a constant in cultural policy. The policy, which must legitimise itself, after all determines that participation in artistic expression such as music, dance and performing arts continues to be a very exclusive leisure activity. Recent research in Belgium confirms that 93 per cent of the population never goes to the opera, 80 per cent of the population never attends a concert or classical music festival, 78 per cent never goes to the theatre, 70 per cent never goes to a pop concert or jazz performance, more than half never visits a museum or exhibition, 47 per cent never goes to the cinema, and one third of the Flemish population does not even use one or more cultural provisions at all.[13]

The groups that are the most difficult to reach are the foreign population and young people. Figures from the Dutch Social and Cultural Planning Office show that the percentage of young people who visit cultural establishments has dropped from 49 per cent in 1983 to 43 per cent in 1995.[14]

In addition to one's social background, the level of education appears to be a very important determining factor for the extent to which one participates in culture; authoritative sociologists have already reported on this extensively.

Apart from the family, the school environment is of course also very important in determining the cultural interests that a child develops. This emphasises the importance of a broad cultural formation at school, not so much through imposing 'art' as a required course, but especially through the manner in which culture 'seeps into' the daily teaching package (the choice of subjects, the manner of teaching, the teacher's attitude, the opportunities that children and young people receive to

12 American research showed, among other things, that music education has a positive influence on children's learning ability. *Nature*, vol. 381, 23 May 1996.

13 T. Jacobs and D. Stoffelen, *Cultuurdeelname in Vlaanderen in 1994–1995*, cultuurstudie 3 (Brussels, 1998) and L. Bollaert and K. Matthijs, *Syntheserapport Toerisme, recreatie en vrijetijd in Vlaanderen anno 2000* (Brussels, December 1999).

14 J. de Haan and W. Knulst, *Het bereik van de kunsten: een onderzoek naar veranderingen in de belangstelling voor beeldende kunst en podiumkunst sinds de jaren zeventig*. SCP Rapport 166 (The Hague, Sociaal en Cultureel Planbureau, 2000).

explore for themselves, the school environment). This approach is, of course, at odds with utilitarian thinking.

Education particularly has the chance to take a step back now and then from social influences and not to go into all issues. In that sense, it is precisely education that can offer compensation for certain trends in society. According to the cultural philosopher Max Wildiers, 'in times when the economic and the technical predominate, the other subjects, the threatened values, must be further encouraged and appreciated. The school must serve as a counterbalance to a one-sided culture, spiritual poverty and ontological emptiness.' In the recent inspection text for the subject *Aesthetics* (June 1999), the same line of reasoning is used:

> Mathematics, economics, the sciences, engineering and others are useful and necessary, but can under no circumstances replace religion, culture, sports, art, literature, music and film. Not one or the other, but everything in balanced harmony next to and together with each other. If education is geared to the material needs of the moment, it will fall short of its goals. Is it not the world of industry that implores education to thoroughly prepare its future employees for their production task, but at the same time acknowledges that it is increasingly finding itself confronted with cultural illiteracy in those same employees? It is the unique duty of education to ensure that such 'secondary illiteracy' does not stand a chance and that art education is promoted.[15]

7. The importance that the government attaches to the active involvement of cultural groupings, instead of taking up this space itself, can go on as one of the most relevant criteria in the assessment of post-war cultural policy.[16] The application of this principle in the field of education further reinforces this point of interest to a considerable degree.[17]

The decision therefore is as follows: increased cultural participation and, more generally, a broadened cultural competence, must form the cornerstone of planned cultural policy in more ways than one. Participation in cultural activities and an intensive perception thereof do not only require a healthy curiosity, but also (fore) knowledge, a frame of reference, mental openness: in short *cultural competence*.

However, encouraging cultural participation must take place on qualitative grounds and must involve the cultural establishments: cultural centres, libraries, associations, training establishments, societies, orchestras, and so forth. They each need to participate in active cultural mediation according to their own nature.

Furthermore, the government must create an incentive whereby the private sector, individuals and groups of people, take on responsibility for culture. After all,

[15] *Visietekst Esthetica*, published by VVKSO, June 1999, 12.

[16] De Groof, J. and Schramme, A., 'Het cultuurbeleid', in Dewachter, W., et al., *Tussen Staat en Maatschappij* (Lannoo, 1995) 426–61.

[17] De Groof, J., *De overheid en het gesubsidieerd onderwijs* (Cepess, 1985) 267.

it is they who give shape to the culture of a people.[18] The government and those responsible for education will furthermore retain an innovative vision regarding culture within the curriculum.

The aim of aesthetic formation[19] cannot be the encyclopaedic gathering of knowledge with regard to art. The specialist term 'training' must be understood literally. It really comes down to awakening the latent aesthetic impressionability of young people by making cultural objects accessible for them.

During this formation, attention should also be paid to objects from *daily life* with the aim of developing the sensitivity to the aesthetic dimension of the material living environment. This includes nurturing good taste, respect for one's living environment and rejection of vandalism. Besides the development of the impressionability of pupils for the aesthetic, the *accessibility to cultural manifestation* itself also makes up part of the objectives of such instruction. That is particularly important for pupils who have less cultural stimulation or who have to make up for socio-cultural deprivation. A well-founded value judgement can only be made if the pupil, when forming a judgement, learns to have an eye for space and time, for the social and historic context in which the work of art was created, for technical and other factors that in one way or another influenced its creation and its outward appearance. That position will also prepare the student to learn to understand and appreciate the *authenticity of a creation*, regardless of the beauty standards of the moment, the prevailing style and fashion and the pure historical relationship. This value judgement can have bearing on the object itself and on the creator thereof, i.e. the artist, whether or not their identity is known. That study can contribute to a better profiling of the artists, of a people or of a period.

Appreciation for one's *own cultural patrimony* continues to be another compelling social duty for education and upbringing. This clearly involves a common good, accomplishments of one's own generation and legacy of previous generations. The preservation of this patrimony demands from the community an ongoing effort to which each citizen contributes. General participation in the perception of the values of the cultural patrimony is a matter of social justice. Knowledge of the components of the *Western cultural patrimony* opens the eye to the wealth of ethnic variations. An appreciative attitude, based on that knowledge, lies directly opposite cultural imperialism and chauvinism.

The broad approach should also give the pupil the opportunity for involvement in terms of his or her own cultural forms. For this, a primary condition is a broad vision with many opportunities for comparison. For that matter, the introduction to other cultures will further understanding of one's own culture. Furthermore, the knowledge and appreciation of the values and achievements of other cultures will

[18] Cf. Preface by De Groof J. to Schramme, A., *Vlaanderen en zijn grote buitenland* (Tielt, 1999), 9–11.

[19] Contribution of the Flemish inspectortate on 'Culture and Education' and aesthetic education.

promote international understanding. In that sense, one can work toward the objectives concerning world patrimony which UNESCO placed in its programme.

We must strive toward a *critical position* with respect to art manifestation, on the condition that in this respect, we depart from a well-founded knowledge. That critical position is necessary in the face of certain side effects such as commercialisation, politicising and indoctrination, amongst others. Recognising the authenticity of the artistic creation is fundamental in that respect. This critical position is held toward all objects from daily material social environment, whereby it should become possible to judge the distinction between kitsch and good product.

4. Attention for Culture in Education: The Development of Cultural Competence

(a) *'Art is not cool'*

8. There is a gap between young people and art, and between young people and culture in general. Amongst young people, the prevailing idea is that art is not there for them, but for adults. Young people regard not only adult lovers of culture and art in a negative light, but also their own peers who participate in culture. The more classical forms of culture have a low status within youth culture.

Also typical of that culture appears to be, to a certain extent, the *anti*-school sentiment. Young people experience system education, the ideology and upbringing as a *fait accompli* but often are too negative about everything that has to do with school and education.

Most young people therefore do not have the codes to interpret art and cultural expressions. It is precisely there that the challenge for education lies: to show them the broad landscape of art and culture and to equip them so that they can find their own way.[20]

Dutch research shows that due to the rise of the *youth culture* (since the 1960s) and the weakened attention to classic culture in education, democratised secondary and higher education has allowed a similar form of cultural transfer to fall to the wayside. The result is a more limited form of cultural competence, a decreasing interest in classical and intellectual expressions of culture, and a growing popularty of art forms that used to be considered amongst the so-called 'lower' culture (pop music, musicals, jazz, cabaret). The pressure to continue being in line with one's age peers will also play a role.[21]

[20] In school performances, cultural institutes often have to contend with this negative association with the school system, and this in spite of the clear spatial distance between the school environment and the cultural environment.

[21] J. de Haan and W. Knulst, *Het bereik van de kunsten: een onderzoek naar veranderingen in de belangstelling voor beeldende kunst en podiumkunst sinds de jaren zeventig*. SCP Rapport 166 (The Hague, Sociaal en Cultureel Planbureau, 2000), 6.

Young people usually do not recognise their own culture in ways parents and teachers would consider 'culture', and *vice versa.* Nevertheless, every generation has its own cultural pattern that is sometimes a continuation of the traditional culture but which radically differs from it in other areas. In this way, the current generation would sooner adopt a distanced and expectant attitude. Many young people do not recognise themselves in the fundamental or political content of a number of artistic expressions. In their world, the focus is on fun, relaxation and enjoying themselves together. Bridging that gap is probably the greatest challenge.

On the other hand, some positive signs are those that point to a renewed interest of young adults for the more traditional forms of culture (including opera, classic theatre, etc) and the attention that these cultural institutions show for young adults in terms of programming and access.

(b) *The multicultural challenge*

9. Another unmistakable development is the issue of migration. The growing number of foreigners in standard education is a social fact. This has given rise to a flood of literature and articles about the problem of cultural integration of foreign young people in education. Certainly, as far as culture in the broad meaning is concerned, this development goes hand in hand with tensions. The individuality of the schools must be reconsidered, and from the policy one is trying to use distribution measures, target group policy, and a better framing (expanded care, and such) to ensure smooth integration. Besides desegregation and active acceptance, the interculturalisation of education is also a fully-fledged principle of the *non-discrimination policy* in education, and this principle is implemented at the level of teacher training. The discussion about cultural diversity has now also begun in the cultural sector.

We hereby assume the following position: culture and art are the pre-eminent instruments of dialogue between peoples. In art, a people places its dreams, its fears, its obsessions, its expectations, its courage, its skill. Again and again, culture emerges as the most direct path from person to person.

A striking element in the policy used in the Netherlands is the placement of multiculturality first and foremost as a hallmark of quality: 'One of the pillars of the cultural policy is precisely the concern for multiformity, for that which distinguises people, without losing sight of that which ties them together. Culture, in short, is more so an unarmed confrontation between many subcultures than an amalgamation thereof.'[22] With this, cultural education, and more generally the topic of youth and culture, come to stand even higher on the list of priorities of the cultural policy.

[22] *Cultuur als confrontatie, uitgangspunten voor het cultuurbeleid 2001–2004* (Ministerie van Onderwijs, Cultuur en Wetenschappen, The Hague, 2000).

The relation between participation in art, level of education and social background is also found in foreigners.[23] Their disadvantage when it comes to participation once again does not so much have to do with financial obstacles as with background traits such as education levels. Furthermore, the participation of foreigners is part of a broader emancipation process that will still take considerable time. It comes down to enabling children and young people of all social layers of the population – native and foreign – to acquire cultural and artistic competence.

Foreign young people must of course also be able share in the diversity of the cultural scene, they must take up a natural place. Then equally evident new cultural forms of expression come into being that form a true enrichment for society. Cultural diversity seems to be a tautology, an 'inherent obviousness'.[24] In concrete terms, the art education programmes, for example, will, given the diverse cultural backgrounds of the students, have to develop evenly diversified attitudes in recruitment, course offerings and assessment. Experience in foreign countries shows that extra resources are needed temporarily to put right existing situations that have gone awry and to optimally put into action the present expertise.

(c) *Active questioning instead of passive transfer of knowledge*

10. The presence of foreign pupils in class further reinforces the fact that it is not the cognitive knowledge that is important but rather the personality-shaping value of art. The subject of aesthetics in the fifth and sixth year of secondary education (third stage) no longer places the emphasis on art history, but on aesthetic experience and training. The focus is on the process-oriented nature in contact with artistic products, and not on result-oriented thinking: 'The subject of Aesthetics must educate to unconditional and active openness toward all expressions of art and culture and that openness should lead to far-reaching tolerance and a critical attitude, it can offer an important contribution to multicultural society.'[25] Because foreign students often have a multicultural background, the curriculum will have to take this into account. That works on two sides: on the one hand, these pupils will find it

[23] J. de Haan and W. Knulst, *Het bereik van de kunsten: een onderzoek naar veranderingen in de belangstelling voor beeldende kunst en podiumkunst sinds de jaren zeventig*. SCP Rapport 166, The Hague, Sociaal en Cultureel Planbureau, 2000.

[24] Ria Lavrijsen, Culturele diversiteit in de kunst (Boekmansstichting, 2000). The author disapproves of the government providing funds to ethnic groups on the basis of their numerical strength. However, she does find that it is necessary for art and cultural policy to take differences of social background into account, as well as the fact that immigrants and 'natives' have different artistic and cultural backgrounds. Reducing the question of cultural diversity in art to a matter of class does not do justice to the process of encounter and confrontation between 'new' and 'native' Dutch citizens, a process that leads to interesting confrontations and new art forms.

[25] *Visietekst Esthetica*, n. 15 above, 15.

easier to connect and on the other hand, their input will broaden the perspective of their fellow pupils regarding the multifaceted nature of culture.

This approach is in line with that of a number of (post-modernistic) social thinkers who, incidentally, question whether you even can reach any conclusions about art. For example, Stefan Hertmans wonders how it is possible to speak of art in an environment of organised transfer of knowledge:

> I am not sure what art is, I am not sure who the person is to whom I am addressing myself or to whom the work of art is directed. I do not know what the work of art wants to say, and I have only vague notions of the context that are involved in the work of art. The only thing that I can describe a bit more distinctly is the mechanism of communication itself, this preoccupation with (metaphorical) transfer of knowledge.[26] Klaas Tindemans of the Flemish Theatre Institute is in agreement and states that a position of radical indefiniteness is important because the work of art is quite simply characterised by indefiniteness.[27]

(d) *Visual culture*

11. With the arrival of film, television and the computer, the number of images and their influence in our society has increased dramatically. Culture pessimists often place this visual culture opposite word culture. The visual culture is thereby equated to intellectual decay, whereas word culture refers to a higher intellectual activity. Nevertheless, image and text can also complement each other. Television also has a positive influence on the knowledge level of children that cannot be underestimated. However, one must be able to recognise quality. Hence the need for image training in education. A child must learn not only to read words, but also to be able to analyse images. It is an important task of education to do something about visual training. Young people must learn to critically deal with imagery, whether it has to do with documentaries, films, photos, paintings or sculptures. A critical attitude is necessary now more than ever because images, no more so than words, are by definition sacred. Images can be false, enticing, mendacious, untrue, superficial, inflammatory, demagogic, degrading or dangerous. Images must therefore be continuously evaluated, corrected and, if necessary, shattered.[28]

[26] Stefan Hertmans, *Waarover men niet spreken kan. Elementen voor een agogiek van de kunst.*

[27] Klaas Tindemans, *Theater maken, theater leren* (State of the Union Theaterfestival, 2000) 5.
According to Wassily Kandinsky, all art is created out of inner necessity. That inner necessity is based on three principles: the personal element, because the artist expresses himself completely in his creation; the temporal element, because every artist is always a child of his time; and finally, the purely artistic element, because all art serves what is intrinsic to art.

[28] Leo De Haes, *Cultuur is oorlog* (Leuven, 1994) 123.

(e) *Attention to culture in curricula and final attainment levels*

12. The emphasis in curricula is primarily placed on the personality-shaping aspect of the subjects with bearing on cultural education: 'Helping pupils develop a full and balanced personality and providing them with a medium to enrich their creativity and develop their sense of beauty and style.'[29]

In the basic curriculum, art education was included in the final attainment levels as one of the five areas of learning along with mathematics, language, practical instruction and physical education.[30]

In the first two years (first stage) and in the third and fourth year (second stage) of secondary education, the pupils primarily have to learn to contemplatively, actively and creatively deal with image and music, especially in the classes of musical education and expressive training. In history classes, they gain understanding of the historical development of culture. In the third degree, the subject of aesthetics is optional (many schools still do not offer it) and one wants to go from elementary introduction and practice to a more in-depth analysis and perception of the language of music, image and film.[31]

School inspections also investigate what the school does in terms of cultural training. Of the 65 secondary schools that were inspected in 1994, according to the school inspections, 10 per cent earned the valuable label 'cultural school' for their vision and approach which truly go beyond the disciplines. In 10 per cent of the schools, not one single cultural component is given noteworthy attention. The remainder lies somewhere in between, often with very valuable initiatives but which rarely involve the entire school district. Culture is, of course, a domain that prompts cooperation beyond the discipline and that requires a stimulating school environment. Further research would be useful in measuring the attention given to culture in education.

5. A SHORTLIST OF EXAMPLES OF GOOD PRACTICES

13.(a) In practice, many teachers have to fight for aesthetic training with school administration or colleagues in order to command respect for their discipline, as well as for the organisation of all sorts of field trips or projects with the students. In contrast to the rhetoric, the subject of aesthetics is often used as cover for the cultural image of the school.

[29] Secondary education curriculum, *Esthetica*, derde graad ASO (Licap, NVKSO, Brussels, September 1992).

[30] Using the media is part of these final attainment levels for art education, and there are also links with language education in the mother tongue (the 'language' of audio-visual, visual, and audio works).

[31] One hour a week is provided for this, corresponding to about 23 teaching periods a year.

13.(b) It deserves recommendation to have professional artists and educators work together in a structured manner in art educational projects to increase the cultural competence of broad yet clearly defined target groups, to promote knowledge of and understanding for the arts. An 'Art and Democracy' non-profit association could support these projects.

13.(c) At least fifty per cent of pupils still do not experience theatre, film, dance, music, a museum or an exhibition with school, and those who do usually do so with their primary school. Nothing much further is done with it: they remain mere isolated activities.

13.(d) To attract more young people to the theatre or opera, a number of cultural institutions offer discounts on admission. However, it often goes no further than this one-sided approach. Too little is still being done about the needs of young people themselves. There exists a need for specific programming for young people.

13.(e) The cooperation between school libraries and local (municipal) libraries leaves quite a lot to be desired. Certainly when it comes to developing municipal libraries into true centres of information exchange, it is important for schools to be able to participate in this. At the moment, too much depends on the personal initiative of individual teachers, and the cooperation is not structurally developed. In Denmark and the Netherlands, there is an official standard for school libraries: for example, at least one book must be purchased per student per year.

13.(f) Some cities organise an annual *cultural fair for teachers*, where they can meet artists, educational staff members and others in charge of all kinds of cultural establishments, alternating with small performances, cafés, and so forth, and an 'Artbank for Image culture', namely travelling exhibitions on modern day expressive art and image culture. The Artbank appears both in schools and in cultural centres, both for primary school children and for young people in secondary and higher education, of all disciplines, levels and systems. The Artbank wants to sharpen the powers of observation in young people and to consciously teach them from a young age how to work with images. The transdisciplinary organisation attempts to encourage after-effects and integration in various subjects.

13.(g) Musecom (Louvain La Neuve) lets students actively interact with the museum collections via a multimedia computer database. This couples the old with the new in the hope of being able to actively involve young people.[32] Museums, after all, should serve as an example with regard to educative working (weekly sessions for children and, during school holidays, the project '*Kunst in kaart*'). For example, the museum game MUSEJA! is an educative game that draws a connection between the various museums in Antwerp.

13.(h) The fact that a more systematic support from the government's side can immediately lead to a great deal of results is evidenced by the initiative called

[32] *Museummakers zoeken vernieuwing, 20 inspirerende experimenten* (Koning Boudewijnstichting, 2000) 22–23.

Canon. In 1995, it was decided to establish a permanent cultural unit, called Canon, within the Department of Education. *Canon* encourages and supports initiatives with regard to culture within education. Notwithstanding the fact that it was a small team, a great deal has already been achieved. For example, there are the *Canon* cultural days and the *Canon* fair week for teachers where all kinds of creative ideas are acquired, experiences are shared and concrete solutions are presened. Each year, the offer is tremendously varied. In workshops, various schools show in concrete terms how they have taken on the challenge. It is always about art and cultural projects that have grown gradually, independent of school schedules and teaching plans and which have developed into major school projects through sustained efforts. The projects *Dynamo 2* and *Meesterstukken* financially support hundreds of initiatives each year. A catalogue distributed to schools at no charge sums up more than 200 projects for which schools can receive subsidies. With the project '*kunSTof?*' secondary classes can have an artist visit for an interactive work session. The teacher chooses the subject of the lesson and the artist interprets it in his or her own way: a mathematical musician, a chemical dancer, a French sculptor… 'The crowning glory' is a stage festival for secondary schools. In five cultural centres, a total of 27 groups compete and the five regional winners can go to the festival of Avignon for free. A more detailed contribution in this respect is included in the section titled '*Country reports*' in the chapter containing the Belgian Report.

13.(i) In the Netherlands, the subject *Cultural and Artistic Education* recently led to various forms of cooperation between cultural institutions and secondary schools in various Dutch cities. For example, the foundation *De Uitlok* was established in Den Bosch in 1999. This foundation introduces secondary school children to the cultural institutions of the city. On '*Uitlok Day*', school children go around these institutions. In addition, the *Sporenplan* is offered, packaged in art discipline transcending mini-subscriptions and with a combination of various art forms from which the students can choose. The foundation *De Uitlok* also oversees the composition and distribution of a booklet, *Het Reuzenrad*, in which the county's cultural institutions introduce themselves to the young people. Perhaps this could be an idea for *Prospecta*, which organises the annual cultural market in Antwerp.

13.(j) The former Dutch State Secretary for Culture, Aad Nuis, together with his colleague from Education, Tineke Netelenbos, wanted to make efforts to strengthen relations between the cultural sector and education. Together, they published the *Culture and School* memorandum in 1997 which called upon schools to give special attention to cultural education in their school plans. In order to make these plans concrete, a sum of six million guilders was made available from the Culture budget. This had an effect: Cultural education has now found itself a clear place in the core objectives and examination programmes, in the development of methods and teaching resources, and in the training and continuing training of teachers. Furthermore, it was decided to organise an annual *Culture Week* during which pupils and their parents can get to know what cultural institutions have to offer.

Finally, it was shown how subjects such as history and geography could make better use of cultural opportunities. Cultural institutions, especially museums, archives and libraries, but also institutions in the field of conservation of monuments and historic buildings, can make a valuable contribution to this. Also in the Netherlands, museums still do not sufficiently profile themselves as centres of knowledge and advice for education. Various projects were developed to explore the possibilities. Throughout all of this, the expertise of the teachers also continues to be essential. Their leading role cannot be taken over by cultural institutions.[33]

The current Dutch State Secretary for Culture, Rick van der Ploeg, already wants to move ahead with the project '*Culture and School*'. He wants to add to it a system of culture coupons. To enable and encourage the undertaking of cultural treasure hunt, students at schools that are going to follow the new subject cultural and artistic training in secondary education, receive culture coupons that are issued together with the free *CJP* (*Cultural Youth Passport*) discount card.[34] In addition, minister Van der Ploeg introduced the three per cent rule. Cultural institutions must spend at least 3 per cent of their subsidy on cultural education and reaching new areas of the public, otherwise 3 per cent will be deducted from their subsidy amount. Those institutions that want to do more can apply for a special incentive budget. This measure already attracted a great deal of criticism from the sector which saw in this a licence to market culture at the expense of quality.

The fact that education and culture in the Netherlands had not been separate worlds for some time is evident from the numerous already existing initiatives. Each year, the supporting authorities already now reach hundreds of thousands of school children. Almost two thirds of the museums are developing special programmes for the benefit of education.[35] Nevertheless, the many information packages and museum promotions that are offered annually only partly meet expectations. The primarily supply-oriented approach of this moment has to make way for an approach in which the wishes of education are better addressed. All of this is only possible through a more intensive cooperation between the Ministry of Culture, the Ministry of Education, the local authorities and the cultural institutions.[36]

33 For example, the city of Leiden has a project called 'Museum en school', which is part of the municipal charter and runs for four years. Connected to this, there is 'Beeldenstorm', the successor to the television programme 'Museumschatten', which focuses on the art collections of Leiden. The museum staff will be given extra training. In the field of cultural heritage too, there seems to be a strongly growing interest in education. Further, various initiatives were taken by theatre and dance companies, orchestras, etc.

34 *Cultuur als confrontatie, uitgangspunten voor het cultuurbeleid 2001–2004* (Ministerie van Onderwijs, Cultuur en Wetenschappen, The Hague, 2000), 51.

35 F. Haanstra and J. Oostwoud Wijdenes, *Trendrapport museumeducatie* (Amsterdam, SCO-Kohnstamm Instituut, 1996).

36 Aad Nuis, *Pantser en ruggengraat, Cultuurnota 1997–2000* (The Hague, 1996) 10–16.

6. A SHORTLIST OF RECOMMENDATIONS

14. The *Scottish Arts Council* has referred to five principles of education policy:

Inclusiveness in relation to that range of art forms;
Integrity concerning the nature of the links between arts and education;
Enlightenment of the self in relation to art form and world;
Empowerment in terms of individual and community outcomes;
Entitlement in terms of individual rights.

These principles are explained, put into context, and embedded in a policy for development and evaluation. These are ideals which we may never fully achieve, but for which we should always strive.
Each Member State should have to define for itself the strategic principles in the matter of 'Art and Education'.

15. May a few policy suggestions be made in this regard?
15.(a) For a successful approach to integration of culture in education the following two issues continue to be important: the vision of the school (the place of art and culture in education) and the concrete position of teachers and the administration. Many teachers still use an outdated notion of culture, whereby culture is on the same level with the traditional arts, the high culture up to the nineteenth century. A dynamic actualisation of the notion of culture is, however, essential in cultural education. It is necessary not to present a fixed 'cannon', but to use the pupil's realm of experience as a starting point. Introduction to modern-day visual art and music is essential in order to be able to enter into dialogue with them.

15.(b) The teacher certainly does not lack possibilities and opportunities to participate in cultural manifestations, but the initiatives are much too *ad hoc* and fragmented to produce a lasting effect. A more integral approach to culture in schools is necessary. Art and culture offer a rich source of inspiration for *all* subjects in education. For history and languages, this is logical. But also in subjects such as geography, attention to the cultural-historic landscape values can enliven the lesson material. This equally applies to a subject such as mathematics, where for example the use of the golden section by the Greeks and the Renaissance architects shows students the usefulness of geometry and numbers. For this reason it seems right for the time being to adopt cultural education as a transdisciplinary final attainment level.

In the Netherlands, State Secretary Van der Ploeg proposes to put together a guide to 'Art and Cultural Heritage in Education' in which teachers, artists, students and parents are invited to show in the most beautiful and illustrative way how the arts and cultural heritage can enliven teaching materials.[37]

[37] *Cultuur als confrontatie, uitgangspunten voor het cultuurbeleid 2001–2004*, n. 34 above, 50.

15.(c) It is important that culture becomes a valued leisure activity for young people. Through institutional promotion, for instance, theatre can occupy a higher place on the list of possibilities for leisure activity. Another way to make young people enthusiastic is to get them actively involved. Research confirms that a mutual interplay takes place between active and receptive participation: those who practice an artistic activity themselves are more insistent and in favour of passive enjoyment of similar art.[38]

15.(d) An important finding is that cultural participation itself decreases considerably once teachers and parental supervision has ceased, as soon as young people become in charge of their own free time.[39] It could possibly be a solution to let children attend theatre or museums not just from secondary school onwards, but to encourage them as early as the fourth year of primary school to visit a theatre or museum at least once per year. This way, they become familiar with culture and the chance increases that they will continue to seek out culture beyond their school years. A greater harmonisation of part-time art education and standard (daytime) education also offers crucial opportunities. However, lesson plans do not have to be detailed minimum plans so that there is little flexibility (e.g. only classical dance and no modern dance forms) and with the result that its place is unclear in the realm of education, especially as far as the objectives or to learn to discover and understand art.

15.(e) In many Member States of the Union, there is especially urgent need for structural agreements between the Minister of Culture and the Minister of Education to make structured cooperation between schools and cultural institutions possible, given the organisational and budgetary consequences.

A progress report at the European level will have to continue to closely examine the mutual reciprocity between culture and education.

CHARLES L. GLENN

Arts Education as Discipline and as Source of Meaning

In the normal course of policy discussion, we might ask first, 'Should the arts be included in the required curriculum of schools?' and then go on to ask, 'What sort of arts education should be provided?' You will see at once that such an approach doesn't work; we must have a clear idea of the content and the approach of arts education before we can reasonably form a judgment about whether it should be made a required subject for all pupils.

That the arts should appropriately be included in the education of those pupils who have a special talent and interest will, I think, be accepted by everyone. Good educational systems and good schools provide room for the cultivation of special interests, and the arts – among which we may include music, visual arts, dance and theatre – surely deserve a pre-eminent place among the interests that are worthy of pursuit. Similarly, we may accept that certain schools place a special emphasis on one or another of the arts, either to develop a high level of competence with the possibility of a subsequent career, or to present the core academic curriculum in a form that will be especially attractive to students who might otherwise be indifferent to it. Thus we have, in the United States, a certain number of elementary 'magnet schools' that use the arts as a vehicle for teaching across the curriculum, as well as some specialized art-oriented schools at the secondary and post-secondary levels. Of course, the latter have long been well-represented in Europe.

The fundamental policy question, however, is the role of the arts in the required curriculum.[1] Should schools be required to make room for the arts in their crowded programmes, and should pupils with no particular interest in the arts be required to study or practice them? If so, what should be the basis for that requirement, and what could we hope that it would accomplish? Is there a way of understanding the

[1] Let us stipulate that by 'the arts' we mean, for the purpose of this discussion, music and visual arts and dance and lyric poetry in forms that rise above popular entertainment, but not literature (including theatre) in general, since these are an inseparable part of the study of any country's language and history.

Jan De Groof, Chantal De Smet and Hilde Penneman (eds.), Art meets Law in Education, 41–51.

role of the arts in education which is sufficiently compelling to argue for their inclusion as a required aspect of the education of all pupils?

In the educational standards adopted in the United States, there is a tendency to attribute to the study of art in schools the function of providing or eliciting 'meaning.' The *1997 Arts Education Assessment Framework* specifies, for example, that by the last year of secondary school pupils should be able to 'place varied and thoughtful personal comments within a compound critical process, with conscious engagement in criticism by explaining meaning; identifying, describing, recognizing critical models; and forming belief systems.' Apart from the obscurity of the prose and the evident difficulty of using such a statement as the basis for actual assessment of student achievement, the reader is – or should be – brought up short by the last phrase, 'forming belief systems.' Is that what mandatory programmes for the arts in schools should seek to accomplish?

The recommendation that public schools promote 'forming belief systems' raises many difficult issues that the authors of the arts standards have not confronted. Will any belief system that students may form be acceptable to the school – and the government that sets the standards – or should art teachers be seeking to direct them toward particular belief systems? In the United States, there are no laws restricting the expression of racist or sexist opinions (unless they are 'fighting words') or requiring that schools cultivate particular values in their pupils, as is sometimes the case in Europe. But already by the eighth grade, according to the arts assessment framework, American pupils should 'use different responses to works of art and design to form, confirm, or change a personal belief system.'[2]

In the arts standards of my own state of Massachusetts, this is described as involving pupils in 'the task of making personal statements about the world and the human condition'. All pupils are expected to use dance, music, theatre, or the visual arts to 'create and/or perform works that show a point of view about social and personal issues'. What is wrong with that? you might ask. After all, as the (advisory) *National Standards for Arts Education* point out, 'All peoples, everywhere, have an abiding need for meaning – to connect time and space, experience and event, body and spirit, intellect and emotion. People create art to make these connections, to explore the otherwise inexpressible.' That is certainly part of what art 'does', and what religion does, and what all manner of rituals and philosophies do. We might well question, though, whether that is a good starting-point for thinking about the role of the arts in schools, whether that entry-point is healthy either for the pupils or for the arts. And we might also question whether, in a free society, public schools should be seeking to modify the personal beliefs of their pupils, including their religious convictions.

Art may indeed often have the effect of stimulating profound reflections, or awakening ideas which are otherwise inexpressible. Is that because the composer,

2 National Assessment Government Board, *1997 Arts Education Assessment Framework*, Washington, DC: US Department of Education (<www.nagb.org>).

the painter, the poet has deliberately set out to convince us of something, to persuade us by some message? It is possible, but not likely. Clever propaganda and seductive advertising seldom rise to the level of art that lasts and gives the deepest pleasure. No, we are deeply moved or awakened to joy by a work of art that says to us, simply, 'Here I am!' Something that the artist has loved, or hated, or worshiped, or desired to celebrate, stirs a response in us that may be entirely different from the 'message' that the artist had in mind. Much of the world's great art, almost all of it before Western modernity, is religious in intention, but I do not have to be an animist or a Buddhist or a Christian in the Orthodox tradition to find it stirring. Great art, and even good art, is seldom programmatic or easily reducible to a 'message.'

No, if we want schools to give their pupils some skill in communicating ideas – meanings – we had better start with the long apprenticeship to writing simple expository prose. Teachers can critique the expository writing of their pupils for its use of solid evidence and sound arguments in a far more precise way than they can critique the 'meaning' of what those pupils seek to express in music, dance, or painting. Surely it is the business of schools to ensure above all that pupils can think straight and express their thoughts in a way that leaves no uncertainty about their intentions. Why should schools encourage children and youth to communicate vaguely-formulated emotions in the guise of expressive 'meanings', before they have learned to express themselves accurately in their native language? It might be excellent therapy, but is it education?

But aren't graphic art, dance, music precisely how the 'creativity' of pupils can best be expressed? And shouldn't schools be encouraging their pupils to be creative? Yes and no. Of course any good teacher attempts to show her pupils how to find new ways to solve problems old and new, to express ideas in fresh and convincing ways. Schooling, in our culture at least, is not primarily about learning to imitate set models, but neither is it about self-expression.

It is not creative problem-solving or creative expression that I would warn against, but the Romantic exaltation of creativity itself as the value that trumps all others. The artist or poet 'inventing himself', possessing an inside track to ultimate truth, and justified in his rejection of the accumulated wisdom and social conventions of countless generations, is in some ways an attractive figure, but not a model for universal schooling. 'Throwing off of the yoke of both Christian and classical discipline in the name of temperament is the essential aspect of the movement in favor of original genius',[3] but it is striking to reflect how little of the greatest art is the expression of temperament. Wordsworth's 'emotion recollected in tranquillity' is something very different from an effusion of feelings or poorly-formulated opinions.

The democratization of the idea that the artist has a lonely destiny of alienation from the stifling demands of bourgeois society has given us a flood of banal self-dramatization and self-invention that leads many youth to believe that finding new

3 Irving Babbitt, *Rousseau and Romanticism* [1919] (Austin: University of Texas Press, 1977) 49.

parts of their bodies to pierce is the height of creativity. The American critic Irving Babbitt pointed out eighty years ago that

> the very heart of the classical message, one cannot repeat too often, is that one should aim first of all not to be original, but to be human, and that to be human one needs to look up to a sound model and imitate it. ... Genuine culture is difficult and disciplinary. ... It is easier to be a genius on Rousseauistic lines than to be a man on the terms imposed by the classicist.[4]

We should not be put off by the word 'imitate'. The form of imitation called for here is not slavish copying, but adaptation, modification, creative rethinking of a model that is worthy to be imitated. The historian Robert Wilken tells us that he enjoys listening, on the radio, to

> interviews with famous and not-so-famous jazz pianists, saxophonists, drummers, trumpeters, etc., and I am regularly struck by how they speak with such respect of teachers and masters, and how to a person they learned to play the piano by first playing in someone else's style or learned to blow the trumpet by imitating Louis Armstrong or someone else. Similarly, one is impressed with how often a performer like folk singer Jean Redpath speaks about tradition as the necessary condition for making and singing folk music. How often we are admonished not to let the old traditions be forgotten. Why? Surely not for historical or archaeological reasons, but because musicians, like painters and writers and sculptors, know in their fingertips or vocal chords or ears that imitation is the way to excellence and originality.[5]

We owe it to our children, and to our pupils, to expose them to the best that has been thought or written, painted, composed, danced, sculpted, or otherwise expressed, so that they will have the means and the inspiration to find their own way – if that is their gift and their desire – of making it fresh and new. Creativity is Mozart rethinking Haydn, and Beethoven rethinking Mozart. But the meaning of creativity has changed in our own time, and not for the better; it has been 'removed from the realm of achievement and applied to another realm entirely. What it means now is an attitude about the self and it belongs not to aesthetics but to pop psychology'.[6] And so schools – at least in the United States – commonly claim that they will stimulate the creativity of our children, while we might prefer that they teach them to spell correctly or to draw accurately or to play an instrument, so that our children will be capable of meaningful creativity as they choose to express it.

But teaching those skills is hard work with often-resistant material. We can understand why art teachers often prefer to stress the fun of creative play and

4 *Ibid.*, 62–3.

5 Robert Wilken, *Remembering the Christian Past (*Grand Rapids: Eerdmans, 1993), 89.

6 Ronald Berman,' Art versus the Arts', in *Public Policy and the Aesthetic Interest*, eds Ralph A. Smith and Ronald Berman (Urbana: University of Illinois Press, 1992), 109.

neglect the discipline that would serve as the basis for genuine creativity later on. The fact is that genuine creativity in any of the arts is not naive self-expression but the result of years of dedication to developing technical skill, skill matured by experience of life until the artist or poet has something worthwhile to express. It can be embarrassing for the admirer of a distinguished poet like Yeats to read his early poems, and Yeats himself insisted that writing poetry that seems effortless is hard work, perhaps two or three lines a day, not a spontaneous effusion.

I said, 'A line will take us hours maybe;
Yet if it does not seem a moment's thought,
Our stitching and unstitching has been naught.
Better go down upon your marrow-bones
And scrub a kitchen pavement, or break stones
Like an old pauper, in all kinds of weather;
For to articulate sweet sounds together
Is to work harder than all these ...'
("Adam's Curze" from *In the Seven Woods*, 1904)

Mozart's father didn't tell young Amadeus to be creative – he taught him to play the harpsichord!

No, the case for art in schools should not be made on the basis that it will make every child creative, or give access to higher forms of meaning than can be expressed and understood in other ways. That those effects may follow for some pupils, even for most, would be an excellent thing, just as it would be fine if every pupil grew into an adult with deep spiritual discernment, but neither is the primary business of schools. Giving all pupils in schools an experience of the arts should be justified on the more convincing basis that, rightly understood, they offer fundamentally educational benefits that no other study can promote to the same extent and, in consequence, are an irreplaceable aspect of a good curriculum.

Art as disciplined attention

I have mentioned how schools may seek to teach the disciplines of writing clear and persuasive prose, of drawing accurately, of producing pleasing sounds from a musical instrument. We might add the art of moving one's body and holding it still in purposeful and expressive ways. All this can and should be taught in school to the limit of each pupil's ability. But I will argue that there is a discipline prior to all these, one which is less familiar yet fundamental. One of the primary functions of the arts in education, from which several secondary functions derive, is the training of *the discipline of attention.*

The schoolteacher and philosopher Simone Weil suggested that 'the development of the faculty of attention forms the real object and almost the sole interest of studies'.[7] While we might reject her apparent dismissal of the content of the curriculum, she points us to an inner disposition without which any amount of knowledge and any panoply of skills, are finally useless. Similarly, Iris Murdoch stressed the ethical centrality of this sort of attention, writing that

> the idea of a patient, loving regard, directed upon a person, a thing, a situation, presents the will not as unimpeded movement but as something very much more like 'obedience.' ... The task of attention goes on all the time and at apparently empty and everyday moments we are 'looking', making those little peering efforts of imagination which have such important cumulative results.[8]

Surely there is nothing more important to teach children, in this distracted age of media saturation, than to *pay attention* to something which is worth that tribute. How difficult children find it to give their full attention to anything that is not ceaselessly changing, to look at something or work at something or think about something for many minutes, much less for hours! But without such sustained attention, they can never rise above the trivial and mediocre.

In giving real attention to a piece of music or to a painting, we quiet the ceaseless babble of messages – commercial, political, social, erotic – that bombard all our waking hours. 'People may be brought to watch and to listen with increasing wide-awakeness, attentiveness, and care,' Maxine Greene has written, 'and they may be brought to discover multiple ways of looking at blackbirds and whales and riverbanks and city streets, looking at things as if they might be otherwise than they are. If this occurs, they will have learned how to move into the artistic-aesthetic domain; and they may have come closer to discovering how to be free.' Disciplined attention may be learned, and exercised, with many different objects – certainly it is part of the method of science – but art is its most privileged sphere. Unlike material presented in the other school subjects, which always points beyond itself to some broader field of knowledge or practice, the piece of music or sculpture is contemplated initially and most fundamentally for its own sake alone. 'This mode of attending, of qualitative perceiving, is fundamental to aesthetic literacy.'[9]

Attention is costly, though, as we can see by the verbs that different languages associate with it. English-speakers 'pay' attention, the French and Spanish more cautiously 'lend' it (*prêter attention, prestar atención*), and the Dutch and Germans 'give' their attention (*aandacht, Aufmerksamkeit schenken*). Scandinavians are even more emphatic: Danes 'bestow' attention (*opmærksom skænke*), using a word which conveys a high sense of giving, rather like the Spanish *entregar*, while Swedes 'devote' attention (*uppmärksamhet ägna*). I am told that, in Polish, one

7 Simone Weil, 'Reflections on the Right Use of School Studies with a View to the Love of God', in *Waiting for God*, transl. Emma Craufurd (New York: Harper and Row, 1973), 105.

8 Iris Murdoch, *The Sovereignty of Good* (London: Routledge, 1991), 40, 43.

9 Maxine Greene, 'Aesthetic Literacy', in *Aesthetics and Arts Education*, eds Ralph A. Smith and Alan Simpson (Urbana: University of Illinois Press, 1991), 159–60, 153.

sacrifices attention. In each case, attention is understood to be something valuable, to be exercised with deliberate intent, unlike clicking aimlessly through television channels or gazing idly out the window of a train.

Simone Weil described attention as consisting 'of suspending our thought, leaving it detached, empty, and ready to be penetrated by the object; it means holding in our minds, within reach of this thought, but on a lower level and not in contact with it, the diverse knowledge which we have acquired which we are forced to make use of'.[10]

John Dewey also emphasized the 'diverse knowledge' that cannot be suppressed when we give our attention to something new, even when we are engaged in an act of artistic creativity. 'The painter,' he wrote, 'did not approach the scene with an empty mind, but with a background of experiences long ago funded into capacities and likes, or with a commotion due to more recent experiences. He comes with a mind waiting, patient, willing to be impressed and yet not without bias and tendency in vision.'[11] In other words, giving our attention to what is before us requires a freshness of perception and an openness to the uniqueness of the experience, but it also draws upon what we have experienced before, including what we have thought about and the cultural tradition into which we have been inducted.

This is why it is important that schoolchildren be exposed to the heritage of great art and music. Of course there is no harm in kindergartners scribbling their pictures or improvising their music, but the developing minds of older children are not blank slates to be written upon in art class any more than at other times. Disciplined attention requires not leaping immediately to whatever association a work of art may suggest, as silly people do. We learn to think about art and – so far as in us lies – to create art ourselves by being alert to what accomplished artists are doing, and have done.

This requires that those who teach, and those who prescribe curriculum, not lack the courage to shape the taste of pupils by praising what has been well done and pointing out the weakness of what has not. There is a curious hesitation among educators today to do so; my colleague David Steiner refers to this as a 'flight from judgment'. While this is manifest in how a whole range of subjects are approached, it may have had its first beginnings in the treatment of art in our wider culture. Shaw tells us that 'a sympathetic observer of the European arts scene in the early 1970s discerned "a phobic caution" about making any attempt to suggest that one work of art might be better than others.'[12]

Using the art of the past as a way to illustrate social attitudes or developments, as commonly occurs in schools, is of course entirely legitimate, but not if this has the result of begging the question of whether some examples are of consummate quality and others mediocre. Educators used to know (how have they forgotten?)

[10] Weil, 'Reflections on the Right Use of School Studies', n. 7 above, 111.

[11] John Dewey, *Art as Experience*, in *The Later Works, 1925–1953*, volume 10: 1934, ed. Jo Ann Boydston (Carbondale, IL: Southern Illinois University Press, 1989), 93.

[12] Sir Roy Shaw, 'Democracy and Excellence', in *Public Policy and the Aesthetic Interest*, (eds.) Ralph A. Smith and Ronald Berman (Urbana: University of Illinois Press, 1992), 89.

that youth must learn to love what is good before they can learn to reason about it. Too often our schools, in their shyness about judgments of value, seem to reflect Jeremy Bentham's famous dictum that, 'Prejudice apart, the game of push-pin is of equal value with the arts and sciences of music and poetry. ... If the game of push-pin furnishes more pleasure, it is more valuable than either. Everybody can play at push-pin; poetry and music are relished only by a few.'[13] Daytime television dramas provide more pleasure than does Shakespeare to those whose tastes have not been educated.

Encouraging pupils to be 'creative' in whatever way seems best to them, without the disciplining of eye and ear, of hand and body, by learning from and imitating worthy models, is not real education. Not only does it fail to teach much that would be valuable to learn, but unfortunately it also teaches pernicious lessons about the significance of effort and of attention.

Too often, Laura Chapman has pointed out, 'we treat art as if it had no content worthy of study in its own right, as if art had no history, no context of meaning beyond that which one can discover oneself through making art or through exposure to individuals whose knowledge of art is presumed lo be trustworthy because they are called artists. The ethical question is whether we believe that the self-proclaimed truths of artists are an adequate basis for education.'[14] No, we do not.

Education in and through the arts is the best way above all to teach the lesson of careful, respectful attention to what is *there*. It can do so, however, only if it is not trivialized by an inappropriate emphasis on 'meaning'. We should not be surprised that art is being asked to bear this burden for which it is so unsuited. A central concern of post-modern societies is somehow to invent 'meaning' no longer available to many of our contemporaries from tradition or faith.[15] The widespread secularization of our educational systems, the unwillingness of many educators to make judgments about truth, about behavior, about quality, has left a vacuum which some hope to fill with meanings that students create for themselves. This is an abdication of the responsibility of adults to guide the young who are placed in their charge;we are reminded of Plato's description of the 'democratic' condition in which the teacher fawns on his pupils, while the pupils have no respect for their teacher (*The Republic* 563a).

To learn to see what an artist is doing in a painting, and something of how she is doing it, and to try one's own hand at producing the same effect, however imperfectly, requires long and close attention and teaches skills that – as Simone Weil contends – are fundamental to a life well-lived. To pay sufficient attention to really *hear* a piece of music, not as a background for other activities but in the foreground

13 *Ibid.*, 88–9.

14 Laura Chapman, 'Arts Education as a Political Issue: The Federal Legacy', in *Public Policy and the Aesthetic Interest*, (eds) Ralph A. Smith and Ronald Berman (Urbana: University of Illinois Press, 1992), 132.

15 See the discussion by Ronald Inglehart, *Modernization and Postmodernization: Cultural, Economic, and Political Change in 43 Societies* (Princeton University Press, 1997).

of one's attention, and then to hear it again and again with the score in hand, and then to learn to play some part of it, is an education in rationality and in character as well as in music. To observe closely how a dancer or an actor creates an effect, the muscular disciplines that must seem effortless, and then to set out to acquire the same intelligent discipline, is education indeed. The skills and the attitudes so learned are fundamentally similar to those needed by the scientist, the statesman, the successful merchant or manufacturer, the effective parent, the good citizen, even by the attentive friend.

The *National Standards for Arts in Education* in the United States represent an unhappy marriage of sensible advice with grandiose claims. Students, the *Standards* claim, will 'develop intuition, reasoning, imagination, and dexterity into unique forms of expression and communication'. Why did the committee that wrote this document believe it was necessary to add 'unique' to an otherwise satisfactory formulation? Of course, every human being is ultimately unique in some sense, and no educational system can or should suppress that uniqueness, but it is surely the primary responsibility of schools to develop competence and understanding and broad cultural knowledge, characteristics that we want every pupil to acquire. Their uniqueness will develop of itself, and all the more if they do acquire real competence and self-discipline. If they do not acquire these virtues, their uniqueness will bring little credit to themselves or benefit to society.

Goethe warned long ago that 'anything that emancipates the spirit without a corresponding growth in self-mastery is pernicious,' and a contemporary art educator has argued – I believe correctly – that 'the good of aesthetic education is the habits it inculcates'.[16] Habits not in the sense of dull routine, but in Aristotle's sense of a settled disposition to do what is appropriate in every situation. The relationship of a well-trained and responsible artist to his work is profoundly *ethical*, and we can hope, through good education in the arts, to give pupils a glimpse and an experience such ethically responsible thinking and creation. And this is another way of saying that they learn to pay, to loan, to give, even to sacrifice, *attention*.

In one of their better moments, the American *Standards* stress that the arts should be taken as seriously in schools as the more conventionally 'academic' subjects.

One of the substantial advantages offered by this comprehensive set of arts standards is that they combat the uninformed idea that the arts are an 'academically soft' area of study. People unfamiliar with the arts often mistakenly believe that excellence and quality are merely matters of opinion ('I know what I like'), and that one opinion is as good as another. The Standards say that the arts have 'academic' standing. They say there is such a thing as achievement, that knowledge and skills matter, and that mere willing participation is not the same thing as education. They affirm that discipline and rigor are the road to achievement.[17]

[16] E. F. Kaelin, 'Why Teach Art in the Public Schools?' in *Aesthetics and Arts Education*, (eds) Ralph A. Smith and Alan Simpson (Urbana: University of Illinois Press, 1991), 166.

[17] *National Standards for Arts Education: What Every Young American Should Know and Be Able to Do in the Arts.*

Art in school is not a matter of messing around with paint for a relaxing hour, but of acquiring a vocabulary, an historical context, a discipline of thought, of planning and of execution. Pupils should be able to communicate proficiently in at least one art form, including the ability to define and solve artistic problems with insight, reason, and technical proficiency. They should be able to develop and present basic analyses of works of art from structural, historical, and cultural perspectives, and from combinations of those perspectives. This includes the ability to understand and evaluate work in the various arts disciplines. They should have an informed acquaintance with exemplary works of art from a variety of cultures and historical periods, and a basic understanding of historical development in the arts disciplines, across the arts as a whole, and within cultures.

This is worlds away from the view popular among arts educators in the 1970s – and perhaps still among many today – that their role as teachers is 'to free the individual so that he may discover his inner self and nurture his individual ability to search for, find, and apply truths in relation to himself'.[18] No doubt it is tempting for the educator to see himself as a sort of guru to the young, a Jean-Jacques nurturing Emile to reject the values of bourgeois society. As religion lost credibility in elite circles in the nineteenth century, art took its place, with great art museums as temples of the new faith. 'The present age', wrote Jacques Barzun a generation ago, 'assumes without question that man's loftiest mode of expression is art.'[19] No doubt many individuals today continue to put their faith in art as a system of belief and a means to salvation, but it is not the business of the schools to promote such beliefs. Surely it is enough if schools can communicate to children and to youth the joys and the deepening of experience available when we give our attention to a work of art, or when we come to understand how it has been created and its historical resonance, or when we participate in that history in a small way by acquiring some measure of the discipline of a painter, a musician, a dancer, an actor, a poet, a sculptor. Surely that is enough, and a very great deal, without asking art education to provide meaning or claiming to enable each child to create something uniquely valuable and significant.

Rightly understood, the study of art in its various forms can play an important part in education, as a discipline of attention, of historical understanding, and of reasoned analysis. The practice of art also can have a place within the program of the school, offering an apprenticeship to careful effort and persistence in doing something well. For some pupils, the practice of art may be their first experience of real success in school, and may give them heart to approach other subjects with the same determination and even anticipation of pleasure in doing something well.

[18] From *Synaesthetic Education*, a 1971 book by Michael F. Andrews, quoted by Samuel Lipman, 'The NEA: Looking Back and Looking Ahead', in *Public Policy and the Aesthetic Interest*, eds by Ralph A. Smith and Ronald Berman (Urbana: University of Illinois Press, 1992), 172.

[19] Jacques Barzun, *The Use and Abuse of Art* (Princeton University Press, 1974), 39.

But the rightful place of art in the curriculum should not be an occasion for the colonization of schools by the Romantic notion of art as the source of ultimate meaning. The art teacher should not give in to the temptation to see herself as a spiritual guide on the pupil's journey of self-discovery, nor should the pupil be encouraged to think that self-expression ranks higher, in the work of the school, than the exercise of critical judgment. John Keats, one of my favorite lyric poets, was wrong: Beauty is not Truth, nor is it moral virtue. Helen of Troy, someone has noted, was beautiful, but she was not true!

In practice, Irving Babbitt pointed out, the identification of beauty with truth rests both on a fluid and deceptive emotionalism. Were we to take art as a moral guide, we would soon find ourselves in the situation described by Plato in books 2 and 3 of *The Republic*, compelled to ban all art that does not teach our preferred message. Of course art can and often does communicate moral messages – good and bad – and schools should help pupils to evaluate those messages, but it is no favor to art to make it carry the burden of being an ethical system or a salvation religion. Let art be art, and let schoolchildren be exposed to as much of it as possible, let it be part of the discipline by which they are shaped into responsible and perceptive adults.

The ultimate product of an education in the arts, it has been wisely suggested, is not the creation of amateurish works of art but 'the development of the disposition to interpret artworks properly and to appreciate artistic excellence'.[20] We would only add that it should contribute as well to the broader disposition to approach all of life with critical intelligence and to appreciate what is worthy of praise in any domain. What more justification would arts education require?

20 Ralph A. Smith, 'Policy for Arts Education: Whither the Schools, Whither the Public and Private Sectors?' in *Public Policy and the Aesthetic Interest*, eds Ralph A. Smith and Ronald Berman (Urbana: University of Illinois Press, 1992), 141.

GAVIN HENDERSON

Towards a Participatory Culture

That the century just past has encompassed the most remarkable changes for the human race is a more than obvious remark, and one that is usually made to highlight the advance of our civilisation – not least in respect of the revolution that is electronic communication. In music, as in other aspects of our culture, technology has brought us increasingly sophisticated means of *reproduction* – photography, recording, telecommunications and broadcasting. It is hard now to imagine a time when people could not just summon up the latest hit tune, not to mention a Beethoven Symphony, at the flick of a switch. Music is more *available* than at any previous time; the rise of inescapable muzak feeds the merchandising of goods and services at every turn, whilst Beethoven might well be pleased to know of the critical mass of superlative recordings that now exists as lasting testament to his every note. Before the advent of recording, if we wanted to hear a given work we would, in all probability, have to persuade friends to play it in piano arrangement, if we were unequal to the challenge ourselves. Perhaps a local brass band might tackle a version of their own or, on high days and holidays, a few favourites would be mixed with other eagerly awaited new works and selections, often in very reduced orchestrations at the seaside and spa. Demand for the new, as well as the favourite classic, was vigorous and choral societies eagerly awaited the latest oratorio from one of the many Victorian composers mostly long forgotten. In place of this sometimes haphazard and usually under-rehearsed tapestry of live performance, we now have racks and shelves of phenomenal recordings, establishing a *heritage* available to all. No one can doubt that this *is* an advance, but music has been transformed from something we make into something we take. In short, music has become a commodity.

As such, we in Europe are amongst the market leaders. Economic statistics are impressive – placing music and the music industry in the very forefront of fiscal wellbeing. The political tide has turned and, whilst we may well have cause to challenge the levels of investment currently committed to grass roots musical development, the sort of commitment now being expressed from within most Governments' thinking is far removed from a remark allegedly made by a senior government

Jan De Groof, Chantal De Smet and Hilde Penneman (eds.), Art meets Law in Education, 53–58.

adviser in Britain when the national curriculum debate on music back in 1988 was first being hatched when he said he 'didn't really know much about such hobbies'.

This is all very well and good, but something keeps recalling those hamfisted attempts at classical arrangements, and the social hubbub and banter around bandstands and pier pavilions ... the weekly choir practice, and bawdy ballads around the saloon bar piano, all of which was on its last legs by the time I was gripping warm ale as an underage *minor* in the backroom of my Brighton local. What *is* a vibrant memory is the excitement of playing in my first youth orchestra on the one hand, and the hot and sticky sense of engagement, as an art student, gathering on Eel Pie Island (on the Thames) for the emergence of a raw new band called the Rolling Stones. It didn't occur to me at the time that this highlighted the divergence that was being compounded on the one hand for publicly resourced access to classical music and the commercial investment and social attraction of pop music on the other. This fundamental separation of the means to music, and the underscoring of high and low in art, will be the serious legacy of the twentieth century. In each extreme the scope for us to participate in the making of music has been marginalised.

In such circumstances, the distinction between the worlds of professional performances, public participation and the role of music education was far less rigorous than it is today. The jobbing musician was less protected by union agreements and employment law, but the range of work engaged in was very much more various.

Super specialisation has brought virtuosic skills to the performance of period instrument work and to the testing demands of much contemporary music. To a student of the baroque flute at Dartington Summer School I once asked if she still found time to play the modern flute, 'No', she said, she never had as she felt it would detract from the ultimate skills she needed to play the baroque repertoire properly. Michael Vyner, on the other hand, once boasted – and quite rightly – that only his orchestra, the London Sinfonietta, was capable of doing justice to a particular new work. What hope, then, for music if it could now only be played through possession of such rare skills – and what of the rock music massaged and marketed through the huge investment of massive technical fit-ups, video production and media hype – what room for participation here?

If we look back at the provenance of many of music societies and clubs, we can recognise a motivation drawn from a desire for people to socialise, to share experience, to mix expert leadership and opportunity for brilliant performance with our inherent desire to engage directly in the spirit of making music. The development of arts centres and fine new halls has ushered in a new breed of professional administrators alongside a raft of regional support to impose strategies and cultural development plans which many will find quite bewildering. If we look back little more than twenty years, however, we can see how far support for the arts in general has grown, but the ownership of such endeavour has become increasingly politicised and idealised, often rejecting the grass roots activity of the societies and clubs that have for so long been a bedrock of a nation's musical life. Regional Arts Boards have grown up (in Britain) to have delegated national status and the danger is that they may lose sight of the voluntary organisations that once formed a key part of their portfolio of interests. This needs watching. City and local authorities are, of course, gradually evolving a new system of arts development but it would be a real tragedy if the small scale, occasional, and usually voluntary, organisation was to be lost in a process of 'hand-me-down'.

However much music may be sold for our consumption via headsets, its real strength lies in its means to bring one another together, to enable individual expression and generally motivate that sense of ritual and celebration that lies at the heart of human meeting and mating. It enables us to participate and contribute in a context less determined by a precise sense of winning and losing than is the case with sport for instance. In the personal doing it renders electronic reception as exciting as a kiss on the phone. We are musical beings, we are made with in-built vocal powers of pitch, volume and tone production, together with an innate sense of rhythm and balance. We may wonder at the extraordinary rise of many wonderful experiences under the generic banner of 'world music' – but the underlying attraction must surely be for a truly living culture in which all concerned feel a tactile sense in which they can take part, and are welcome to do so ... and how frustrating are the rows of fixed seating in our western auditoria for an audience which soon transforms from passive attendance through a compulsive desire to dance, clap and engage in the ritual. How these halls exemplify the specific distinction between the customer and the performer, as the architects and planners do all they can to compete with the armchair consumption of the digital hi-fi and home-delivered pizza. Little do they appreciate that the spirit of Shakespeare's Globe, the Georgian Playhouse, the eighteenth-century pleasure gardens, the classic Italian opera houses, the Victorian music halls, the Proms (both schools and BBC), and parks concerts (even in the absurdity of the English climate), all share a common factor of relative discomfort, far removed from the anaesthetised cocoon of the home, but driven more by the touch, feel and smell of live engagement, something so manifest in contemporary rock festivals and club life, but also prevalent in the attraction of other social extremes such as Glyndebourne, Garsington and the Royal Opera House Crush Bar in the UK and many similar examples throughout Europe.

So how does this all relate to music education? One could elaborate on the social values of music which have been so seriously side-stepped in the last twenty years or so, whilst tracking the rise of a youth culture so desperately in need of an alternative to vandalism, glue-sniffing and drugs on the one hand but expressing itself, sometimes vibrantly, via graffiti and rap on the other. It wants to be heard but finds little beyond the market salesmen to listen. There is much talk of late about the so-called 'Mozart Factor'; – wherein music can be compellingly demonstrated to enhance a child's cognitive powers of learning, memory, numeracy, co-ordination, confidence and ability to interact with others in circumstances far beyond strict musical confines. Maybe we should embrace Hegel's theory of how much the human experience tends towards the condition of music? In the eighties the market economy determined a eunuch climate of accountancy culture, to be followed in the nineties by a sequel of consultancy culture set in hot pursuit of the 'vision thing' – now as we turn the millennial corner may we at last recognise the potential of the artist's vision, and appreciate that little can match the purity of vision expressed in childhood. I am often drawn to Picasso's remark on looking at some children's artwork 'Ah', he said, 'when I was their age I could draw like Raphael – it has taken me all my life to draw like them.' He spoke at a time when children were less driven by a dependence on television and we must spare a thought for the boy, Bart, in the cult TV cartoon services 'The Simpsons', when his father, Homer, chastises him for watching TV instead of doing his homework – 'Why should I listen to you' asks Bart, 'when that set has given me so much more time than you ever have?' A far cry from Wagner's portrayal of the ancient city of Nuremberg in which the entire populace is engrossed in the quest for a fine new song and voice to match it ... with the venerable sage Hans Sachs declaring that, 'We ignore the arts at our peril.' Such scenarios are noted in the sense of a 'living culture' as opposed to a 'heritage culture' – it was a telling moment when the Department for National Heritage in Britain was retitled as it is today emphasising the once dirty world 'Culture' rather than 'Heritage'. It is surely something of a paradox that the very immediacy and ready access of recording and broadcasting has, through its commercial exploitation, ensnared a market fixation on the retrospective and collectable pop and classics – so easily analysed and repackaged by the accountants than ... dedicating its energy to the risky excitement and challenge of the new. For the new we must now depend upon subsidy and patronage, and within such support the artists are enticed into a protected world where the demand for innovation breeds its own surround of critical, bureaucratic and academic assessment, far removed from the will of public demand and a ready desire to participate.

Works of genius have undoubtedly emerged through this stage of patronage and our culture would be the poorer without them: but in the main the system has produced work that can best be described as 'interesting' rather than 'communicative'. Consider the nineteenth century and early twentieth century avant-garde – Beethoven, Berlioz, Liszt, Bruckner, Wagner, Mahler, early Schoenberg and Stravinsky, who came through despite the prevailing culture of their time and were therefore never sheltered from the need to communicate directly with their audiences. Consider the enduring power of their works and you have some idea of the potential new music might have now if the funding system did not favour innovation at the expense of communication. It is a fact of life that Germany subsidises its culture four times more per capita than we do in Britain, but this doesn't excuse us spending money on new music in the wrong way. More 'communicative' new music is performed to full houses in venues in Germany, but ironically this is not the direct result of German funding policies. This is the expression of German audiences defying their own arts funding system which is still primarily concerned with supporting the hard line avant-garde.

I believe we can take heart from this and recognise some shifts in our own culture. That will, in due course, challenge the policies of much of artistic bureaucracy.

Children have begun to compose – just as they have drawn the pictures which Picasso so admired. The adherence to ultra complexity, sophistication and super-intellectualisation has no place in the early striving of such youthful expression. The composers who have led such work have come to respect the first imperative of communication and in many cases have found much stimulation for their own work. The composer Virgil Thomson was once asked for his opinion on electronic music. 'Oh', he said as rapier response 'electronic music is in its infancy, and all you can do is coo at it'. Well, now it has grown up to meet a Media Menopause in which the new digital age, internet and interactive exchanges have ushered in a global culture of participatory potential which a latter day Hans Sachs would surely once again tell us to ignore at our peril. Already our children have appetite and skills in this world which, I suspect, far exceed those of many of us gathered here today. I speak for myself and apologise to those who would exclude themselves from such accusation… but to applaud the notion of a new sense of interpersonal creative energy as stimulated by the world-wide web.

But let us return here to the concert hall and the oft discussed need to build the audience of tomorrow, how shall we find the new generation of music lovers to fill these very seats which so frustrate the lovers of world music events? Some twenty years ago, the marketing initiatives of orchestras and opera companies in Britain began to derive outreach schemes and education programmes to interest young people in the work of their respective organisations. Composers would go out to schools and talk about their music, and they soon devised programmes for the children to take part in; the results were often introduced to concerts as preludes to the main programme and then whole events grew from such work – notably for instance the community operas at Glyndebourne… not a venue conspicuous for its need to fill empty seats. The Royal Opera could be found in Arndale Shopping centres and the Royal Ballet took on the toughs of a desperate estate in Bristol, whilst the ENO's Bayliss programme made the Dolphin Opera in Plymouth from which the BBC culled a documentary that should be part of a compulsory induction programme for every Minister for Home Affairs, and to every Education Minister, as demonstration of a means to combat truency. Work which was initially a marketing side-show to an orchestra's or company's main cut and thrust has now become part of the core. Great concerts will not be replaced, but another exciting and stimulating role has emerged as conduit for people of all ages, but children in particular, to once again take ownership of their place in music and make it for themselves.

We could easily be subsumed in the needs of an established educational infrastructure, like the boy with his finger in the dyke. But that is the proper responsibility of core funding from the Education Authority, a responsibility which our Government in Britain has at last demonstrated a will to address. Our job is to address that strange and neglected pathway between the worlds of formal education and of public performance by the established arts organisations. Often the most inspiring work is led by an individual, a maverick perhaps. These are people not often found in an institutional context but who may well be encouraged into partnerships.

We also need to be looking at needs for training the animateurs of tomorrow and supporting partnerships to provide in-service training and encouragement for the many teachers who have struggled for so long at the margins of a school's preoccupation.

Returning to my opening remarks about the versatility of musicians in the days before ultra specialisation and the intensive market of recording and broadcasting. It seems clear that the musician of tomorrow, indeed today, must now embrace many skills. Bernard Shaw remarked: 'those who can, *do*, and those who can't, *teach*'. This is a differential that will increasingly vanish. I have been anxious, in setting the new mission for Trinity College of Music, that our policy of 'Music Plus' should encourage all students to think of a career that will combine a range of opportunities ... in which community music will mean much more than taking a few concerts into schools. The clubs and societies will have much scope to join in securing a tapestry of work for indiginous musical leadership. It is a process that is happening at all levels – as we can see from the new arrangements for players in the London Symphony Orchestra to undertake teaching and animateur work for as much as 50 per cent of their time; the planning – for a new music centre in Gateshead (in the north of England) brings community music making and education together with a Northern Sinfonia that will have teacher-players also working in conjunction with folkworks and a specific culture based on participation.

It is the spirit of a culture based on everyone's ability to feel a sense of being a part of the work that gave rise to, and sustained much of, what we now attend and listen to as our Heritage. The context in which so much great art has been made is far from the market place – and belongs to a world of ritual and celebration, both secular and sacred ... a word curiously re-emerging 'on-line' and in the new youthful underground of club culture. The avant garde of the twentieth century is the new establishment, whilst the cutting edge has become a domain in which the popular and accessible are seen as challenging the old order ... a world in which people truly want the art of the moment.

INGO RICHTER

Drawing the Teacher as a Nude: The Freedom of the Arts in the Classroom

Recently the following case happened in a small German town; too bad that it was not brought to the courts. The wall of a school-building (it was a *Gymnasium*) was to be decorated with a fresco. This decision was reached by the teachers' conference with the participation of the students and the parents; the city-council had approved. The students of the upper classes were asked to do the fresco themselves. It was a large project and it looked like great fun. First drafts had to be made, and the school organised a competition. Every student was asked to submit a draft for the fresco. Anton, a 17-year-old, came up with a nude. It was an excellent drawing, but it was obvious that the drawing represented the art teacher. It was not a malicious picture; on the contrary, it was flattering. The art teacher showed it to the director, however, and Anton was excluded from the competition and dismissed from the school. Students and parents protested, and he was readmitted after a couple of days.

1. Freedom of the Arts

The German Basic Law guarantees the freedom of the Arts in Article 5 III: 'Wissenschaft und Kunst, Forschung und Lehre sind frei.' The wording of the constitution is that the arts *are* free, unconditionally and without any reservation. But, what is art? Is the student's drawing a work of art, to be protected by the constitution?

There are some questions to ask and to answer:

(a) *Can a student's work be a work of art? Or is the freedom of the arts reserved for professionals?*

Certainly not. The constitution protects the creativity of everybody. It is a human right and not a privilege for professionals only. Therefore, without any doubt: a student's painting can be a work of art protected by the constitution.

Jan De Groof, Chantal De Smet and Hilde Penneman (eds.), Art meets Law in Education, 59–62.

(b) *Can a nude be a work of art?*

Of course, the naked human body has always been shown on paintings and modelled in sculptures. We cannot think of the history of art without nudes. Nevertheless, in all countries governments and courts have tried to ban pictures of the naked human body, using the obscenity argument. The recently ended twentieth century, for example, is full of court decisions in obscenity matters, particularly relating to films, of course. But, in our case obscenity was not an argument. What obscenity finally is might be unclear, but the naked human body as such cannot be obscene. Insofar as that point is concerned we can find a consensus in the jurisprudence.

(c) *Does the constitution ask for a certain quality?*

This is a very difficult question. If we say 'no', everything can be a work of art, if only somebody says so. If we say 'yes', the courts have the power to decide what art is. Finally only an artist can say what art is. The German courts tried to solve the dilemma, ruling that every serious undertaking to create a work of art should be protected by the constitution. But this definition is somewhat circular: 'Art is what seriously pretends to be art.' But, quality is not the question in our case. Nobody said that it was not a fine drawing. But, what is serious? Anton did not really mean to propose his nude for the fresco. It was provocative or fun, or both. He produced a work of art in drawing the nude, but his work was not seriously aimed at the purpose of the competition. This poses a kind of problem. Can we deny the protection of the constitution to a work of art if this work of art is not meant to fulfil the purpose of commission? Personally, I think not. Even under these conditions it has to be protected under the freedom of the arts.

2. The freedom of the arts within schools

It was not a public competition with free artists taking part, it was a competition of students within a school. The decoration of the wall was part of the educational programme of the school, it was a special matter of instruction. This raises the fundamental question, if constitutional rights are guaranteed in schools at all, or whether school is exempted from the constitutional rights because of its educatioal aims. If we put the question like this, it is easy to answer: yes, of course the constitution is also valid for the school and the students do not shed their individual rights on the threshold of the school as 'Tinker' put it. But, 'Tinker' does not solve our problem. In the US Supreme Court decision of the *Tinker* case, students wore black armbands in schools to protest against the Vietnam War and the Court gave them the protection of the First Amendment of the US Constitution, 'Freedom of speech'. But, this was not a decision on the instructions in schools. Wearing armbands on the occasion of school attendance is different from making use of free speech during the lessons. The parallel to our case would be if a student answers a teacher's question during the lesson and that he seeks the protection of free speech for his answer. He would get it. Freedom of expression also covers speech within the classroom, protects the students and what they say during the lessons. Their *answers* can be wrong and they can risk getting bad marks, but the *opinions* can never be wrong.

The same then should also be valid for the freedom of the arts. If art education is part of the educational programme and if students produce works of art in the classroom, they are protected by the freedom of the arts under the constitution.

But the student in our case missed the point. Instead of making a proposal for the fresco, he made a painting of his teacher as a nude. We resolved this problem before: even in this case the work of art should be protected by the constitution.

3. Limits of the Freedom of the Arts

(a) *Educational goals*

Schools always try to restrict individual rights, saying that their exercise was disruptive for the school or the educational process. I will not explore this in great detail, because it cannot be an argument in our case. The solution of this problem in German constitutional law is that restrictions of constitutional rights for educational reasons have to be laid down in the law. Therefore we find restrictions of the freedom of the press, the freedom of assembly and the freedom of association in the school laws: but there are no restrictions of the freedom of the arts. So, if the nude painting were a disruption of the educational process or a danger for the educational goals, without any legal basis there could not be any sanction against the students. But in fact the painting was not a danger for the educational process. A gifted teacher would have said: 'Wonderful, thank you. Too bad that we cannot put it on the wall', instead of running to the headmaster.

(b) *Personality rights*

But the personality rights of teachers who are not so gifted also have to be protected, and this is a well-known conflict. A painter paints somebody who feels offended by the picture. A writer barely disguises his victim, who claims that it is libellous and asks for a book ban or for compensation. The most famous conflict between the freedom of the arts and personality rights in Germany was the *Mephisto* Case. You will all know the story because it became a famous film by Karl Maria Brandauer in the 1980s. Klaus Mann, a son of Thomas Mann, had written a book on Gustav Gründgens, the famous actor and producer, director of the Prussian State Theatre in the 1930s and close friend of Hermann Göring and other notables of the Third Reich. Gustav Gründgens' adopted son tried to have the book banned after Gründgens' death and won, because his personality rights prevailed over the freedom of art, even after the death of the offended Gustav Gründgens.

Can the picture in our case be an insult of the teacher? The nude was said to be flattering to her. Can she nevertheless feel insulted? I think it is not so much a question of insult, but a question of privacy. There might be some people who might like to see the picture in public, even if it is a nude, but most people do not want to be exposed to the 'public eye', even if it is a positive picture. At least, it is their decision if they want to or not. In our case the student submitted the painting and made it public, even if this took place within the school. The other students could see it, the jurors saw it: it is the violation of privacy. As there is no prevailing interest of art in this case, as there was not an artistic, but a provocative motivation on the side of the student, the teacher's personality rights must win. An adequate reaction to this violation of personality rights would have been exclusion from the competition, or even some kind of extra work, such as drawing another ten nudes. Dismissal from the school was too harsh in this case. It was reversed for good reasons.

Education and the freedom of the arts. We do not find many cases in the jurisprudence, compared to the freedom of speech. Why is this so? Are words more dangerous than pictures? Or do the schools and the art teachers handle such cases with more calm and humour compared to teachers in the social sciences?

Creativity

CHRISTOPH WULF

Image and Imagination. Towards a Historical Anthropology of Images. Perspectives for Art Education

What is art? What is art education? What is the relation between art education and education in general? These are difficult questions to answer. I would like to suggest the following definition for art education: art education has to do with images and pictures; art education has to further the individual's creation and understanding of pictures and images. If we accept this definition, the question 'what is an image?' is of central importance for art education. From the standpoint of educational anthropology I would argue that art education has to do with all kinds of images, and not only with images which traditionally are part of art. Today such an enlargement of our understanding of art education is very important, since we can no longer clearly define what art is and where the boundaries between life, art and culture can be drawn. Therefore art education is education to deal with images, to create and understand them and to use their potential for the development of children and young persons.

If art education focuses on images, we cannot limit it to art. Before there was ever a societal subsystem called art, there were already images. Today there is a great variety of images. Among them there are images which belong to a history of the image before the age of art, where the images were in a close relationship with the sacred, for example in the case of cave images. There are perhaps also images which belong to a period after the age of art. We may see the beginning of this period related to the rise of technical and electronic reproduction of images and the destruction of their aura. In any case, the new media contribute to the overproduction of images today.

During many centuries the lack of images was criticised. Comenius spoke, for example, of children's thirst for images and of education's need to take this into consideration. This situation has changed. Rather than the lack of images, the problem is the flood of images in socialisation and education. Too many images may destroy the potential of the image, since they cancel each other out. Today there is almost a need for anaesthesia towards images, in order to avoid losing the capacity to perceive them and to remain sensitive towards them.

Jan De Groof, Chantal De Smet and Hilde Penneman (eds.), Art meets Law in Education, 65–76.

The German word 'Bilden' means to develop, to form, to shape, as well as to educate. Thus, 'Bildung' – education – is connected to the idea of forming. Let us say that to educate is to shape according to a mental picture or image – the German word for picture, 'das Bild', would confirm this association. But what exactly is a mental picture or image? For a long time, despite its relevance, educational science largely ignored the meaning of image. With the 'iconic turn', however, this appears to have changed. 'What is an image?' has at last become a fascinating question in cultural studies, and has also more recently become a focus for research in educational science. What is contained in the mental pictures one has of childhood, or in one's preconceived image of the gap between generations, of school or of the organisation of learning? For a long time the connection between sight, and the creation of images and inner pictures aroused little interest. Moreover, the relation between phylogenetic and ontological images, between collective and individual pictures or their sequence and structure, has been largely ignored. The question connects vision with image and fantasy, body with culture and history. How does an individual's imagination, his/her 'inner world of pictures', relate to a cultural picture-world or collective imagination? These questions point to the historical/cultural, pedagogical/anthropological foundations of upbringing and education and thus open the way to a whole new field of investigation in educational science.

Imagination, fantasy, the capacity to picture

Imagination is certainly one of the most mysterious of human faculties. It permeates all levels of life, manifests itself in many different ways, yet is tangible only in its concrete manifestations, and seems to defy clear definition. Imagination refers to the ability to picture objects in one's mind, even when the objects themselves are not there, in other words, the faculty of inner vision. It is first referred to as a concept in Plato's *Politeia*. In book 10 of *The Republic*, painting is defined as the imitation of 'an appearance as it appears'.[1] According to Aristotle, to fantasise is 'to visualise (*pro homaton gar esti ti poiesasthai*) like a memory artist chooses particular images.'[2] Fantasy is that which produces appearances (*phantasma*) within us. 'The Romans replaced the concept of 'phantasia' with 'imaginatio'. 'Imaginatio' refers to the active power of internalising pictures, of imagining. Fantasy and imagination signify the human ability to internalise outside images, in other words to transform the outside world into an inside world, as well as the faculty of creating and changing different origins and meanings for those internal picture-worlds.

In imagination, inside and outside worlds overlap. Both Maurice Merleau-Ponty and Jacques Lacan have emphasised the importance of this chiastic structure for perception and the creation of images. Any concept of vision that assumes a

1 *Pros to phainomenon, os phainetai.*

2 Aristotle's *De anima* III, 3.

self-identical object and an 'empty' seeing subject must fail. There is always already something in seeing

> which we can only approach by feeling for it with our vision. The things we look at, in fact we never get to see 'naked' because sight itself encloses them and dresses them with its own flesh ... Sight ... enfolds things visible, caresses them, then unites with them. As if there were a pre-established harmonious relationship between things and sight, indeed as if it already knew of them before it actually saw them, sight moves in its own hectic and imperious way, yet the sights it sees are not arbitrary – I do not peer into chaos, I see things – so that in the end, one can hardly tell whether one's vision or the things one sees hold the upper hand.[3]

Not only in vision does an overlap take place between one's sense-perception and the outside object that our sense perceives, but also in touch and hearing and above all in smell and taste.

Thus, human vision is not unconditional. On the one hand we see an anthropomorphous world that is on the basis of the physiological conditions in our head. On the other hand our vision is determined by historical, anthropological and cultural factors. Thus, for example, the invention and spread of writing has affected our sight to the extent that we really no longer see in the same way as in oral culture. Similarly, the new electronic era and the acceleration processes associated with it, are changing our perception. As research in Gestalt psychology has shown, imagination plays a part in the simplest of perception such as, for instance, complementary vision. The same can be said for one's cultural frame of reference which attributes meaning to the things one sees. All seeing is both made possible and limited by history and culture. It is therefore changeable, contingent and open to the future.

For Lacan, sight is rooted in the imaginary. He attributes imagination to a prelinguistic physical state, in which the individual is not yet aware of his/her own insufficiencies and limitations. On this view, imagination is rooted in the early stages of an individual's life, when at first the infant has such a strong sense of identification that it does not yet perceive the mother as 'different' from itself. The infant is fascinated by the physical wholeness of its mother's body which it perceives as a mirror of its own sense of completion and power. Yet this very experience of its mother's perfection soon leads the infant to the realisation of its own incompletion and dependency on others. There, too, in the experience of incompletion and finality, lie the origins of the sexual subject. For Lacan, the imaginary, with its world of pictures, preorders the symbolic world of language. Picking up on this view, Cornelius Castoriadis defines the relation between the two realms as follows:

> The imaginary needs the symbolic. Not only to 'express itself' (that goes without saying), but in order to exist at all, in order to become something more than merely virtual. The most elaborate of delusions, as well as the

3 Merleau-Ponty, M: *Le Visible et l'Invisible* (Paris, 1964) 193.

> most hidden and unclear fantasy consists in 'images', yet these themselves have a symbolic function, stand for something else. The symbolic of course equally depends on imagination (*capacité imaginaire*), for it relies on the ability to see in one thing another, or indeed to see one thing as another. Yet ultimately, imagination depends on the basic ability to visualise or reproduce things or relations (that are not now perceivable or perhaps never were). Therefore we shall speak of an original or radical imaginary, as the common root of actual imagination as well as of the symbolic. What we mean here is the most elementary ability to mentally picture an image.[4]

Despite major differences in his argument, Arnold Gehlen's attempt to locate imagination points in a similar direction:

> at the core of dream motion or at times of dense vegetative life, like in childhood or in relations between the sexes, wherever the powers of ripening life can be traced, there are indeed, in changing images, certain arch-fantasies of a pre-existing concept of life, which contain within themselves the tendency for an increased level of form and current. These are the manifestations of an immediate vital ideality, that is, within the substantial vegetans, a tendency towards higher quality and quantity – though one might question this distinction.[5]

Gehlen interprets fantasy as the projection of surplus drive. Yet might not fantasy pre-exist surplus drive in order for 'life drive to find satisfaction in its images'?[6] In any case Gehlen clearly links imagination to human incompletion, residual instinct and the gap between stimulation and reaction. Thus it is connected to human need, drive, motion and desire for satisfaction, though not to them alone. Human flexibility and openness-to-the-world confirm the need for cultural shaping. Imagination's part in this process is so central that one might justifiably refer to man as 'a fantasy-being as much as a rational being'.[7]

Despite differences in their points of view and arguments, Gehlen and Castoriades agree that the imaginary is a collective faculty through which society, culture as well as individuality, are revealed. Developing Merleau-Ponty's later work on the chiasmus between human body and perception, Jacques Lacan went on to show the extent to which the imaginary influences the everyday perception of any social subject.

Magic, representation, simulation

Pictures and images are always ambiguous. The suspicion that they originated long before the development of consciousness, out of fear of death or a fear of having to

4 Castoriades, C: *Gesellschaft als imaginäre Institution* (Frankfurt, 1984) 218.

5 Gehlen, A: *Der Mensch: Seine Natur und seine Stellung in der Welt* (Wiesbaden, 1978) 325.

6 Flügge, J: *Die Entfaltung der Anschauungskraft* (Heidelberg, 1963) 93.

7 Gehlen, A: *Der Mensch*, n. 5 above, 317.

die, is perhaps not too wide of the mark. Dietmar Kamper suggests that the purpose of images is to cover up the wound at the root of human existence. Yet this goal is unattainable: every attempt to conceal a memory is at the same time a reminder. Thus, all mental pictures are in essence 'sexual', even though their motive may be deeply religious. With Roland Barthes, we may call images 'death of the subject'.

> Through fear, picturing plays a central part in distraction from human desire. [...] It stands for original sin. At first, imagining serves to reassure the individual that regardless of uncertainties, its mother's voice will always be there. It accompanies us from the sacred to the banal. For indeed, reproduction is an important step in the overcoming of fear. The original image is supposed to get lost in imagining ... but it remains.[8]

From the point of view of cultural science there are three different kinds of image:

- image as magical presence;
- image as mimetic representation;
- image as technical simulation.

Of course there are many overlaps between these different kinds of image, yet it makes sense to distinguish them, for this allows for the identification of different, sometimes contradictory iconic characteristics.

Magical, cult, and sacred images date back to an era when images had not yet become works of art. Hans Belting considers these in his book *Likeness and Presence: History of the Image Before the Era of Art.*[9] However, he deals exclusively with presentational cult pictures since the end of the Antique age. Images that bestow the gods' magical presence we call divine figures or icons. These can be found, for instance, in archaic cultures. Early depictions of fertility goddesses engraved in clay or stone belong to this kind. In his well-acclaimed book, *The Anthropological Structure of the Imaginary* Gilbert Durand designs a cosmos of images, many of which are 'magical'.[10] He distinguishes an 'order of day' and an 'order of night', dedicating a section of the book to each category. The third section deals with images that stem from what he calls 'transcendental fantasy'. Durand's attempt to characterise and structure collective pictorial imagination highlights the fluidity of transitions from images as presence to images as representations. Philippe Seringe's study of symbols in art, religion and everyday life points in a similar direction.[11] We see the distinction between presence and representation

8 Kamper, D: 'Bild' in: Wulf, Ch. (ed): *Vom Menschen: Handbuch Historische Antropologie* (Weinheim, 1997), 592.

9 Belting, H: *Bild und Kult. Eine Geschichte des Bildes vor dem Zeitalter der Kunst* (München, 1991).

10 Durand, G: *L'imaginaire. Essai sur les sciences et la philosophie de l'image* (Paris, 1994).

11 Seringe, Ph: *Les Symboles. Dans l'art, dans les religions, et dans la vie de tous les jours* (Paris, 1985).

finally blur. Seringe provides a brief interpretation of animals pictured in imagination. From images of farmyard and domestic animals (such as bulls, cows, horses, donkeys, lambs, rams, goats, cats, dogs, rabbits) to other land animals (elephants, camels, etc.), the realm of the imaginary extends to birds and fish as well as plants (the Tree of Life, palm trees, cedar trees, oak; flowers, roses, lilies, lotus; cereal, fruit etc.). The imaginary also encompasses the cosmos and the elements with images of fire and light, of smoke, clouds and dew, water, earth, rock, caves and grottoes, air, sun and moon, etc. Images of constructions (palaces, houses, gardens, gates, sculptures) as well a more abstract things (names, numbers, spirals, labyrinths) also belong to the realm of the imaginary, highlighting time and again the 'in between' nature of images. Illustrating the world, turning it into pictures, images turn the world into a home for humans. For what could be more threatening than a world without images, where any image would be engulfed and destroyed by either darkness or blinding light?

Plato describes images as representations of things that they themselves are not. They show something, express or describe something, relate to something. In Plato's view, painters and poets do not, like God, create ideas or objects, they merly present the appearance of things. Painting and poetry are not limited to the artistic presentation of things, but rather to the artistic presentation of the appearances of things. Thus, it is not their business to portray ideas or truths, but to represent fantasies, semblances, and appearances as these appear. This explains why in principle the realm of painting and mimetic poetry is the already visible.[12] Here we are speaking of the images and illusions of creative mimesis, where the difference between the model and its representation is insignificant. The aim is not to create similarity but to show the semblance of an appearance.[13] For Plato, art and aesthetics constitute one realm, where the artist or poet is master. The artist cannot create being as such, and does not share the truth claim to which philosophy is bound, and which lies at the basis of the Politeia. Thus, the realm of art and aesthetics gains a certain independence from the interests of philosophy, the search for truth and knowledge, and the question of what is Good and Beautiful. As a consequence, however, art is excluded from the Republic, which does not accept the incalculable character of art and poetry.

The process of artistic creation aims at the outward shaping of an internal image as pictured by the painter or poet. The model, according to which a created image is shaped, being of a different nature than the creation, progressively dissolves in the development of that image. Throughout the process, changes, omissions, additions and other such deformations occur, so that in the end, there is only a limited similarity to the original idea. Mostly, the models of an artist's images and drafts are unknown; either they have been lost or forgotten, or they never existed. At the

[12] Plato, *Politeia*, 598a.

[13] Zimbrich, U: *Mimesis bei Platon* (Frankfurt/M., 1984).

centre of the artistic process there must be an image which, related to models and earlier images, is created through the course of transformation and innovation.

What is the relation between the model (*Vorbild*) and its likeness (*Abbild*)? Does the former create the latter? How are we to understand the connection? Already, in Antiquity, Phidia's celebrated depiction of Zeus led to speculation about whether there was a model, and if so, where? Since there cannot have been a precedent, however, this image of Zeus must have been new. It came about in the working of the material, through the artistic process itself. Anyone who sees the statue recognises the image, even though there is no earlier model of 'Zeus' that one might know. Zuckerkandl went so far as to claim that every work of art is 'an image in search of a model, created in order to find within the human spirit its model, and thus fulfil its purpose, that of becoming an image'.[14] The image is not unambiguous; it is more of a question than an answer. Put through the work of art, a question to which the observer may answer in many different ways. The structure of the work of art conjures up images, strings of meaning and interpretations which all contribute to its complexity. The mimetic terms are displaced: a work of art is no longer seen as the imitation of a certain model. Rather, there is a relationship of representation; imitation takes place between the work of art and the observer.

Technical simulation determines the third, new kind of image. There is a growing tendency today to turn everything into image. Even the most opaque bodies are being transformed, losing their non-transparency and spaciousness, becoming see-through and transient. Processes of abstraction lead to images and pictures. They are everywhere; nothing is more alien and overpowering. Images make 'real things' disappear.

Parallel to the printing of texts, more images than ever before are recorded and supplied. Photographs, films and videos have become tools, gradually contributing to a common memory of images. Whereas texts need to be supplemented by the necessary participation of one's imagination, one's capacity to picture, imagination, on the other hand, is now being restricted by the production of 'picture texts'. While the number of people actually producing the images is constantly decreasing, ever more people passively consume these unstimulating ready-made pictures.

Pictures and images constitute a particular kind of abstraction. Their flat two-dimensional nature is at odds with, indeed eliminates, the multi-dimensional space around them. The electronic character of television pictures allows for ubiquity and acceleration: at the speed of light, images can be transmitted simultaneously around the world. As a consequence, the world is miniaturised, experienced explicitly as a succession of images. Pictures and images constitute a new form of product which can be subjected to market principles. They become marketable products even when the objects to which they relate are not themselves tradable goods.

Caught in constant exchange with each other, images are mimetically interrelated. Fragments of images are picked up and put together differently, creating

[14] Zuckerkandl, V: 'Mimesis', in: *Merkur*, 12, 1958, 233.

fractal images forever forming new wholes. They move and refer to each other with a rate of acceleration that itself makes them resemble each other in 'mimesis of speed'. Their two-dimensional planeness, as well as their electronic and miniaturising qualities, make different images come to resemble each other. A fundamental restructuring of present-day picture-worlds is thus underway, creating a kind of promiscuity of images.

Images grab the observer and immerse him in a whirlpool of impressions that threaten to drown him. Both fascinating and terrifying, you cannot escape them; images dissolve things and transport you into a world of appearances. This leads to an inseparable connection between power and invasion. The world, both political and social, is aestheticised. Images look for models to turn into, transforming through this mimetic process into new fragmented images, divorced of any frame of reference. Fascinating, these images lead into an ecstatic game involving simulacres and simulations: never-ending differentiation parallels an implosion of difference – unlimited similarity. The images themselves constitute the legacy (McLuhan) in a world of appearances both fascinating and delightful.

Contaminating like a virus, pictures and images multiply at the speed of light. Mimetic processes produce ever-new images, creating a world of appearances further and further removed from 'reality'. As a world of art and poetry, this world of appearances is not subordinate to the realm of politics. Rather, it tends to rob other 'worlds' of their reality content, turning them, too, into worlds of appearance. Life becomes aestheticised. More and more images are produced to which no reality outside of themselves corresponds. This finally leads to an image-game where everything is possible – political questions are subordinate. This tendency towards a 'culture society' is ambivalent: if everything is but a game of images, arbitrariness and non-commitment are unavoidable. The picture-worlds created in this self-relating mimetic process, lead in turn to the aestheticising of life. As the realms merge, the distinction between life and art, imagination and reality, seems to dissolve. Life becomes a model for the world of appearances, which itself becomes a model for life. The visual develops hypertrophically: everything turns transparent; space capitulates to image-like surface; as if there were but the present tense of accelerated images, time is condensed. Images attract attention and desire, above and beyond all differences. Yet at the same time, by always referring to something absent, they evade desire. People and things yearn for dissolution in images. Desire fires into the emptiness of electronic signs.

Images are becoming simulacra. Thus, political debates are often led solely for the purpose of being transmitted on television. What appears as a political controversy has actually been carefully geared towards being presented in images. Television pictures are a medium for political debate; this aestheticisation of politics is unavoidable. The viewer watches the simulation of a political controversy that is set up so as to appear authentic. Yet nothing but the simulation itself is authentic! The viewer's convictions and expectations are manipulated; everything is devised in and for a world of appearances. If this succeeds, then so does the controversy. Only as simulation can the intended political effect be achieved in television. In fact, such make-believe is often more effective than 'real' political discussion.

Simulacra are on the look out for models, which they themselves create. They have become trade marks that influence the character of political controversy. It is gradually becoming impossible to draw a line between reality and simulacra; the dissolution of this boundary leads to new pervasions and overlaps. Mimetic processes circulate models, copies and after-images. Images no longer aim to resemble models, but to resemble themselves. The same applies to people: the individual strives to become like him/herself, a mimetic result that can only be achieved against the background of extensive differences within one same subject. Mimesis becomes the determining power of images, their fractal multiplication in a world of appearances.

The inner world of images

A social subject's inner world of images is defined (a) by a culturally conditioned collective imaginary, (b) by the unmistakable and unique images from his/her own individual history, and (c) by the amalgamation, overlap, and mutual transformation of these two image worlds. In recent years, pedagogical research in biography has gained important insights into the role and function of these inner picture-worlds. In what follows, I propose to distinguish seven types of inner picture-world: regulators of behaviour, orientating images, images of desire, of will, of memory, mimetic images and archetypal images.[15]

Images as regulators of behaviour

The question is if, and if so to what extent, are structures or patterns of behaviour inherited? The gap between stimulation and reaction is undisputed in humans, yet this does not exclude the possibility of influence through inherited images or patterns of behaviour. In recent years, ethnology has made significant progress in understanding how trigger-images can affect such elementary human behaviour as eating and drinking, reproduction, and the raising of new generations.

Orientating images

Through socialisation and upbringing, young people are transmitted thousands of images to guide and orientate them and enable them to lead their lives. Many of these images are very clear, catchy, easily reproduced, and therefore, socially speaking, extremely effective. They are public images, shared by many. They connect

[15] Flügge, J: *Die Entfaltung der Anschauungskraft*, n. 6 above, 155.

people, conferring on them a sense of community, affiliation, belonging, collectivity. Globalisation extends these networks of images far beyond the borderlines of national cultures, creating transnational forms of consciousness.

Images of desire

Drive-determined fantasies and images of desire tend to be similar in structure, though their concrete expressions often vary. These images are crucially important for the adjustment of human behaviour and dreams. They often aim at the satisfaction of desire, though at the same time contain the knowledge that wishes cannot all come true.

Fantasies of will

Whereas images of desire are directed towards having and enjoying, fantasies of will tend to be projections of doing. Such will-determined desire expresses human surplus drive, the root of human work and culture.

Memory images

Memories determine a person's particular character. They are partly accessible and manipulable, partly unavailable to the interventions of consciousness. Some originate in perception, others are based on imagined situations. Images from memory combine with new perceptions and contribute to shaping these. They are the result of a selection process, whereby unconscious effacement and consciously motivated forgetting (e.g. forgiveness) both play a role. Memories constitute a person's history, they are linked to the different times and places of his/her life. Memory images relate to pain and happiness, connect to failure and success. In remembering, memory images resurrect the past and soothe from the inexorability of time.

Mimetic images

Real people or imaginary images can serve as models for human behaviour. Plato referred to the fact that as models, images stimulate our own mimetic capacity. According to him, humans – especially children and youths – cannot resist the urge to imitate. Therefore, in terms of a theory of education, Plato's view was that one should consciously exploit images that it would be of value to imitate, and carefully exclude any which could have a bad influence. Aristotle on the other hand believed people ought to be able to learn resistance through confrontation with undesirable images. These opposing views have re-emerged over the relevant debate about the effects of violence depicted in modern media.[16]

[16] Gebauer, G. and Wulf, Ch: *Mimesis. Culture–Art–Society* (Berkeley: The University of California Press, 1995).

Archetypal images

C. G. Jung defines the relevance of archetypal images as follows:

> Every important life experience, every great excitement [...] touches the inner treasure-house of these [archetypal] images, conjuring them up within. Given enough self-contemplation and mental capacity, an individual will become aware of these images as such, and therefore not merely act but also think what he/she experiences, in other words live out the myth and the symbol.[17]

Jung's somewhat dubious account for the origins of archetypes and 'collective unconscious', ought not to prevent us from recognising the fact that every culture develops powerful models and images of fate that influence the course of human action through dreams and cultural events.

CONCLUSIONS

Human flexibility is illustrated in the fact that the inner image-world can take on so many different forms. All are the result of imagination, which encompasses all levels of human life, whether in perception and feeling, or in thinking and doing. Even human eccentricity is due to imagination, for it refers to the capacity to position oneself outside of oneself, and from there to relate back to oneself. Such self-reflection is often expressed in the relation of images to images.

Images manifest one's capacity to picture, their different figures show cultural multiplicity. This is shown in the above-mentioned different kinds of imagery. Images reveal magic, representation and simulation, changing the character of these, while affecting the quality of the imagination they articulate.

Art education necessarily works reflectively with images. This does not mean to reduce an image to its meaning, but rather to bend it backwards, to turn it round; to linger with the image and perceive it as such; to represent to oneself its qualities of shape and emotion and let these take effect; to protect the image from too hasty an interpretation through which it would be transformed into language and meaning, yet as an image, drained and emptied; to bear out uncertainty, ambiguousness, complexity, without calling for clarity. The meditation of images: imaginary representation of something absent, mimetic creation and change within the current of inner images. Art education requires one to work on one's inner imagery; not only to bring it out in speech, but to let its image-content unfold and develop. To deal with images is to expose oneself to their ambiguousness. In order to do this, one must get in tune with an image and offer it full attention. With the powers of one's imagination, one must create the image as an inner picture, protecting it from other inner

[17] Jung, CG: *Psychologische Typen* (Zürich, 1958), 311.

images that flow; with the powers of concentration and thought, one must 'hold on' to the image. For an image to emerge is the first step, to hold on to it, to work with it, to let it unfold in imagination are further steps towards consciously dealing with images. To reproduce or create an image in imagination, to carefully linger with it, is no smaller an achievement than that of interpreting it. The duty of art education is to bring together these two aspects of working with imagery.

FRANS DE RUITER

Mozart from the Box of Bricks. 'Sense & Nonsense of Artistic Curricula'

This chapter is about the undesirability of unjustifiedly desired legislation, with as a subtitle 'Curricula and mobility against the rocks'.

Many publications and contemporary policy-makers base themselves on Manuel Castells' (Cat.) book: The Information Age – Economy, Society, Culture (1996/98).

He describes:

- *a historical transformation through integration of different forms of communication in an interactive network, leading to the development to a network society;*
- *new possibilities of information – and media technology in relation to a global economy, leading to a new worldwide society based on networks and new connections between people and organisations.*

The results being:

- *the economy develops to an economy of knowledge;*
- *the loss of social cohesion;*
- *mobility;*
- *cultural context operating through the media;*
- *in the cultural area: a meta-language consisting of an integration of textual, oral and audiovisual forms of communication in one and the same system;*
- *hybrid forms: new integrated forms overcome conventional borderlines in the digital media-culture;*
- *digitalisation which produces new mixed forms between television and the internet; CD-roms have text, sound, music, images in a new synthesis; video techniques and film meet each other; there are combinations of interactive design and visual arts;*
- *hybrid forms which have the possibility to produce and to distribute information in any form (game, film, CD-rom, internet) and to change fundamentally existing forms of art, media and entertainment.*

Jan De Groof, Chantal De Smet and Hilde Penneman (eds.), Art meets Law in Education, 77–81.

Via one platform we have access to audiovisual news, education, public authority, a virtual museum or a shopping mall.

What, then, is the difference between a tv-company, a publisher or an animation on a website, if they are only separated from each other by one or two clicks of the mouse?

There comes a cultural convergence, and interdisciplinary mixture between visual and applied arts, music, architecture, industrial and graphic design, fashion, television, radio, but also, e.g., computer games, software development, online education, publicity, libraries.

These crossovers are more than the sums of the subjects. The borders between artists and individual consumers are fading.

It is always both/and no longer either/or.

Significant developments in the arts over the last decennium on our way to the twenty-first century are:

- broadening of the repertoire;
- renewal of the performance practice;
- explosion of creativity: in composition, e.g., we see traditional, atonal, citation and row techniques; electronic, analogue, digital and interactive music; minimal, repetitive and free tonal music; music about music; besides jazz, traditional and popular music;
- new technology;
- multi- and interdisciplinary work;
- completely new ways of using space and time;
- professionals have a combination of jobs at the same time and/or different jobs in the course of their lives.

Training and education

Training and education in this area should teach the actual state of the arts, as well as contribute to the development of the arts. The process leading to the product is more important than the isolated product itself.

At this moment the majority of curricula consist of a list of elements, such as the main subject(s), general studies (such as theory, history, paedagogics, sociology), secondary subject(s), most of them compulsory.

In the future there will rather be a system of core curricula and optional extras (partly compulsory, partly free). Curricula will deal with the arts of the world, with the entrepreneurial artist and the overall landscape of the arts in all its varieties. (See in the Annexe below an example of an interdisciplinary project.)

There is an ever-growing need for clearly described qualifications before students enter the system, and at the end of their studies; aims and objectives should be very clear on top.

Important criteria are *the history* of the student before entering the (semi-) professional system or the preparatory systems, *the results* achieved so far, *the growth-capacities* of the student and *the artistic potential.*

Each student needs an individual curriculum from a given situation into the new situation, towards the prospective results, taking the individual tempo of development into account.

The judgement, evaluation and assessment of the study progress should reflect all these elements. Similarly the comments and marking of the final exam and good advice for the future.

This all because we are confronted with some who know and have the capacity to pass everything in a brilliant way; some are good at a lot of things, others not so, and some are limited in all areas.

Mobility has many pitfalls

In general, even useful mobility is inhibited by different legal approaches in each country, both sending and receiving. A whole system of residence permits, tax-systems and grant problems encourage not travelling at all.

The reasons to study abroad can be disparate. Many take the qualifications to use them at home, others stay in the guest country, others mix their intentions and final decisions. The ambitions are either to aim at an international career, or to start working on the local labour market.

Ambitions also vary from one-dimensional, such as a solo-career, or more social, aimed at ensemble or group work, or aiming at a real societal professional activity, as a paedagogue or coach/repetiteur, or straight into multi/interdisciplinarity.

In dealing with mobility we always have to take the great many differences into account as far as the respective part of the world, country, region or city is concerned, the typology of the aimed-for study programme and the comparison between institution A (the guest institute) and institution B (the institute of origin).

There are no rules, only individual cases when dealing with students in the arts.

Arts education and legislative aspects

Nothing will function if the same rules are applied in all circumstances, leading to inflexible rules and rigid legislation. To achieve a manageable classification of the arts education system, as expressed in curricula and diplomas, an ECTS or other equivalent Diploma system does not apply. They are too one-dimensional to function. They can be helpful, however, if they are part of a multidimensional box inside the laws providing the legal framework.

In any case, the law should provide the right for every child and adult to participate in education and training in general, and also in the arts, especially in the regular school system.

In particular those aiming at a professional career in the arts (as performer, creator, teacher, facilitator) should have the right to be admitted to professional establishments where one will be trained for an arts career, on the basis of proven skills and sufficient progress, given the combination of age, skills, progress, attitude and motivation.

There should also be a legal framework for mobility, exchange, etc., but not on the basis of credit points or Diplomas; they do not mean anything and only have a relative importance, such as in the profession:

- 'can you play, sing, act, dance, paint, sculpt for me?';
- auditions are more important than diplomas;
- assessment of works (tapes, images, scores, exhibits) are more decisive for a career than any diploma whatsoever.

Formalities do not work.

Practical remarks

Leave it to the responsible institutions to judge if plan A from student B from institution C is valuable, productive enough to be accommodated in institution D, with the prospect of aims and objectives E, to be achieved for being successful in career F. We should try to make laws on the basis of this canon. And further:

- establish a group of designated institutions of international excellence with acknowledged programmes in all or certain areas;
- create a situation wherein students, who want to attend these institutions and are accepted, should not experience any impediment/hindrance in studying abroad (these internationally recognized excellent institutions and teachers/professors will only accept the highest quality, so the number of participants will by nature be small);
- construct the most simple mechanism: the 'sending' country pays for the costs of the student (max. 10.000 euro); the receiving country for the training and education (on average, the same amount).

Summary

Arts Education is not, nor should it be, a system in itself, but should follow/be a forerunner in the cultural landscape and:

- be flexible;
- not depend on rigid legislation;
- set its own rules;
- be extremely critical of itself and permanently ask itself vital questions;
- provide individual solutions for each participating individual.

Annexe

Sonic Acts 1999
Labyrinth: from Monteverdi to dj Moondance, and back

A contribution to the development of the arts:
- Monteverdi
- Lamento d'Arianna
- Amsterdam water-city Venice
- Lamento is about: to stay behind
- Water is farewell, arrival, departure, greeting
- A sound lab of mechanical instruments and tools
- A space and image lab: colours, architecture, smell
- A lab for storytelling

Locations:

Wharf Wallfish	: Farewell from the prenatal phase
Boats	: Farewell from the location
The Stone Head	: Farewell from the lighthouse
The IJ	: Farewell from the Central Station
St. Nicholas-church	: The impure sounds, the diving men, beauty
Tower of the Weepers	: Monteverdi + recomposed
Ship – museum	: Songs of distress, farewell songs, songs of the tears of the bride
New Metropolis	: Farewell from the old technopolis
Marine Wharf (dinner)	: Farewell from starvation and thurst
Paradiso	: Farewell from old, new and old & new music.

GORDON H. BELL

The Place of Creativity in School Curricula

The creative development of pupils and teachers in Western primary and secondary schools has attracted considerable attention in the modern history of educational institutions. But the translation from rhetoric to reality has been far from consistent and far from complete.

Such ambivalence may be traced to ambiguities and inconsistencies in the underlying norms and values of European cultures. Their interpretation in legislation has created a gap between statutory theory and practical implementation and as a consequence, a continuing deficit of achievement over aspiration is apparent.

An account of the role and function of creative impulses in school curricula may therefore be understood as a reflection of the related policy dilemmas, shifts in policy priorities, changes of policy direction, competition amongst values, and the perceived urgency of issues of the moment.

Policy dilemmas and priorities

Certain key concepts have dominated thinking amongst policy makers and practitioners alike. The compromises and accommodations reached have yielded contradictions which have their roots in a central dilemma between providing education and funding schooling.

'Educating' is a very different enterprise from 'schooling'. These concepts play a logically distinct role in the languages of European nations and denote a fundamental tension between instrumental values (schooling) and intrinsic values (educating). Valuing teaching and learning activities for their own sake and valuing them for some further end in view have very different implications for the framework of institutions designed to incorporate these values whether as schools, courts, police, welfare, or related agencies.

The gap noted earlier between the formal provision of a structure and the implementation of policy is variously estimated to lie in the range 15–25 years. Criticism of policy initiatives as 'innovation without change' derives not only from problems

Jan De Groof, Chantal De Smet and Hilde Penneman (eds.), Art meets Law in Education, 83–94.

arising from this time lag but also from the relative neglect of research based evidence to inform a legislative programme. The appearance of organizational dynamism through constant modifications to existing structures veils the actuality of reform as distinct from the rhetoric of innovation. Placing legislation before effective evaluation compounds these difficulties.

Such contradictions in the management and maintenance of educational institutions as between education and schooling, evaluation and legislation, innovation and reform severely constrains systemic creativity. The consequent restrictions arising in the curricula of institutions defined by this process are wide ranging and significantly limiting for the creative development of individuals, whether as parents, teachers, researchers, or pupils (Bell, 1990, 1999).

The sense of urgency to secure more effective change and reduce these gaps in school curricula has intensified in recent years. But the perceived need to achieve swift outcomes has impacted upon the desire to co-operate because of the extended timescales this would require. Meanwhile, the imperative to compete to secure economic advantage has introduced further contradictory influences, especially in the context of partnership in a European Union.

The accompanying emphasis upon cost/benefit approaches to the delivery of public services has led to greater accountability for providers. The recent emergence of policy priorities to do with educational 'quality' and 'standards' has further focused interest on quantifiable measures. This has meant closer scrutiny of the implementation of legislation and a narrowing of attention to certain subjects in the curriculum perceived to be more closely aligned to material outcomes.

The so-called '3Rs' – reading, writing and arithmetic – has gained a formal status as 'core' subjects in some countries. This priority has consolidated a previously informal hierarchy of subjects that permeated all levels of education and training from kindergarten to university. This bias has further disadvantaged areas of the curriculum associated with the development of qualitative and interpretative knowledge, skills and attitudes.

This prioritization of instrumental over intrinsic values has led in turn to the relative marginalization of social and pastoral concerns to do with the maintenance of peace and security and the development of social cohesion. The prevailing belief amongst policymakers has been that a secure grounding in key skills to do with literacy and numeracy acts as an effective precondition for active citizenship. The opposing viewpoint asserts a developmental, multi-sensory approach based upon concepts of motivation, readiness, needs and interests (Oppenheim, 1999).

Ideologies of education

The passage of legislation arising from such dilemmas and the policy priorities that have determined the direction of policy, can be traced to underlying systems of belief that have a long and turbulent history.

These underlying ideologies can be described in terms of competing conceptions of an ideal; in particular an ideal of intelligent citizenship secured and developed through state funded institutions. The framing in statutes of selected interpretations of certain key concepts and their representation in schools have in turn determined the place and function of creativity in the curriculum. Three key concepts can be identified as playing a significant role in this process; concepts of democracy, concepts of the educated person and concepts of the teacher.

It was Herbert Read in his seminal book *Education Through Art* who pointed out that the kind of culture we can acquire through State institutions is determined by the nature of libertarian and authoritarian conceptions of government within which they are set. And it will be clear from current membership of the United Nations formally defined in terms of 'democratic' governments that there are widely varying assessments of their actual status and relative worth.

Evaluative judgements of this type can be traced to prevailing assumptions of the nature of citizenship. In the Western tradition the core values of the French Revolution; liberty, equality and fraternity are exemplary instances of these assumptions. The pre-eminence of the first of these principles described in terms of 'freedom' has, for example, largely framed the Constitution of the United States.

This complex mix of social concepts and moral principles and their linkage to the concept of education has been penetratingly revealed through Isaiah Berlin's celebrated essay on 'Two Concepts of Liberty'. Here he notes an ambiguity in our uses of this concept which contains a negative component (freedom from) and a positive component (freedom to).

The case of the 'happy slave' illustrates this crucial dilemma for the politics of education. Do we force children to be free through education in order to maximise happiness or do we content ourselves with providing the conditions under which children are free from sources of unhappiness? The practical implications for education in general and the specific implications for creativity are very different.

Such issues lie at the heart of the debate about the place of creativity in the curriculum, for they define a conception of the ideal self which is presupposed in the model of the ideal citizen. The underlying logic can be summarized in the negative sense as grounded in a primary and critical evaluation being made of the present or actual self. 'Freedom' is then judged in terms of the extent to which this definition of the situation is hindered or constrained. This meaning is captured in the phrase 'Man is by nature free and everywhere in chains.'

By contrast, the positive uses of 'freedom' can be understood in terms of the 'ideal' self not being compatible with the 'actual' self. Bringing this system of wants and desires into harmony would realize the 'real' self. Providing the conditions through education or schooling for actualizing the real self is the central challenge for achieving positive freedom.

Describing and analysing the appropriate enabling conditions have occupied philosophers of education from Plato to Dewey. Securing the relevant conditions by means of legislative programmes and school environments has determined the policies and priorities of politicians and practitioners throughout the ages. Indeed the history of educational theory and practice can largely be described in terms of the values and enabling conditions advanced for (positive) freedom to be achieved.

However, the claims made by proponents of the pedagogy of negative freedom seeking to achieve the optimal conditions for realizing the 'natural' hence 'free' self, stand in stark contrast to the teaching and learning thought necessary for the 'ideal' self to be developed through the notion of positive freedom. The central case of creativity – the creation of the self – is crucially determined through the interpretation (and ultimately the legislation) that is placed on the uses to which these concepts are put by parents, politicians, practitioners and pupils. But as Karl Popper remarked, too much freedom leads to too little, highlighting the well known paradox of freedom which defeats itself if it is unlimited.

Meanwhile, we might note that schools are custodial institutions and in the negative sense of freedom act as a constraint on 'natural' creativity. Through appeals to the positive sense of freedom, we seek to justify compulsion with reference to the realization of the ideal self. We also acknowledge that restrictions on freedom through the collective exercise of power and authority must operate (provisionally) as a necessary condition for initiation into citizenship. Acceptance of this reasoning is assumed to provide sufficient justification for the benefits of freedom as a social principle to be secured.

On this account, the conditions for maximising creativity are inseparably connected with a disciplined and regulatory framework of rights, rules and duties – providing both the basis for a statutory framework and a central justification for the construction of a 'curriculum'.

If we now turn to the second key concept underpinning the place of creativity in school curricula, we are confronted with competing interpretations of the concept of the educated person. Whilst we have noted that there have been many prescriptive definitions of the nature of the educated citizen and the conditions necessary for this ideal to be realized, there are few analytic accounts of the uses to which it is put in a language.

Richard Peters' application of the assumptions and techniques of linguistic philosophy has provided an exhaustive and compelling account of the necessary and/or sufficient conditions for the meaningful application of this concept in the English language.

Peters (1966) argues that the concept of education in its specific sense refers to a process of initiation into worthwhile activities that have a cognitive core, have an intention to develop knowledge and understanding in depth and breadth, are valued for their own sake, and are governed by ethical principles and procedures.

The meaning of the term 'educated person' is therefore determined by the logic of the criteria which govern the use of the term 'education', namely that individuals are transformed by what they know, are committed to use their knowledge in guiding their conduct, and recognise that the knowledge they gain is valued for its own sake as much as it is valued for its uses.

The critical issue arising from the practical application of this analysis is the range of interpretations to be derived from the notion of 'worthwhile' activities. For example, given that this account supplies an analysis of the logical conditions under which meaning arises in the use of these concepts, what are the psychological and operational outcomes that flow from them? How worthwhile are creative activities in the school curriculum? We shall return to these questions after we have considered the third key concept, the concept of the teacher.

If we examine the diversity of ideologies that shape the education systems of European nations there is a well researched view that teacher education and training is at a crossroads. It is a variant of the education/schooling distinction and the debate is represented by two dominant models. The first, described as the 'bureaucratic-managerial' approach, regards the teacher as a technician transmitting prescribed information. The second, 'professional' approach describes the teacher as having an active role in collaborative planning for policy development.

The content of training programmes for each of these models reflects conceptions of the ideal teacher. The educational possibilities arising from these sharply contrasting conditions for teaching and learning to take place are radically distinct. For they offer very different opportunities for the creative activities of all participants in the development of schools whether as pupils, parents, practitioners or policymakers.

Current values and the justification of policy

From this brief survey of current ideologies in education, certain themes dominate. I suggest that the central debate can be described in terms of contrasting concepts of literacy, what I shall term functional literacy and cultural literacy. The place and function of creativity in the curriculum can, I believe, be understood against the background of these competing conceptions of schooling.

One may become functionally literate by mastering the basic skills of being able to read and write and add up. Throughout Europe there is the idea that schools are failing to secure these basic skills and that being poor and disadvantaged is perpetuated by not being taught effectively enough to acquire these skills in a predetermined time scale. But being educated in this minimal sense can also mean being uncivilised, intolerant and unimaginative. Basic skills are a necessary but not sufficient condition for becoming an educated person.

By contrast, the notion of cultural literacy signals that beyond these basic competencies to read, write, and add up are visual, aural and tactile skills that seek to achieve a balance between intellectual and emotional capabilities. These are the competencies that liberate and enable individuals to transform their modes of thinking, acting, and expressing themselves in ways that would otherwise impoverish and limit their lives.

Cultural literacy is centrally to do with a disposition to reflect critically on the basic attributes of being a person, having a purpose, and having an identity.

Creativity, aesthetics, history, and the literary, visual and performing arts are the keys to this capacity to think critically for they celebrate the role of the imagination in becoming human.

Underlying these conceptions of literacy are justifying values which have their roots in the three key concepts explored above. The institutionalization of these systems of belief which form the curriculum of schools has been examined by Mitter (1991) who provides a summary analysis of European trends in teacher education. He proposes that there are five main determinants of the role of the teacher in the 1990s:

- the *economic* aspect, which indicates the teacher's income;
- the *social* aspect, which explains the status of the teacher;
- the *formal/legal* aspect, which defines the position of teachers within the administrative structure and affects the amount of their freedom (or restraint) within the political order;
- the *professional* aspect (in the narrow sense of this term), which describes the teacher's everyday activities;
- the *socio-educational* aspect, which determines their place in the education system reflecting dominant expectations in a given society.

It is through the socio-educational and socio-economic standpoint that we may track the place and function of creativity in school curricula. For it is through the values that define the nature of the activities that are provided that we may judge how worthwhile creativity is judged to be. At the heart of this evaluation are evident tensions between the demands of nationalism and internationalism in the political order, cultural and intercultural definitions of self, and individual and collective claims on democratic decision making.

McLean (1990) in examining these issues identifies the way school knowledge traditions are regarded in the different countries of the (then) European Community. He suggests that there are three main competing ideologies; Encylopaedism based upon universality, rationality and utility; Humanism centring upon morality, individuality and specialism; and Naturalism based upon philosophical, psychological and sociological evidence on the way human beings develop towards mental and physical maturity. From this analysis it will be clear that a variety of interpretations and implications arise for the concept of creativity.

Thus far we have largely assumed a relatively close coupling of the formal/legal arrangements that define school curricula. This perspective is based on the assumption that nations can determine the systems of control that administer schooling in terms of both process and content. However, recent advances in information and communications technology and trends towards the globalization of economic structures can be judged to be undermining the capacity of national authorities to secure compliance.

These drivers of change, independent of nation states, can be attributed to a cluster of factors arising in four main areas:

- *Technicalization of the world of work*: a shift from unskilled to highly skilled workers requiring governments to raise the general level of qualifications and review school curricula;
- *Transformation of the school population*: through increased cultural diversity, modified family structures and integration of special needs pupils in mainstream schooling;
- *Rationalization of systems*: budgetary pressures reducing the unit of resource, introducing quality control procedures and shifting responsibility to local financial management;
- *Internationalization of education and training*: to respond to the needs of a common market including new information technologies and links with the world of work (Vonk, 1995; Seltzer and Bentley, 1999).

Three further sources of influence can be noted; urbanization, privatization, and environmental management. Each one of these has an impact upon the perceived relevance of creativity for pupils and teachers and affect its relative status amongst school based activities.

Experts tell us that up to the year 2015, the annual increase of the world's population will be 89 million. One of the most challenging consequences will be urbanisation and its impact on the environment. In ten years' time, half of the world's 6.6 billion people will be living in cities. At present there are 14 megacities with more than 10 million inhabitants; in 10 years this number will have doubled. In 1953 there were 83 cities of more than one million people; today there are 280 and in twenty years there will be 500 (Von Hentig, 1997).

Alongside these trends, budgetary pressures leading to the rationalization of systems have increased opportunities for the private sector to participate in what was previously considered to be the sole responsibility of public authorities. This effect is particularly apparent in the UK where for the first time private commercial companies have taken over the running of local education authorities and the inspection of schools.

Finally in this survey of socio-economic influences, we might note the increasing impact of global environmental issues on the politics of schooling with consequent effects on the place and function of creativity in the curriculum.

Creativity and the role of the Arts

Creative and responsible citizens whether as pupils or teachers throughout the Western world will be seriously challenged to address these issues. Indeed if schools and colleges in their present form survive to cope with this situation, it hardly seems sufficient to rely solely upon what has previously been described in terms of functional literacy.

The idea that basic skills should come first and that functional literacy is a precursor to or precondition of citizenship stands in danger of substituting socialization for education (Oakshott, 1972). The additional prospect of instrumentalising young people and exposing their varying abilities and rates of development to predetermined stages of bureaucratized learning offers up the prospect of stigma and de-motivation.

If we discount these concerns by assuming the common sense view that pursuing numeracy and literacy from an early age are worthwhile activities, current tendencies throughout the Western world show that their dominant status displaces equally worthwhile activities from the standpoint of intelligent citizenship.

Not least amongst these worthwhile activities are the arts and the formation of attitudes and beliefs so crucial to the early stages of pupils' learning that develop amongst other things tolerance and understanding of cultures other than their own.

Whilst the arts have a unique and special role to play in these concerns, it is clear from surveys of current practice that various forms of exclusion operate in schools and teacher training institutions which restrict opportunity and have both intended and unintended consequences for the place of creativity in school curricula.

Chief amongst these restrictions is access to the Arts in the fullest sense. By that I mean that there is a significant difference between 'Education in or through the Arts' and the 'Arts in or through Schooling'. Most frequently in school systems across the world we encounter the latter – 'Arts in or through Schooling'. This usually means limited opportunities for pupils and their teachers to experience certain aspects of visual art and to have restricted access to music.

By contrast, we could mean:

- visual and performing arts, minimally music, art, drama and dance;
- designing and making minimally three-dimensional design, including crafts, technology and the built environment;
- written arts, minimally poetry making, creative writing, and the literary arts including story telling.

It is very rare to find all of these elements in the curriculum of schools or in every form of teacher training.

Some reasons for this marginalization are grounded in the spectrum of philosophical, empirical and political issues explored previously. The apparent reluctance of decision makers to affirm the arts as independent, teachable and accessible elements of a well balanced curriculum represents an unwillingness to accept the relevance of the arts for the purposes of schooling. As the arts are central examples of the role and function of creativity in the curriculum, a closer scrutiny of this phenomenon will be necessary.

The 'relevance' argument appears to take three main forms: relevance for future prosperity, relevance for the future of schooling, relevance for having a future worth having.

Concerning the relevance of the arts for future employment, in the USA the Arts in Education are now designated as a core subject on the grounds that they are indeed recognised as highly relevant (Educate America Act, 1994). This commitment is expressed in the formal conclusions of a recent conference on business and the arts:

> *Three Good Reasons Why Arts Education is Basic*
> 1. *An arts education contributes to the quality of education overall and builds critical thinking skills.*
> 2. *An arts education builds specific workforce skills that business values.*
> 3. *An education in the arts builds values that connect children to themselves and to their own culture and civilisation.*
>
> (Business and Arts Conference, Getty Institute for the Arts, Los Angeles, 28 October 1996.)

In terms of the relevance of the arts to future prosperity, in the USA a recent national report on non-profit making arts organisations (*op. cit.* Getty Institute) estimated that the Arts generate:

- $36.8 billion annually for the national economy;
- 1.3 million jobs;
- $25.2 billion in salaries;
- 6% contribution to Gross National Product.

In the UK what are referred to as the 'creative industries' generate annual revenues of £57 billion and employ more than 1.7 million people (DCMS, 1998). In the decade 1981–91, the number of people employed in the cultural industries grew 34% (Further Education Funding Council, 1996).

But the broader relevance of the arts to having a future worth having hinges on the view one might take about the relevance of the work culture itself. As one commentator has pointed out:

> *so much energy in the present school and post school system is channelled not into creative directions, but into nurturing conventional patterns of work… and as people have more of their lives for their own autonomous concerns, the wasteful struggle for 'better jobs' will come to seem that bit more pointless.* (White, 1997)

Nevertheless, we will be painfully aware that the modern-day dictators have all used the arts for the brainwashing of their people. Creativity, aesthetics and the arts are no good in themselves. However, their relevance on the account provided may be justifiably derived from being combined with the right sort of politics and used in training for responsible citizenship (Von Hentig, *op. cit.*).

Creativity in theory and practice

Against this background, the concept of creativity has a variety of uses to which it is put. Like 'education', 'democracy' and 'liberty', it is an honorific term conferring status on the contexts of its application. However, in the field of education and schooling it assumes Janus like qualities – facing in one direction it appears in a negative role, facing in another it can be seen to have a positive function.

The range of its positive applications denotes a capacity for encouraging enterprise, tolerating uncertainty and justifying risk. It refers to the conditions necessary for unlocking talent, exploring conventional rules and their unconventional possibilities, and finding novel solutions to problems and issues. In these ways it promotes a disposition to think strategically using both lateral and linear forms of reasoning. Perhaps above all, the place and function of creativity in the curriculum calls attention to the development of the imagination recognizing that without imaginativeness having a conscience and acting morally would not be possible.

In short, creativity represents a valuing of originality in all its forms. However, this need not necessarily entail unconstrained freedom, lack of discipline, neglect of traditions nor be for the gifted few. Neither is creativity to be found solely in the arts, indeed it can be considered to be a process fundamental to excellence in every aspect of school organization including the curriculum (DFEE, 1999).

What then does all of this mean in practice? First, and foremost, creativity in the curriculum promotes a fundamental human right – freedom of expression. Secondly, the limitations of current conceptions of schooling are broadened, made less restrictive and commit everyone to an educational agenda. Thirdly, restricting the creativity of individuals whether as teachers, pupils or policy makers is self-defeating whether in the context of negative or positive forms of freedom.

A recent OECD report on improving the innovation capacity of schooling systems in eight countries across the world had this to say:

> *Young people leaving school at the end of the twentieth century require a range of skills and competencies only some of which are imparted by the traditional academic curriculum. In work and in adult life they need to be able to think flexibly, to relate well to people, to solve problems and to communicate effectively.* (CERI, 1998)

The implications of this judgement are being actively pursued in a number of countries, not least in Japan which has embarked on a national teacher development programme based on the principle that to facilitate the development of creative children, the imaginativeness of teachers must be enhanced first. The new objectives in Japan are to encourage diversity and creativity, to widen teachers' perspectives, and to promote new approaches to teaching.

This is but one example of how countries are responding to the challenge of improving schooling. Underlying these policy initiatives is a theory of good teaching that is fundamentally related in the Western world to conceptions of democracy and to preparing future citizens for their roles in a civil society governed by law and ensuring that they acquire an ability to access its institutions.

Underlying this theory of good teaching is a thesis. The thesis is that improving the quality of schooling and raising standards in what it is to be educated as distinct from being schooled, is more effectively achieved by developing more creative contexts for teaching and learning. This thesis can only be tested through collaborative action and research – a commitment few decision makers have either had the inclination or time to pay serious attention to. The place of creativity in the curriculum is therefore uncertainly poised between cultures which value power as a condition of knowledge and those that prioritize knowledge over power.

References

Bell, G. H., 'Art Education as Action Inquiry' in Bloomfield, A (ed.) *The Creative Self in the New Era, Aspects of Education, 42*, (The University of Hull, 1990) 6–23.

Bell, G. H., 'Education and Schooling in the Arts', European Journal of Arts Education Vol 2 Issue 2, 59–67. (European League of Institutes of the Arts, 1999).

Berlin, I., *Two Concepts of Liberty* (Oxford: Clarendon Press, 1958).

Department for Culture, Media and Sport, *Creative Industries Mapping Exercise* (London: DCMS, 1998).

Further Education Funding Council, *Art, Design and Performing Arts: Report from the Inspectorate* (London: FEFC, 1996).

McLean, M., *Britain and a Single Market Europe: Prospects for a Common School Curriculum* (London: Kogan Page, 1990).

National Advisory Committee on Creative and Cultural Education, *All Our Futures: Creativity, Culture and Education* (London: Department for Education and Employment, 1999).

Oakshott, M., *Education:* 'The Engagements and its Frustration' in R. F. Dearden, P. H. Hirst and R. S. Peters, *Education and the Development of Reason* (London: Routledge and Kegan Paul, 1972).

Oppenheim, T., *Schooling the Imagination*, (Atlantic Monthly, 1999) 74–83.

Organization for Economic Co-operation and Development. *Staying Ahead: In-service Training and Teacher Development* (Paris: Centre for Educational Research and Innovation, 1998).

Peters, R. S., *Ethics and Education* (London: Allen and Unwin, 1966).

Popper, K., *The Open Society and its Enemies*, Vol 2 (London: Routledge, 1966).

Read, H., *Education Through Art* (London: Faber, 1956).

Seltzer, K. and Bentley, T., *The Creative Age: Knowledge and Skills for the New Economy* (Demos: Redwood Books, 1999).

Von Hentig, H., *Our Children and Our Culture*, Forum on Children's Culture, European Conference (Copenhagen: Royal Danish School of Educational Studies, 1997).

Vonk, J. H. C., 'Teacher Education and Reform in Western Europe' in N. K. Shimahara and I. Z. Holinsky (eds) *Teacher Education in Industrialised Nations* (New York and London: Harland Publishing Co, 1995).

White, J. P., *Education and the End of Work*: *A New Philosophy of Work and Learning* (London: Cassell, 1997).

ÁLVARO ZALDÍVAR

Academic Aspects of Higher Arts Education

This talk has had the privilege of being preceded by one given by Professor Embid Irujo (see his chapter below) who, with his expert knowledge on the subject, spoke about the legal structure of arts education in Spain; and at the same time bearing in mind that it is to be followed by a talk by Professor Daniel Vega Cernuda, (see his chapter below) who is well-versed in this field and who will draw on his vast experience to talk about comparative aspects of arts education in Europe, in this chapter we need to concentrate on a brief but critical look at the main academic elements of higher arts education in Spain. By this we mean only those subjects that, when not integrated within the University system (for example, Fine Arts in whose Faculties painting, sculpture and restoration are taught), should be considered as being part of higher arts education, based on the development of the LOGSE, with their highest qualifications being equivalent, to all purposes, to a University degree, even though its organisation and management are still part of the general education system (primary, secondary and vocational training).

Thus, we shall be concentrating on subjects which the LOGSE includes in the section on Arts Education – Section II, devoted to Special Subjects Education. But since Arts Education includes music, theatre and dance as well as fine arts and design, with as many similarities as differences between them, we shall need to narrow our area down even more and extract only the subjects relating to music and the stage – drama and dance. These are the most closely related, because of their origin and traditional coexistence in the former 'music and speech centres', with their traditionally (and justifiably) unified teaching staffs. In fact, for certain specific aspects, for justifiable reasons of space-saving, we shall concentrate on music education as a pattern and the basis for our brief reflections.

Having defined the reduced scope of our analysis, the narrowness of which lies not in any lack of interest in the other subjects, but in the rigid constraints of a succinct but, at the same time, necessarily effective explanation, it should be remembered firstly, and this is a convenient starting point, that special system arts education – in other words, that of Authorised Higher Schools, Conservatoires and Centres – has to provide its students, as laid down in article 38 of the LOGSE, with

Jan De Groof, Chantal De Smet and Hilde Penneman (eds.), Art meets Law in Education, 95–102.

an artistic training of such quality as to guarantee the qualification of future professionals in these arts. This concise but demanding definition should, especially when considered and applied in its maximum regulatory status, be the basis for the norms, criteria and relevant actions which, from a purely academic point of view, we shall group into two main blocks: the profile of the students and the profile of the teachers.

We should remember, before we begin, that we are currently in the middle of a process of reform for these subjects (with the introduction of the new higher grade of music and dance having been postponed several times, although the latter did not even have an 'old' higher grade, unlike music; and with the teaching of the renovated drama subjects now fully underway, albeit in its early stages), and thus, what is being analysed here based on recent history and current experience cannot be applied, either directly or fully, to future circumstances which, it is to be hoped, will improve in all fields. We must certainly hope that this development of tomorrow will have learnt the lessons of yesterday (and to a certain extent, those of today), in which problems and shortcomings have played a leading role in this oratorically present as well as eternally preterite sector in the practical budgetary and legislative aspect of Spanish educational life at the close of the twentieth century.

As a brief preface of what we shall now be looking at, the following two aspects stand out: with regard to the students, their complex heterogeneousness – in age, educational/cultural level, professional expectations, etc. – which without doubt results in excessive individualism that primarily seeks personal solutions and hopes for solo success; with regard to teachers, nothing is more relevant than their inadequate treatment and professional consideration, in a no-man's-land (due to a lack of suitable regulation) between general and special system education and between primary/secondary and higher education (university or otherwise). This generates a deep-seated feeling of ill-being which is only relieved and compensated for by teachers' strong artistic vocation, thus avoiding further problems.

To the above we might add, as a no less significant conclusion, that in fact we are talking about something we do not know for certain, given the lack of reliable studies in which, among other aspects, the students' entry into the profession is evaluated, which is the ultimate object (remembering the previously mentioned article 38 of the LOGSE) of arts education in accordance with the new regulations governing the educational system. This is an evaluation which needs to be concerned with concrete results in the professional world as well as with opportunity and the quality of the resources that centres propose and develop in order to achieve this.

With regard to this, close study of 'Higher Music Schools and Entry into the Profession' is recommended, a survey carried out by the Association of European Conservatoires within the framework of the Luxembourg Meeting of November 1995, whose main statistical results have been commented on in an article I wrote for *Melómano* (no 6, January 1997, 50–3). In this study, which began with the optimistic result of 83 per cent of those surveyed in favour of considering their students' entry into the profession as part of their role as a higher educational-artistic institution, there are also pessimisti results such as 62 per cent unaware of the existence in their respective countries of public or semi-public bodies or even associations to help musicians enter the profession. I shall quote just one more figure, no less enlightening: 58 per cent of centres acknowledge that they do not have reliable statistics for studying the professional situation of their former students.

Obviously, the generally sad situation summarised above becomes frankly depressing with regard to the case in Spain, beginning with the very small number of centres which took part in the survey. This lack of collaboration was due to excessive shame, or the traditional apathy which can perhaps be explained when we consider that then, as now, most of the Higher Conservatoires of Music are not exclusively Higher Centres, and thus confusion easily arises with their lower elementary-professional levels, whilst dance still does not have a higher qualification as such – with the old system, studies finished at the professional level.

Similarly, we may point out, in this general overview, a serious problem with higher music, drama and dance education in Spain in that it is made up of just one cycle: this not only makes the existence of intermediate qualification impossible between the baccalaureate – general, music or dance – and the higher music, drama or dance qualification (equivalent to a *licenciatura* (degree)), an intermediate qualification which in line with other qualifications, also in arts education, but in the visual arts, would enjoy full equivalence with a university *diplomatura*; but it also adds unfair extra stress for the students – if they do not complete the higher level, they will have the same qualifications as when they entered (which might mean none at all, since the LOGSE allows entry by an entrance test, without the need for academic requirements such as the baccalaureate or intermediate grade).

Sadly, we must also point out two aspects that strongly condition expectations for the future for this type of education: firstly, the slow development of a basic set of regulations (e.g. there is still no regulatory framework for agreements with universities to provide third-cycle studies to graduates from conservatoires and higher drama schools, so that, for the moment, admission remains at the discretion of each individual university); and secondly, this slowness seems to be infecting the Educational Authorities who, while enjoying full powers in educational matters, are the ones who will really provide concrete solutions (perhaps suitably different, perhaps too different or excessively similar) for this type of education, and its teaching and learning establishments.

Students' profile

We have already commented on the heterogeneousness of students, with ages lying between seventeen and forty (or more, as some of them are employed as teachers in elementary/professional centres, since to qualify, they were only required to possess a teacher's certificate, and there is no upper age limit in Spanish higher education establishments), and cultural levels ranging between pre-baccalaureate and postgraduate – there are even cases of third-cycle students, including PhDs, completing their artistic/creative training or finally fulfilling their true musical vocation. And they can be found in the same general or specialist class, even though they may have widely differing musical backgrounds, having studied different subjects and courses: for example, between a specialist instrumental qualification, such as percussion, and a theory/creative qualification, such as composition, there may be some twenty subjects and courses, fewer or more, respectively. In addition, in line with the current regulations known as the 1966 syllabus, the situation of higher grade students is permanently in 'a state of doubt': doubt about whether they really do belong to this level – since some are studying subjects that are legally included in the intermediate level but are required for higher level qualifications – and even doubt about the real higher level of their speciality: the requirement of only an entrance test for the corresponding 'speciality' is seriously problematic in a syllabus that actually has more titles than specialities, as is the case, for example, with a higher qualification in solfeggio and theory of music, transposition and accompaniment. This strangely does not provide in any of the three subjects quoted any course higher than that which is already required for the same title at the intermediate level, with the result that the effectively higher level of this speciality merely consists of the subjects common to all higher qualifications (pedagogy, teaching practice, etc.).

Risks apart, when trying to predict what will happen from the current state of development of the new syllabus arising from the LOGSE, perhaps the heterogeneousness of the students will be maintained (since the entrance test allows access for those who have passed the baccalaureate and the intermediate grade, as well as those who have not (the latter will take an extra test), and there is still no upper age limit). This will then depend more on each individual centre, since the entrance test system gives the examining body a certain capacity to standardise the new intake over and above the official academic requirements, at least more so than in the current 1966 syllabus. The LOGSE can also provide the new syllabus with the hope of reducing the excessive individualism of the students, a serious flaw which I mentioned at the beginning, which is fostered in the 1966 syllabus thanks to the system used to draw up the syllabus: students construct their own individual 'study course' by choosing the subjects and courses which, within the bounds of what is permitted in an often incompatible table of requirements and conditions, they wish to study each year in line with their own particular needs or possibilities. The isolation produced by the impossibility of feeling part of a particular 'intake', in that one is not placed in an academic year, but in a series of scattered courses and subjects, typical of a student's situation under the 1966 syllabus, will doubtless disappear – or at least we hope so – under the new LOGSE syllabus. It provides for four or five academic years with a predetermined number of subjects in each, depending on the speciality, each with its optional subjects, so that students can 'feel' suitably integrated in a genuine intake and a real speciality. It certainly would not come amiss, either, to encourage choir, orchestra and chamber music activities, not only essential for the training of a musician (and not just a soloist!), but also ideal environments for interaction and character-building.

Teachers' profile

I have already mentioned the first main complaint, totally justified, of teachers in non-university higher arts education: the unsuitability of their situation and the inappropriate management they are subjected to – with practically no special treatment beyond that of the make-up of teaching staff in other fields – under elementary and intermediate general education. This is obviously based on a fundamental contradiction: the requirement of a degree or equivalent qualification to teach subjects leading to a qualification that is to all effects at the same level as a degree: if the first part of this contradiction is valid, then logically these teachers should form part of the secondary or equivalent level of education. If the second part is valid, however, it is obviously absurd that this level of arts education is not treated as the higher level.

This almost paradoxical situation and, we hope, the fact that there is an attempt to underline the higher status of this type of education, with all its consequences, are mirrored in supplementary clause four of Act 9/1995 of 20 November, concerning the participation, evaluation and governing of educational establishments, since this states that 'higher arts education establishments shall promote research programmes in their appropriate fields'. A simple reminder of what is stipulated in Article 1 of Act 11/1983 of 25 August, concerning university reform ('the public service of higher education is the responsibility of universities, who carry this out by means of teaching, study and research'), once again poses the question as to whether higher education establishments can still be so outside the ambit of the university system, and therefore, whether the solution for higher arts education establishments is to be found outside one of the following two options: either they are integrated into the university system or they are set up – through specific regulations – as independent bodies equivalent to a university.

We need to strictly emphasise this concept of 'independence', in other words, autonomy, to give it its correct name, as an essential feature of higher education. Since university autonomy (which 'requires and makes it possible for teachers, researchers and students to comply with their respective responsibilities, with a view to satisfying the educational, scientific and professional necessities of society' – Article 2.2 of Act 11/1983) is already ratified by the highest level ruling, higher arts education establishments must be included, either within the university system by virtue of the quoted legislation or, perhaps preferably, achieving their own autonomy by virtue of a regulation of their own (also previously mentioned) which, with the status of an Act, would finally resolve the contradictory situation of this type of education, its teachers and students, within the Spanish educational system.

However, if we look at the immediate progress that the LOGSE has made up to now with regard to the basic academic aspects of non-university higher arts education, in particular related to music, drama and dance, and in spite of the fact that some of these regulations, applicable to the whole country, have been approved since the publication of the previously mentioned Act 9/1995 (which, let us remember, significantly stressed the research aspect of these establishments, research which in Act 11/1983 is understood to be inseparable from autonomy in order to comply with their responsibility – see above), we are surprised, if not shocked and even disgusted, that this type of education is still treated as if it were not higher education, strictly subjected to the maximum legal level of predetermination and supervision that the educational administration possesses and exercises on elementary and intermediate general education.

Paths to a solution

The regulations developing from the LOGSE, the Royal Decrees establishing the basic aspects of the syllabuses for the higher level of music, drama and dance education, give rise to a substantial academic backing for the main path to a solution to have been proposed up to now: the 'Report on the Viability of Proclaiming an Act to Regulate the Organisation of Higher Arts Education in Spain under a System of Autonomy', an excellent report drawn up by Professor Antonio Embid Irujo, Professor of Administrative Law at the University of Zaragoza, and an acknowledged expert on Educational Law. This report was commissioned by the Spanish Association of Higher Arts Education Centres (ACESEA), a body efficiently chaired by the Director of the Real Conservatorio of Madrid, Professor Miguel del Barco, to which almost all the music and drama higher education establishments belong (until the new higher grade is implemented, dance establishments can only be professional). The Association has studied, unanimously approved, and published this report and its conclusions as its own. In these conclusions, following a historical analysis of aspects of arts legislation in Spain and of the current solution in a society as artistically advanced as Germany, various solutions, more or less viable and advantageous, are proposed, including, of course, that of integration within the university system. In the end, the Association opted, with good reason, to propose, as the optimum solution, that these establishments and this type of education be organised with full autonomy and equivalence to the university system, but constituting their own educational status: Higher Arts Institutes.

Indisputably in these norms of basic academic development (in order of proclamation, as follows: Royal Decree 754/1992 of 26 June, for the basic aspects of the higher grade syllabus – the only one taught in Spain – for drama studies; Royal

Decree 617/1995 of 21 April, for the basic aspects of the higher grade syllabus for music; and finally, Royal Decree 1463/1999 of 17 September, establishing the basic aspects of the higher grade syllabus for dance), when comparing their respective specialities, subjects and other didactic aspects, the essential unity of music, drama and dance studies, the three disciplines brought together in Professor Embid Irujo's report, it is plain to see within Higher Arts Institutes, which logically should make room for other artistic disciplines, but quantitatively and qualitatively speaking, that these three institutions should form the basic nucleus of the Higher Institute.

It can clearly and repeatedly be seen, in the specialities of music, drama and dance, how often musical elements are profitably interwoven with others clearly connected to drama, and how they similarly link with body movement and dance; they are permanently interrelated. It is worth remembering that in certain higher music education specialities, elements related to movement and dance are emphasised (especially in teacher training: pedagogy, or the pedagogy of language and musical education option); or how essential elements of poetic forms are integrated; similarly, the value placed on modern audio-visual techniques (when training future creative artists: the composition speciality), etc.

This same integrative aspect is equally evident in drama studies, where we find, within the various options of the performance speciality, one option 'directed towards the training of performers, studying in more detail aspects in which the body is the fundamental instrument of expression'. There is also another option 'directed towards the training of performers, studying in more detail aspects in which song, dance and music are the fundamental elements of expression'. With dance, too, this doubly demonstrated interrelation is equally evident, when the general objectives of this discipline's specialities refer to 'studying in more detail acting techniques and new stage movements' or else 'getting to know and use music as part of the creative process'. A simple review, albeit too extensive to explain here, of the subjects contained in the different basic music, dance and drama syllabuses, clearly indicates this close union, just as even the most superficial knowledge of professional life in these three arts shows the permanent links existing therein, in which some disciplines stand out; a prime example of this is opera, where one cannot even say which is the principal discipline among its blend of content and requirements, in this case even more allied with some of the disciplines related to the visual arts.

So, to sum up, we need to stress the importance of the Embid Irujo Report's proposed solution; and to its valuable contribution to knowledge and legal aspects, and to its unanimous approval and subscription by the authorities of practically all the establishments directly affected, let us add here one more modest point in its favour: to enable the development, academically harmonious and fruitful, of non-university higher arts education, that is to say, music, drama and dance, which apart from enjoying its own legitimate environment, also possesses such clear common references in its subjects and specialities, student and teaching body, and professional profiles, both teaching and otherwise, that collectively they are enhanced. And it is this complementary enhancement that will without doubt guarantee successful compliance with the important mission assigned to this type of education: to give top level academic and artistic training to the professionals of the future that society has the right to expect.

PIET CONVENTS

A CANON as an Example or About the 'What' and 'Why' of a Government Initiative

The participants of the congress entitled 'Arts meets law in education' are also provided with a practical example, by which the reason for an initiative by the authorities is explained and by which is shown what such an initiative is all about. In fact, an example is used to illustrate the importance of art and culture in the wide field of education and in the realization possibilities of this integration at any educational level.

For this example, an appeal was made to CANON, the Cultural Unit of the Education Department of the Flemish Community in Belgium. CANON is represented by Piet Convents, senior staff member.

A COMPLICATED STORY MUST BE TOLD FIRST

The educational situation in Flanders is determined – among other things – by two important elements directly affecting the possibilities of the Education Department when it intends to take initiatives aiming at the integration of art and culture in education.

The first element is the freedom of education in Belgium. This means that anyone can take the initiative of providing education. As a matter of fact, there are three main educational networks in Flanders: Community education (organized by the Flemish Community), subsidized official education (organized by provinces, cities or municipalities) and subsidized private education (organized by private initiative and consisting of denominational (mainly Catholic) education, non-denominational private education and independent schools applying specific teaching methods).

On the other hand, the authorities are committed to provide anyone with high-quality education. For this purpose, compulsory education up to the age of 18 and the attainment targets and developmental objectives apply, among other things. Attainment targets and developmental objectives are the minimum educational goals to be realized at the different education levels. Each education provider must be able to show that the pupils are able to attain these final targets or that the

Jan De Groof, Chantal De Smet and Hilde Penneman (eds.), Art meets Law in Education, 103–113.

educational goals can be developed to a sufficient extent. Attainment targets and developmental objectives have been introduced in elementary education (nursery school and primary school) and in the first grade of secondary education. They are still being designed, developed and discussed for the second and third grades of secondary education.

The tension between the freedom of education and the commitment for high-quality education for anyone leads to the education providers having the freedom to lay down the contents and form of education in their own way to the extent that the minimum educational conditions must be realized and that the authorities must respect this freedom to determine the contents and form.

If the authorities want to make an additional effort to integrate art and culture into education – on top of the minimum conditions laid down – they can only play a stimulating role and arouse enthusiasm.

... la pena de ser ciego ...

The following statement about beauty is chiselled in a side-wall of an old citadel high up at the Alhambra of Granada:

Dale limosna, mujer,
que no hay en la vida nada como
la pena de ser ciego
en Granada.

Give him alms, Madam,
because nothing in life is as bad
as being born blind
in Granada.

The Education Department of the Flemish Community established a modest Cultural Unit for stimulating the integration of art and culture in the wide field of education.

As a matter of fact, the authorities are convinced that art and culture provide life with an irreplaceable and essential addition. They know that learning about, of, with and from art implies an essential and unique enrichment of the individual. They think that anyone should have the opportunity to develop artistically. They find the artistic development as important as any other development form. They consider artistic integration, art education and art training in education to be an absolute necessity and a fundamental right rather than alms. They ... (and we could add many reasons here, but that would make this brief contribution too long).

In short, they know that nothing is as bad as being born blind in Granada; and let us think of that image again. In other words: a fully fledged life must also include the development of all skills, the exploration – as encompassing as possible – of the world that surrounds us and the broadest possible integration of the observations and discoveries made. Art and culture are included here. That is why art and culture also have their place in education as a whole and not just in art education.

For that reason, the authorities would like to invite all education levels and all teachers and school boards to strive for creative integration of art and culture in the classroom. They invite CANON – the Cultural Unit – to concentrate on this and to help them realize this task.

What and why?

CANON, the Cultural Unit of the Education Department, was set up in January 1995. The name refers to the different meanings and fields of the word 'canon': from a collection of good examples about the ideal proportion in monumental art up to a kind of song, in which two or more voices start the same melody, one after the other. In our work we try to have these different aspects of the word featured and we want to link up the 3 meanings with a single purpose: giving culture an active place in education.

The basic philosophy of the CANON Cultural Unit comes down to supporting, encouraging and exchanging examples of good practice. Moreover, this philosophy is based on a thorough study of the interaction between culture and education. Among other things, this resulted in the research project entitled Education, Culture, Creativity and Art – in 1997/98 – supported by both responsible Departments: the Education Department and the Welfare, Public Health and Culture Department.

Four items occupy a central position in the operation of CANON:

- considering creativity as a necessary and logical complement of the intellect;
- activating attention for art and culture in the world of education;
- coordinating the cultural offer; and
- stimulating the positive image and impact of art and culture in education.

Here, special attention is paid to:

- supporting teacher training (professors and students);
- supporting the attainment targets and developmental objectives for art training and art education;
- supporting art and culture in the education sectors in which the attainment targets and developmental objectives are not applicable yet.

Art education in general includes a duality:

- on the one hand, it is a means to develop self-expression, required for any individual;
- on the other hand, special artistic talent must be fostered.

Here, it is important to consider that our work must be more than a single shot. Eventually, it must be integrated into education as a whole.

Projects

CANON's recurring projects and their evolution.

DynaMo²

DynaMo² can be called CANON's 'mother project'. As the title indicates, the basic purpose is to launch dynamics in schools. Each spring, all 4,000 schools in Flanders receive a DynaMo² catalogue, in which many organizations introduce their activities and offer for schools in five fields: business/democracy/health/ecology/arts. Individuals, such as artists who can offer activities to schools, are also included in this catalogue.

DynaMo² provides all schools with the possibility to have projects in a field of activity financially backed up; they develop this project themselves in cooperation with professional agencies whether they are featured in the catalogue or not. The major field of work is the artistic field, aimed at art and culture; however, the other four fields turn DynaMo² into a broad social project. Schools can also work thematically across the fields and for instance artistically interpret a democratic or business theme. It is crucial here that the projects proposed always be in line with the school and living culture of the applicant in conformity with the larger autonomy and more demand-oriented nature of the schools. This is how the schools' own initiatives are emphasized instead of the consumptive use of the many ready-made projects offered in various fields.

An expert jury with insight into the different fields of work annually makes a selection of the project proposals submitted. These projects receive a subsidy by the CANON Cultural Unit. On average, about half of the applications are positively assessed. The amount of the support is determined on the basis of the estimated costs the schools are to submit. However, one always takes it for granted that the schools themselves also co-invest in the projects they would like to realize.

Masterpieces/CANON culture days for teachers

These two projects – the CANON culture days and Masterpieces – alternate. Masterpieces are organized every two years in November. The Culture days for teachers are held in the years in between.

Masterpieces

For a whole month, a few dozens of art and cultural centres offer some 'free seats' to teachers. Next to a real 'VIP' treatment at an art event, the 'masters' are involved in an instruction project, counselled by a specialist, aiming at classroom practice. By means of active work sessions, Masterpieces aim at providing teachers working methods that can be applied in their own practice. On top of this VIP treatment, anyone participating in a Masterpiece also gets a masterpiece. For the 1997 edition, this was the art reproduction entitled *Pierrot Lunaire*, a painting by Frank Maieu.

For the 1999–2000 edition, all participants received the CD entitled 'Le Carnaval des Animaux' by Camille Saint-Saëns, executed by Walter Boeykens' Large Ensemble. These initiatives come with a kit containing course suggestions, in which the different domains – image, music, drama, movement, media – of art training as applied in primary school are featured.

Culture days for teachers

The CANON culture days for teachers intend to start dialogue and exchange. Teachers of all education levels introduce examples from their own practice regarding cultural-educational projects to colleagues. The enthusiasm and equally the problems they were faced with when developing the projects and finding creative solutions may lead to inspired initiatives and own initiatives by other teachers. Representatives of Cultural Centres are also involved in the dialogues. They add their experiences with culture and education to the whole picture.

In the third CANON culture days edition (1998), attention was concentrated on the transfer to the participants' own practice. The selected projects introduced were models aimed at providing an answer to the frequently recurring question of how the experiences of colleagues can be converted to their own genuine school situation. Another point of attention in this edition was the weight school boards attach to culture in their school as a whole and the space they create for that purpose.

Backing up art training

The CANON Cultural Unit devotes quite some attention to backing up art training at all levels of education. By means of all kinds of initiatives, teachers and pupils learn how they can convert the attainment targets for art training and art education to the practical courses. More in particular, the attainment targets and developmental objectives for primary education deal with five aspects: image, movement, drama, media and music. For the first grade of secondary education, art education is mentioned and it features music and visual arts training.

Arts working days

Teachers in nursery and primary education, and also students in teacher training, can attend a training session of two days, in which some self-selected, active and creative workshops are offered in the five art fields. These workshops are supported as far as contents goes by an explanation about the position and significance of art training in primary education.

Art working days' participants are stimulated into applying the acquired insights and skills in their own education practice or apprenticeship. Subsequently, they are invited to a one-day follow-up session, during which they can exchange experiences with colleagues.

The third part of this initiative consists of another continued training of two days, in which the integration of art training into other fields of learning such as mathematics, language, world orientation or physical education occupies a central position. A follow-up project for the art training work days is being prepared for the near future.

ho'bo

The CANON Cultural Unit provides support, not only for teachers, but also for lecturers of teacher training colleges, when getting acquainted with new teaching methods in the field of cultural education. In the 'ho'bo' project – in cooperation with 'Kunst in Zicht' (i.e. 'art in sight') – lecturers and specialists examine the position art education and culture occupy in the teacher training curriculum; the name 'ho'bo' (in Dutch) stands for contemporary project for the enhancement and support of attainment targets and developmental objectives for art training in nursery, primary and secondary education through the teacher training colleges. This initiative – that originated from questions in teacher training – was extended to the students of these training programmes from the 1999–2000 school year on. During an active project week, they learn how to work with the art training methods, together with their lecturers.

Art kicks

In the 'Kunstkicks' (i.e. art kicks) CANON publication, written by journalist Anna Luyten and featuring photographs by Lieve Blancquaert, the art education attainment targets are submitted to a whole range of different individuals of our society: 100 famous personalities, 'Fascinating Flemings' – from a car mechanic to a philosopher – freely talk about their experiences and visions on the art education attainment target for the first grade of secondary education. This is book full of ideas that show that educational targets are part of everyday life.

Art posters

Based on the art training attainment targets, the CANON Cultural Unit developed a first series of five posters by children's books illustrator Gerda Dendooven in 1996; they may contribute to working with art in the classroom. The posters are very attractive for children of the first and second grades of primary education, but they also contain a number of texts from the Parliament of Flanders Act on the attainment targets the teachers can use in their work.

In late 1997, a second series by writer–illustrator Gregie De Maeyer was published; it is meant for the third grade of primary education and it zooms in on the cross-fertilization between art training and the other subjects. Gregie also wrote a booklet entitled 'Juf and Aagje' to go with the posters. The third series of art posters – this time designed by illustrator Mathilde Geens – mainly illustrates the art attitudes for preschoolers.

Learning how to learn with art training

'Leren leren met muzische vorming' (i.e. Learning how to learn with art training), written by André Blondeel and Alix Van Ransbeeck, is a handy piece of reading and working material concerning the contents and application of art training in the classroom. Next to a basic text, some practical work files in each field of art training are included; these files illustrate how a teacher may flesh out an art training lesson. Moreover, the book invites the reader – by means of a large number of examples – to involve the world of art and culture in his daily classroom practice.

Art postcards

In order to make the link between art training in primary school and cross-curricular work in secondary schools, the CANON Cultural Unit developed a series of art postcards. Based on the attainment targets of the first grade in secondary education, these twelve postcards are a source of information for teaching across the subjects in a creative way. 'Water' is the starting point of a series of teaching suggestions, in which this theme is treated each time in another subject from a cultural point-of-view. Seventy five thousand teachers in secondary education received the cards for free with the educational magazine *Klasse* and – subsequently – they can collect and exchange many additional ideas on a website developed especially for this purpose by the teacher training department of Ghent University (URL http://simsim.rug.ac.be/water).

Right you are

In cooperation with the Minister for Equal Opportunities and supported by 'De Standaard' publishing company, a series of ten books for first readers was developed in 1997. The 'equal opportunities' theme was incorporated into each story in a playful and non-pedantic way. The books were offered for free to all primary schools in Flanders. In cooperation with 10 voluntary groups of teacher training students, the CANON Cultural Unit developed a text leaflet with teaching suggestions to go with each booklet.

The year after, a CD entitled 'Groot Gelijk' (i.e. right you are) was also produced for the first grade of secondary education, in which well-known Flemish artists musically treat themes such as bullying, multiculturalism and poverty. The CANON Cultural Unit also developed a text leaflet to go with this CD.

Golden Owl for Youngsters

Following the example of 'De Gouden Uil' (i.e. Golden Owl), the well-known literary award in Flanders and the Netherlands, the Welfare, Public Health and Culture and Education Departments of Flanders and the Netherlands joined forces with the 'Taalunie' (i.e. Language Union) and the 'Stichting Lezen' (i.e. Reading Foundation) to develop a 'Jonge Gouden Uil' (i.e. Golden Owl for Youngsters). Adolescents from schools in Flanders and the Netherlands initially selected their own juries. Afterwards, a reading and assessing period took place across the schools, in which the various reading experiences of the pupils were extensively discussed. At the final happening of the 'Jonge Gouden Uil' debates with the authors take place and the prize is awarded by the young juries. The CANON

Cultural Unit counsels and supports this project on behalf of the Flemish Education Department; its fourth edition was held in early 2000.

With flying colours
Art as a lever for social and cultural emancipation?

The project entitled 'Vlaggen en wimpels' (i.e. with flying colours) addresses a number of primary schools with more than 50 per cent migrant children. Artists concentrate on a single school for a whole year and develop a project one day a week together with the pupils and teachers. The project aims at confronting the pupils with each others' culture and way of life by means of creative methods. For this project, the CANON Cultural Unit of the Education Department works together with the 'Koning Boudewijnstichting' (i.e. King Baudouin Foundation), the Minorities Policy Unit of the Education Department and the Centre for Amateur Art.

Going with this project, 'Steunpunt Intercultureel Onderwijs' (i.e. Support Centre for Intercultural Education) of Ghent University is conducting a project investigation that led to the development of 'Puur uit de Buurt' (i.e. purely from the neighbourhood), a working instrument for schools intending to realize a similar project in their school culture.

Museum projects
The idea that many art education projects run the risk of lacking a long-term effect due to their topicality led to developing a number of 'permanent' projects to be developed in several Flemish museums. The museums involved will be logistically and financially supported by the CANON Cultural Unit to develop a project that fits their own character. The museum project already resulted in two concrete initiatives. At MIAT (i.e. 'Museum voor Industriële Archeologie en Textiel' or Museum of Industrial Archaeology and Textiles) in Ghent, a number of 'Speelkasten' (i.e. a kind of play box) were developed, especially designed for the museum and closely related to the collection as far as design and contents go. Simultaneously, the 'Speelkasten' make children and youngsters familiar with a historical era in an innovating, playful and active way.

The second Museum Project at 'SMAK' (i.e. City Museum of Contemporary Art) in Ghent proved that a museum also displays modern stuff. Children and youngsters helped to develop the audioguides for the young museum public. By means of sharp comments and considerations, the visitor is guided through the permanent collection of SMAK and is presented with another way of looking at the works of art. The 'Speelkasten' and the audio guides can be used by a group in a school context as well as by individual visitors, which bridges the gap between a school visit and a 'regular' museum visit to a considerable extent.

Crown It
'De kroon op het werk' (i.e. 'Crown It') is a performing arts festival for pupils.

Theatre projects of secondary schools are introduced to a large audience in the form of a competition. Through provincial theatre projects at the Flemish cultural centres, the CANON Cultural Unit gives pupils the opportunity to develop themselves in a creative manner. The final day – when the provincial winners compete for the main prize, a cultural trip – is the apotheosis.

Spoiling days

The name 'Verwendagen' (i.e. spoiling days) has an ironic touch but it also has a literal meaning. On each spoiling day, about a hundred teachers are really spoilt with words, images and food; they sit at a nicely decorated and rich table with six special guests from the world of art and the media. One single question is asked (and sometimes answered) on this occasion: 'Which teacher ever aroused inspiration?' As a matter of fact, each of them was also a pupil – in the old days – in which a teacher brought out the budding talent. This is an important message for the teachers involved.

CANON's one-year projects

By means of the one-year projects, the CANON Cultural Unit intends to align with the contemporary trends in the world of art and culture. That is why these projects are truly varied and they can even develop into recurring projects.

A shot of art (artists for youngsters)

In this project, secondary education pupils (aged 14/18) work with a professional artist within the school context. For a fairly long period, this artist is supported to enable him/her to work together with the pupils on an artistic product that may lead into a performance or an exhibition in a large and more public forum than the school. By means of the cooperation, the CANON Cultural Unit wants to provide the pupils with the opportunity to express their own ideas in a professional way. No doubt, this cross-fertilisation will provide the required creative impulses.

'kunSTof' (artist in the classroom)

The basis idea of 'kunSTof' (i.e. a pun in Dutch, meaning 'knowing your subject' as well as 'art or' as well as synthetic material) is to approach the subject matter differently. The CANON Cultural Unit provides 100 secondary education teachers with the opportunity to consider and treat their subject – from motor mechanics to mathematics – from a different angle. In the space of a minimum 2 or a maximum 4 hours, an artist approaches the subject matter from another, unexpected angle. His/her vision and work with the pupils may lead to new impulses, fresh ideas or a project.

CANON concert

In order to open the new school year festively, the CANON Cultural Unit receives a hall full of teachers for a concert. This is a nice musical evening that provides everyone with the opportunity to meet the classic CANON. Concerts at St. Baaf's Cathedral and at the Opera in Ghent have already been held, each time in cooperation with 'Festival van Vlaanderen' (i.e. Flanders Festival).

CANON nature day

The CANON nature day – an initiative of the CANON Cultural Unit together with the Environment and Infrastructure Department – emphasises the broad interpretation the CANON Cultural Unit gives to the term culture. In all kinds of working groups, teachers examine various project strategies they can apply in their own school when developing creative environmental projects.

Roots-blues

Four schools get the opportunity to indulge in the blues culture. By means of a special CD-ROM programme, the pupils look for the roots of contemporary music and the links of the blues with what happens in the classroom. Simultaneously, a musician forms a band at the school. No doubt, this will eventually lead to a great presentation.

KLASSE

This is the monthly education magazine, edited by an independent team for which the Education Department is responsible. *Klasse* consists of 3 different magazines: *Klasse voor Leraars* (distributed for free to all teachers in Flanders), *Klasse voor Ouders* (meant for parents of children in primary education and in the first grade of secondary education, disseminated by the school free on request) and *Klasse voor Jongeren* (directed at youngsters aged 14 to 18 and distributed through the same channel as *Klasse voor Ouders*).

The main subject in these 3 magazines is always the same and no doubt this has a positive effect on the communication between the different groups involved in education.

Since March 1997, the CANON Cultural Unit has had its own permanent column: 'CANON met Klasse' in *Klasse voor Leraars.*

The CANON Cultural Unit can always be reached by mail, telephone, fax or e-mail.

CANON
Cultuurcel Departement Onderwijs
Afdeling Informatie en Documentatie

address:
Hendrik Consciencegebouw – 5A
Koning Albert II-laan 15,
1210 Brussel
Belgium

CANON	Tel: +32 2/553 96 63	*canon@ond.vlaanderen.be*
	Fax: +32 2/553 96 75	
Staff:	Erna Schelstraete	
	Jan Staes	
	Piet Convents	
Secretariat:	Déanne Durant	
	Sonja Demesmaeker	

European Patterns and Comparative Analysis

MICHAEL WIMMER

Recommendations: Towards European Patterns on General Cultural Education

When I started to prepare this chapter I accidentally watched a feature on TV about Nikolaus Harnoncourt on the occasion of his 70th birthday. During this feature Mr. Harnoncourt gave a practical example of cultural education. He did not just conduct the orchestra, he also explained his personal view of the music on stage and for the audience, his very specific approaches to this kind of music and how he tries to realise his thoughts and emotions together with the musicians.

When they played the concert overture 'The fairy tale of the beautiful Melusine' by Felix Mendelssohn-Bartholdy I became enchanted, so I decided I had better not start with the recommendations on the future of cultural education which you probably already know, and of course also follow, but discuss my new passion for the beautiful Melusine whom I cannot forget because of Mr. Harnoncourt.

I did not know the story of Melusine before, so I consulted my books and what I found was a story of a mermaid, also called 'Mère Lusine', ancestress of the house of Lusignan in Poitou, which dated back to 967.

This is the story. During hunting the Earl of Raymond unintentionally killed his uncle. Afterwards he met three young girls, one more beautiful than the other. The most beautiful was Melusine. She promised to help him, if he would marry her, but he had to promise not to ask her where she came from and never to meet her on a Saturday. After the marriage Melusine helped him a lot: because of her Raymond became the owner of a huge property where they built a castle named Lusignan. They became parents of 10 sons, but all of them looked a little strange, for example 'Geoffroy au grand dent' with the teeth of a boar. However, all of them were strong, brave and successful.

One day, when Raymond started doubting, he asked his brother to watch Melusine to find out what she did on a Saturday. His brother discovered that on Saturday Melusine became a mermaid. You can imagine how surprised Raymond was, but he feared to acknowledge the strangeness of his wife and also that he had broken his promise, so he decided to keep silent.

Jan De Groof, Chantal De Smet and Hilde Penneman (eds.), Art meets Law in Education, 117–122.

But times were hard in those days and when Geoffroy set fire to a cloister and all of the monks, together with one of his brothers, died, Raymond, remembering what his brother had seen, blamed Melusine, now in his words a miserable worm, for this disaster. With this accusation he destroyed the relationship between him and Melusine. Melusine had to say goodbye and flew away in her mermaid guise while Raymond, realising that he had made a terrible mistake, started a pilgrimage to Rome.

So, that is the story I found. And I was really affected by the significance of this historic occurrence, which you maybe do not see yet, or do you? What I am going to attempt to explain is that the story of the beautiful Melusine has to be seen as the story of cultural education in Europe.

The story begins with a terrible mistake. Raymond has killed his uncle, unintentionally we are asked to believe. Looking at our educational systems we are witnessing a mistake of a similar kind. Our educational systems are educating, but at the same time they are also destroying. What does not fit in to the current framework of the school curriculum is of no value. It does not exist for the school, or even has to be abolished, but it exists in the bodies, in the hearts and in the brains of the young people, not being just school children, but also being engaged in all kinds of extra-curricular youth culture activities.

It was during another European conference on 'A Creative Culture' about a year ago, where the participants stated that 'our educational systems are dominated by too narrow a view of children's abilities, which are primarily focused on particular styles of deductive reasoning and verbal and mathematical thought'. But it is more than evident that young people are equipped with a much wider range of intellectual abilities that are systematically not taken into account during normal school lessons.

In this connection I recommend to you the Convention of Children's Rights of the United Nations Children's Fund. Looking at the aims of education you can find: 'Education shall aim at developing the child's personality, talents and mental and physical abilities to the fullest extent'.

I am not going to repeat what we all already know, that times are changing quite rapidly, but if it is true that our school systems have been developed on the basis of an industrial economy and that we still tend to think and act in the same direction, then there is something fundamentally wrong. And that is why Melusine has to come in.

Melusine promises a lot. She promises Raymond, easily recognisable as the representative of the old educational system, to undo his mistake and to start a common and fruitful life by developing all his abilities to the fullest extent. And it seems to work quite well, if there were not two problems.

The first problem is the ten sons. They are different from what we, and probably also Raymond, consider to be normal. They look and act unusual: they have the teeth of a boar and they set fire to a cloister. Quite unusual.

In cultural education terms we also have a lot of promises around; for example, many studies tell us that children would become more intelligent, more social, less criminal or less likely to become drug addicts when sufficiently exposed to cultural education.

That may or may not be. Personally, I do not believe in this argument. There are too many culturally well-educated people looking quite strange, not to say ugly, and setting fire wherever they can. Cultural education is important for its own sake; more, it is indispensable, but it is no guarantee for anything. In any case, cultural education cannot be seen as an excuse for political ineffectiveness.

Maybe I am speaking mainly from an Austrian point of view, but it becomes more and more counterproductive for me when representatives of cultural education argue that they would solve the problems that are created systematically within the other areas of the curriculum. Cultural education would be the only remaining advocacy of comprehensive personal development of young people, while colleagues teaching the other subjects would destroy these efforts. This would result in a monster.

Thanks to the Council of Europe, Ken Robinson from the University of Warwick, a key person in the field of cultural education in Europe, carried out a survey on the status of cultural education in Europe. The information he obtained officially from the educational departments of the national ministries included where and how many music or fine art lessons per week are given in individual countries. Up to now we know almost nothing about the content of these lessons, and what are the specific contributions of cultural education to what young people are learning on the whole in school. So my assumption in this context is that we have a problem of legitimating cultural education, not only in competition with other subjects (that is mainly the problem of the teachers who do not want to lose their jobs, which is understandable) but from its unique learning approach, which is difficult in a world where the argument of immediate usefulness is followed.

It was quite alarming for me when, together with some colleagues at the conference, we participated in a discussion on future perspectives of Arts Education in New York. The most elaborate arguments towards more and better cultural education in school did not come from the experts, but from representatives of the economic sector. Their message was quite clear: the industrial economy is over and with it the traditional educational systems. The major growth areas in the world economy are driven by the generation of new ideas, by capacities of innovation and creativity, and by the ability of individuals to adapt to new demands and changes. So what they need are very new qualifications provided by new educational settings, and in these settings cultural education would have to play a major role.

So far we have considered the commission of economics, but we also have to treat the other problem. It is the problem of Saturday. You remember: Raymond was not allowed to meet or even watch Melusine when she wore her fishtail. Obviously this fishtail fundamentally affects the image of the human body, but do we have a similar effect in cultural education terms?

I am convinced that we do. I think that there is a secret around, at least a taboo. My assumption is that the fishtail in the story stands for the arts in Arts Education.

Why, you may ask? In my daily practical work with schools I often wonder why we speak of Arts Education without taking into account the arts. Arts Education consists of drawing, painting, singing, dancing, etc., which is undoubtedly important, but not necessarily a genuine artistic approach.

More than that. There is something I would call a deeply rooted hate–love relationship between education and the arts, and within this field of tension the harmonising endeavours of the superego of education regularly wins against the chaotic id of the arts. The arts, especially those not yet sedimented as part of our cultural heritage, are enigmatic and manifold, often nasty, ugly, irritating, crazy and complicated – and they are also unique and terrific. As life goes on I am tempted to say that young people know this quite well. Maybe that is one of the reasons why artists normally find an easier access to youth culture than educators, who stick to the mediation of values in cultural clothes in a well-structured framework which is normally the opposite of life.

In our educational systems this structural repression of that which makes the arts vibrant is a pity, because the arts are probably the only remaining school of perception. They allow us to learn to differentiate, to distinguish and how to proceed with the different and with the strange.

The fishtail of Melusine on Saturday is strange. More than that, even when watching very closely you will never fully explain it. You have to accept it; it is important just because it *is*. Strangeness is an indispensable part of our life and we have to learn how to deal with it. How to deal with these kinds of things, for example with emotions, with farewell, with death is not fully explainable. Is this an issue to which school can contribute in personal development, or must it be repressed because it is too dangerous?

Perhaps what Melusine wants to tell us is that you cannot solve the educational problems by forcing the arts in the old system. But Melusine represents the offer to bring to bear their specific abilities, up to now systematically neglected in school. And she gives us the advice that you had better change the whole week by Saturday than make its attraction more of the same.

Raymond did not believe in his own promise: he did not believe in the arts, and he lost. But at the very end he understood and began a pilgrimage.

Recommendations

Maybe we should also start a pilgrimage, not towards Rome, but towards common patterns of general cultural education as reflected in the title of this chapter. To make the journey a little less arduous, I have some recommendations. They were developed about a year ago when we started the experiment of establishing a common European network on Arts and Education.

1. First of all, we should forget all hopes of reforming educational systems solely on the national level. The (at least) EC-wide freedom of personal traffic, together

with the freedom of residence makes European approaches in the field of education indispensable. This is true also in the field of the arts. The arts are by their very nature transnational. If you try to keep the arts within certain (not only geographical) boundaries you will destroy them.

2. Take the arts seriously. The arts are an important, an indispensable part of our societies, and they should become a more prominent factor of our general educational systems too, not only in a so-called cultural ghetto, but as an integral part of all learning processes. An important prerequisite is the good relationship teachers are developing towards the arts, especially towards contemporary art forms. How many teachers do you know regularly reading contemporary literature, listening to contemporary music, watching contemporary dance performances? But you are sure that they should act as cultural mediators in the cultural institutions schools undoubtedly are?

3. We need to promote flexible curricula in our schools. Existing school curricula tend to be based on firm and often impermeable divisions between the individual disciplines, but cultural development often happens at the points where areas of expertise overlap: culture happens on connection. The most exciting developments are happening through interaction of science, arts and technology. We should allow for and encourage these kind of collaboration and that means more project-oriented and interdisciplinary learning settings within our school systems.

4. We need to promote more open relationships between schools and cultural institutions. Artistic archives, libraries, exhibition halls, museums, concert halls, theatres and other cultural institutions provide an enormously rich resource which should be drawn on fully in invigorating the education we provide for our young people. It should be in the interest of both sides to have close and positive relationships forming the attitudes, abilities and attributes of pupils and students, not only towards arts and culture.

In this connection I would recommend you to look more closely at the newly developed curriculum for cultural and *kunstzinnige* education in the Netherlands. Supported by a voucher system, young people are invited to visit cultural activities normally outside school, which are of interest to them. The assessment is based on an art file, which the students have to deliver. There are at least three incentives: students become acquainted with cultural activities; cultural institutions are providing attractive mediation activities; and teachers have to find new relationships towards the cultural world in which young people are engaged. And as an important side-effect the state, in the shape of public schools, gives up the definition of culture.

5. We need to promote new conceptions of young people's abilities and intelligence and new methods of assessing them. The traditional educational systems – as I already mentioned – are narrowing young people's personalities on particular styles of deductive reasoning and verbal and mathematical thought, but there is powerful evidence that young people have a wider range of intellectual abilities in

other domains normally structurally repressed in school. In more flexible learning settings we should also take into account these abilities and find new methods of assessing them.

6. We need to explore new forms of training for teachers, artists and others. Training systems for teachers give too little attention to creativity and the arts. Unless we have a supply of motivated and well-trained teachers, all of our policy aspirations for cultural education will come to nothing. Cultural education relies upon a creative engagement between teachers and taught, within which teachers themselves must have room to develop their own creative capacities.

Equally the training of artists tends to ignore opportunities in education. Professional training systems for artists are, for the most part, focused on the nineteenth-century model of artistic production: i.e. of virtuoso artists driven by solitary genius. New modes of creative production in the arts are much more collaborative, and often much more rooted in the use of new technologies.

7. All cultural institutions need to develop educational as well as cultural policies. That means not only insisting on the highest possible artistic quality, but also developing new strategies for engaging with audiences, for example working together with schools and other educational institutions, and with it broadening the base of participation in its work and enabling the creative work of others. That means the development of new strategies to articulate responsibility in a common process of cultural development.

8. To give the pilgrimage a common feeling you are warmly invited to join the arts and education network. This network has been developed over the last year as an international platform for creating new policies for arts and education on all political and administrative levels. It provides a forum to negotiate the variety of existing directions and contents at the interface between arts and education and to promote the creation of a new diversity of methods in this new policy and expert field on a European level.

As one of the founding members I can tell you that in this first year we have had really fascinating discussions; recently in Vienna, about 100 colleagues from all over Europe worked on the issue of 'Arts in context'.

If you join the network you may meet Melusine with her full proud fishtail, not only on Saturday.

JERRY BOOTH

Towards Manageable European Patterns on the Arts Education

In a speech at the College d'Europe in September 1999 Jaques Delors quoted Henrik Brugmans:

> *L'Europe, c'est la terre des hommes continuellement en lutte avec eux-mêmes, c'est le lieu ou aucune certitude n'est acceptée comme verité, si elle n'est continuellement découverte. D'autres continents se vantent de leur efficacité, mais c'est le climat européen qui rend la vie dangereuse, aventureuse, magnifique et tragique, et par la, digne d'être vecue.*

Delors himself later says:

> *Certes eduquer, c'est avant tout transmetter aux etudiants ce que l'humanité a appris sur elle-même. Mais c'est dans le même temps, fournir les outils permettant a checun d'affronter la nouveaute et l'alea.*

In Bologna in June 1999, the Council of Ministers, committing themselves to the creation of a European Higher Education area set out a number of objectives, among them:

- easily readable and comparable degrees to boost employability and the international competitiveness of our system;
- 2 cycles with progression to the second dependent on successful completion of the first;
- a system of credits relating to contexts within and outside higher education;
- co-operation in quality assurance to develop comparable criteria and methods;
- a European dimension in higher education, especially in curriculum development, inter-institutional co-operation, mobility schemes and integrated programmes of study, training and research.

Some people fear that harmonisation will destroy the diversity which characterises Europe and especially European arts education. Others feel that the European Commission's education programmes are ill-adapted to the needs of arts

Jan De Groof, Chantal De Smet and Hilde Penneman (eds.), Art meets Law in Education, 123–124.

education. They perceive developments such as modularity and new funding regimes as attacking the values of individualism, questioning and rule-breaking central to the arts and arts education. Here in southern Europe Nordic and Anglo-Saxon structures are not always seen as appropriate reform solutions. The incorporation of arts institutions into the university sector in the UK and Nordic countries is still seen as destroying the most valuable characteristics of arts education, and this perception has been shared by some in the UK.

On 12 October 1999 in the House of Lords, Viscount Falkland, apologising for raising their Lordships' hackles by mentioning France, went on to say that the French:

> realise that it is important to encourage artists of all kinds, not only to do what they do but to challenge the barriers which face them; indeed to encourage them to be iconoclastic, to take risks, to push the barriers forward forward, indeed to fail – always a problem with artists.

Earlier in the same debate the painter Patrick Heron's article titled 'Murder of the Arts Schools', written in 1971, was also quoted.

> A disaster of massive proportions is going unnoticed in the press. I'm referring to a development of major national significance, which every painter and sculptor I know has bitterly opposed since its inception; namely, the Government-decreed, and therefore forcible, absorption of nearly all the country's biggest and most important colleges of art by new polytechnics.[1]

Nearly 30 years after this dire warning of imminent disaster, it seems that this particular prophecy of doom was rather overstated. In the light of that experience it seems unlikely that the proposals endorsed at Bologna will mean the banishment of a Europe dubbed by Delors *le continent du doute, du doute metaphysique, du doute de nous-mêmes*?

European arts education will continue to challenge and question, and in that spirit some will doubtless criticise moves towards transparency in a European higher education area. However, they will need to take care that they are not perceived as defending unsustainable and reactionary practices.

1 *Guardian* 12 October 1971.

PIERRE KUENTZ

L'Enseignement Supérieur des Arts en Europe une Enquête d'ELIA

A travers une enquête, basée sur un questionnaire, Elia (European Ligue of institutes of the Arts), a entrepris de collecter les informations permettant de donner une vue d'ensemble de l'enseignement supérieur de toutes les disciplines artistiques dans les Etats Membres de l'Europe des Quinze.

Une étude approfondie et systématique des informations existantes avait, tout d'abord, été entreprise par Irene Magill; mais les éléments résultant de ce travail de compilation se sont avérés inutilisables trop de données étant inexactes ou dépassées ou largement incomplètes, les lacunes, selon les pays, ne correspondant pas aux mêmes secteurs ou aspects.

Citons pour exemple les résultats d'une enquête menée par O.E.S (Gesellschaft for Empirische Studien bR, Maiworm & Over, Kassel), grâce au soutien de la Commission Européenne et publiés en novembre 1995. La méthode utilisée pour collecter l'information est malheureusement très criticable: nous ne savons rien sur le genre d'établissements consultés ni surie mode de sélection permettant une représentation proportionnelle de la réalité 'nationale'. C'est la raison pour laquelle aucun chiffre ne peut être considéré comme pertinent ou fiable, et les pourcentages donnés ne peuvent valablement servir ni pour décrire os répartitions a l'intérieur d'un même pays ni pour faire des comparaisons entre les différents systèmes nationaux.

Nous avons ainsi constaté qu'il n'existe aucune étude fiable sur l'enseignement supérieur des arts. Or, il est plus que Jamais nécessaire de disposer de renseignements exacts à l'heure ou les étudiants, les enseignants et les artistes se déplacent librement en Europe sans connaissance réelle des différences et similitudes existantes.

D'autre part, les modifications apportées, actuellement, aux dispositions régissant l'enseignement des arts dans de nombreux pays, risquent d'accroître les disparités présentes s elles ne peuvent s'appuyer sur une vue d'ensemble dégageant les tendances qui se dessinent ailleurs.

L'enquête entreprise par ELIA s'est volontairement limitée, dans un premier temps, aux seuls Pays Membres de l'Union Européenne, mais ne comprend pas le

Jan De Groof, Chantal De Smet and Hilde Penneman (eds.), Art meets Law in Education, 125–128.

Luxembourg qui, n'offrant pas d'enseignement supérieur pour les arts, n'est pas concerné. Pour chacun de ces pays, le même questionnaire à été adressé aux organismes de tutelle des enseignements des disciplines artistiques représentées au sein d'ELIA: les Arts plastiques, l'Audiovisuel, le Design, la Danse, la Musique et le Théâtre. Seuls les enseignements destinés à des étudiants qui veulent devenir des 'artistes praticiens' intéressent cette étude: les enseignements théoriques, tels que 'l'Histoire de l'Art' ou 'l'Esthétique', Si la pratique d'un art ne constitue pas la matière principale. n'ont donc pas été retenus.

Un seul et même questionnaire a été adressé à chaque autorité de tutelle. Il nous a semblé, en effet, qu'au niveau ministériel nous pouvions espérer trouver des réponses qui soient suffisamment globales pour permettre de larges synthèses et autoriser des comparaisons pertinentes, les informations non disponibles à ce niveau pouvant ultérieurement être obtenues auprès d'établissements sélectionnes.

Son contenu aborde les aspects suivants de l'enseignement supérieur des arts:

- l'Enseignement Artistique dans le contexte général de l'Enseignement Supérieur
- le profile des Etablissements: liens institutionnels, degré d'autonomie, financements
- le profile des Enseignements: niveau de recrutement, niveau des qualifications
- le personnel enseignant: statut. avantages sociaux et obligations de service
- les modalités de la pédagogie et de l'évaluation des acquis
- les étudiants: avantages et contraintes de la vie quotidienne et des études.

Le questionnaire a été réalisé en allemand, anglais, espagnol, français, et italien.

Des personnes-relais membres d'ELIA, dans chaque pays et pour chacune des disciplines, ont été invités à nous apporter leur aide pour:

- définir les destinataires du questionnaire et donner leur avis sur les modalités retenues
- vérifier les traductions afin d'éviter les 'crissements sémantiques'
- se mettre à la disposition des responsables ministériels pour leur faciliter les réponses
- trouver des sources complémentaires d'informations, si nécessaire
- sélectionner, dans ces cas, des établissements susceptibles de nous les fournir
- donner leur avis sur la présentation des résultats de l'enquête concernant leur pays.

Un tel groupe de travail illustre parfaitement les avantages d'une structure comme Elia, qui regroupe on son sein des représentants de l'enseignement supérieur de toutes les disciplines de tous les pays européens. Il convient toutefois d'en indiquer également les limites, Car, en effet, les membres d'Elia sont des collaborateurs bénévoles pour lesquels les responsabilités attachées à leur fonction de chefs d'établissements sont nécessairement prioritaires Aussi leur disponibilité est-elle parfois restreinte et occasionnelle; ceci ne facilite pas l'établissement du calendrier de réunions de concertation ni la programmation du déroulement des opérations par étapes.

Le retour des questionnaires nous a valu quelques surprises. Contrairement à notre attente, les réponses des ministères ne comprenaient souvent pas les informations globales que nous pansions pourtant plus facilement accessibles auprès des administrations centrales. Certains ministères ont demandé à des établissements choisis par eux de répondre au questionnaire à leur place, mais sans pour autant ajouter les données globales dont ces établissements ne pouvaient disposer. Pour combler ces lacunes nous avons sollicité ces renseignements auprès des 'agences nationales de statistiques universitaires'.

Dans l'ensemble, la collecte de l'information a été beaucoup plus difficile que prévue.

Les résultats de l'enquête, traités par ordinateur, seront diffusés sous la forme d'une publication et d'un accès sur internet; ces présentations comprendront

- la description des enseignements supérieurs des arts dans chacun des pays,
- des comparaisons entre pays, pour chacune des disciplines, selon les différents chapitres du questionnaire.
- des considérations plus générales que les synthèses et comparaisons auront permis de mettre en lumière.

Les textes seront accompagnés de graphiques permettant une visualisation rapide des donées les plus marquantes.

Nous disposons aujourd'hui, d'informations complètes pour la Belgique flamande, le Danemark, la Finlande et la Suède, et de réponses partielles pour l'Autriche, les Pays-Bas, le Portugal et le Royaume-Uni. Elles nous ont permis de réaliser un 'pilote' qui est envoie d'être soumis aux autorités nationales concernées, pour contrôle et accordé définitif.

Un bilan provisoire peut, ainsi, être tenté concernant d'une part, les modalités de l'enquête, et d'autre pat les premières constatations qu'elle nous a permis de faire:

- *l'information collectée* prouve qu'une telle étude était nécessaire et qu'elle est réalisable; elle a convaincu même ceux qui au début n'y croyaient Pas. Le travail, il est vrai, ne s'est pas tait sans difficultés: seule l'expérience en relations internationales d'une structure comme Elia a permis d'éviter les erreurs constatées dans les études précédentes Mais le bénévolat, mode de fonctionnement habituel des associations, a ses limites; la collecte des informations concernant des pays comme la France, l'Italie ou l'Espagne ne pourra, sans doute, passe faire sans une aide financiaire de l'Europe, car ces pays ont des systèmes d' enseignement supérieur infiniment plus complexes que ceux de la zone nordique rassemblés dans notre 'pilote' et cela nécessitera des déplacements et un travail d'analyse beaucoup plus important.
- *l'analyse des informations* permet de constater l'existence en Europe de deux zones dont l'une, au nord connait un système d'enseignement supérieur simplifié et homogène, où es statuts des établissements, les types de diplômes, etc, sont

les mêmes pour toutes les disciplines, y compris celles des ans: et une autre au sud, qui présente, pour chacun des pays, une très grande diversité concernant les ministères de tutelle, le statut des établissements, celui des enseignants et des étudiants, les diplômes, etc, et où les dispositions peuvent varier non seulement entre les disciplines mais également entre les diverses filières au sein d'une même discipline.

Les tendances qui se dessinent sont l'extension du système simplifié du nord européen qui, progressivement, gagne du terrain, et une prise de conscience, au sud, de la nécessité de simplifier et homogénéiser l'enseignement supérieur afin de faciliter les échanges internationaux et les changements de filière au sein du pays; mais de nombreux freins sont encore a vaincre: les traditions nationales, les efforts financiers que nécessite l'intégration dans le système d'enseignement supérieur de disciplines ou filières non encore admises, et, surtout, le fart que les dénominations des diplômes sont d'une très grande diversité chacune taisant référence au type d'enseignement ou de contenu et non à la seule indication du niveau d'études, tel que cela se pratique dans les pays anglo-saxons.

L'enquête d'Elia n'est pas terminée: elle a déjà permis de rassembler suffisamment de données pour constituer un 'pilote', mais l'étude ne pourra progresser sans la participation de tous les partenaires concernés qui devront apporter leur critiques constructives à ce projet dont l'urgente nécessité est, désormais admise par tous.

DANIEL VEGA

Higher Music Education in Europe and the Specific Situation in Spain

I shall be concentrating on higher education in music, frequently linked to a type of education such as dance and drama, to which the same analysis and conclusions may be applied with regard to their organisation in a good many countries, and certainly in the Spanish system, as this type of education is included in the General Education System Planning Act (the LOGSE).

Denomination of institutions

Centres which offer musical education or similar training adopt a wide variety of names. The A.E.C., the European organisation to which these higher education centres belong, is identified in its initials as the *Association Européenne des Conservatoires, Musikhochschulen et Académies de Musique*. To be more accurate, one would have to add today *Music Universities* and *Faculties of Music*, a status into which many former conservatoires have evolved.

This diversity of terminology is accompanied by a diversity of concepts, structure and operation. The most misleading term is that of 'conservatoire', which in some cases

- denotes non-higher professional music education centres (e.g. Germany);
- or refers to music education centres of all types and levels (Spain, France, Italy, England, Switzerland (before the reform in progress)).

Musikhochschulen (Higher Music Schools) are the higher music education institutions in Germany, in Austria up to 1998, when their designation changed to Universities, and in Switzerland after the reform in progress.

Music Academies are the higher institutions in the majority of eastern European countries, with University status *per se*, or because of their dependence on a University: the Akatemia Sibelius in Helsinki, the Polish academies in Warsaw or Cracow, former Yugoslavia, etc.

Jan De Groof, Chantal De Smet and Hilde Penneman (eds.), Art meets Law in Education, 129–136.

The designation of *Music University* is less common and takes in the three in Austria (Vienna, Graz and Salzburg) and the one in Bucharest.

Faculty of Music is another concept that is gaining wider application and which includes these institutions in a University of the Arts (e.g. Utrecht).

The nature and structure of these centres is considered from two viewpoints: (a) legal and (b) academic.

Legal status

The designation almost always defines the legal status, except in the case of the 'conservatoire'. In order of legal identity and status (highest first), they are:

- *Music University,* with full rights and autonomy. There are institutions that do not have this designation, but they are to all effects equivalent to a University in their respective countries: Oslo, Tallin and the higher Belgian conservatoires (except that the latter do not grant Doctorates).
- *Music Faculties* dependent on a general university (Helsinki) or a university of the arts (Berlin, Utrecht and others in the Netherlands). Some English institutions claim this status (The Royal College of Music, London, the Birmingham Conservatoire) or state that they are linked to a University (Manchester) where Doctorate studies are undertaken.
- Institutions with university status equal to that of University faculties (Music Academies in Eastern European countries), or equivalent (the German *Musikhochschulen* or Swiss conservatoires redesignated as *Musikhochschulen*, and the National Conservatoires in Paris and Lyons).
- Institutions with non-University status. It is Usually in southern European countries that these are to befound to different extents having a minimum degree of autonomy and legal status recognised; if indeed we can talk about such conditions in the strictest sense, given their limitations.

The two Portuguese Escolas de Música in Lisbon and Oporto depend on their respective Polytechnic Institutes, which in turn do not enjoy full University status.

Italy has had, up to the present time, a traditional and obsolete conservatoire system. This is now in the process of legal reform and a Bill has been debated in Parliament and the Senate, which is now waiting to be referred back to Parliament for definitive approval. This declares, with the unanimous agreement of both Chambers, that centres of

> *higher artistic and musical training and specialisation... are endowed with legal status and enjoy statutory, academic, scientific, administrative, financial and accounting autonomy in accordance with this article (2.4), and they are no longer bound by State and Public Body accounting norms, but shall respect their relative principles.*

In Spain, the Higher Conservatoires are pathetically dependent on the same departments that manage primary and secondary education (Primary and Secondary State Schools and Institutes). These departments are to be found on the bottom level of the scale of the Ministerial organisational chart: Minister > Under-Secretary > Secretary General > Director General > *Deputy Directorate General for Arts Education + Provincial Director of Education*, (the Madrid Higher Conservatoire manages to be directly assigned to an even lower level: the Territorial Deputy Director of Education), which in many aspects act through Inspectors. The conflicts and distortion in the way they operate are never-ending. I shall come back to this question later.

(B) Academic situation

(a) *Organisation*

The composition of subjects which these centres include is diverse. In some cases they include Drama (Austria) and/or Dance (Paris, Frankfurt, Copenhagen).

Academic organisation enjoys different levels of self-government, which are in direct proportion to the legal status of the various institutions: the higher their legal status, the more academic autonomy they enjoy.

Organisation in faculties or departments is not identical, but it follows more or less coinciding patterns, depending on the scope of the fields they include. In the vast majority of cases, the faculties and departments are established and organised by the institutions themselves; in other cases, by the administration they depend on. This is the case in Spain, where the academic organisation of the departments is established from above by the State education administration, which even decrees the syllabuses, entrance tests to the higher level etc., with an absolute minimum, and controlled, academic autonomy for the conservatoires.

(b) *Degrees and diplomas*

The benchmark of the academic level of institutions lies in the degrees and diplomas (authorised by degrees) that are obtained by the students.

Top of the academic ranking are the diplomas from organised institutions such as Universities or Faculties, who administer and confer doctorates themselves.

Equivalent to certain levels of University diplomas are those from the other centres (except Italy for the moment). Not all lead directly to Doctorates with their own resources (e.g. Paris, which prepares its Doctorate through the University of Tours).

It is common for centres to award diplomas that are equal or parallel to University diplomas, with Universities reserving the right to award Doctorates, as is the case in Belgium and Spain, and even Germany where the Doctorate in Musicology is awarded by a University. In Portugal, of the four possible University diplomas, the Escolas de Música award the first two.

The Spanish situation is both striking and illogical: her higher conservatoires, with a level of degrees and diplomas equivalent to the *Licenciatura* (the degree immediately preceding a Doctorate), and whose mission of research is recognised by Law, 'enjoy' a totally inappropriate legal and administrative status for this category of education.

A GENERAL PROBLEM FOR EUROPE

Following the 'Declaration of Bologna' by the European Ministers of Education, there has been a proposal for its introduction into our area of education as far as Higher Education is concerned (the declaration refers to any type of higher study). The A.E.C., in its conference in Bucharest (5 to 8 November, 1998), decided to send educational authorities a letter requesting the initiation and study of this process. This 'Declaration of Bucharest' can be summed up as follows:

(1) Acceptance of the establishing of a co-ordinated system of higher education based on two cycles. (The use of the English terms 'undergraduate' and 'graduate' was met with some reticence by the German members).

(2) This structure is perfectly applicable to the higher level of our teaching.

(3) The Association believes that for European musical education to function at its optimum level, all members should be able to take part, through mutual recognition of student exchange, transfer and further training, in the framework of these cycles. In this context, the Association urges countries such as Spain, Portugal, Italy and Greece to recognise the application of these two cycles to musical education.

(4) The Association offers to place its considerable experience with institutions at the disposal of the various countries.

By way of a corollary, the application of this standardisation will bring about the proper use of ECTS, which otherwise will be grossly distorted by terminology and content discrepancies.

MUSIC EDUCATION IN SPAIN

Since this year's ELA Conference is being held in Spain, I think it would be a good idea to tell you something about the current situation in Spain with regard to Music Education.

(A) *The system*

Music education in Spain is built on three levels:

- elementary grade (8 to 12 years old, usually);
- intermediate (12 to 18 years);
- higher (18 years and over).

The first two grades are taught in Music Schools or elementary Conservatoires (first grade only) or professional Conservatoires (elementary and intermediate grades). The higher conservatoires are reserved for higher music teaching. Admission from one grade to another is effected by examination.

In Spanish Universities, there are three types of diploma: *Diplomatura* (after 2/3 years), *Licenciatura* (4/5 years) and Doctorate, after two years of preparation and a doctoral thesis. Higher Conservatoires award the qualification, after 4 to 5 years of study, of Professor Superior, 'equivalent to all effects to a university Licenciado (B.A.)'.

In spite of this, I have already explained the limited legal powers of the institutions that teach these subjects and how the authorities they depend on are at the lower end of the scale, a sign of the low esteem shown by the educational authorities for arts education. In the AEC Conferences and General Assemblies that I have attended, the opening session has always been chaired by the host country's Minister of Education, sometimes by even higher officials. In Spain, the only Education Minister to condescend to address and receive the corresponding Spanish organisation (ACESEA) was Mrs Aguirre; the other Education Ministers of the 1990s (Messrs Solana, Rubalcaba, Suárez Pertierra, Saavedra and Rajoy) did not manage to reply to proposals and offers of collaboration (total deafness towards calls from representatives of music Education on the part of a so-called Ministry of Education and Culture, something astonishing in a civilised country). The present Minister, Mr Rajoy, replied in April 1999 to a letter from the Chairman of the AEC (in which the Administration was urged to find a solution to the situation) through a Director of Schools (see above for the ranking of this post in the Ministerial organisational chart).

(B) *Proposed reform: Some historical notes*

Given the gap that exists between the organisation of music education in Spain and that of its European counterparts, the need for reform is not something that should be subject to discussion within the framework of an evermore structurally and operationally convergent Europe.

In 1995, the Spanish Association of Higher Arts Education Centres (ACESEA) drew up a project for the reform of this type of education, to which Professor Embid Irujo, Chairman of the Spanish ELA, gave legal form and substance, following an excellent historical study of the legal precedent. The Administration, the Ministry of Education, ignored it and would not be drawn into discussion because it did not want to, alleging that it was a project that had not been drawn up by the Ministry – and perhaps also because of political reasons. When the Ministry of Education asked some 'experts' for a ruling, one of them committed the serious error of proposing the French system of higher conservatoires without taking into account the high degree of decentralisation in Spain, and the other based his findings on accepting as proved what needed to be proved: that everything was to continue as it was but, under different names.

The former Minister of Education, Mrs Aguirre (May 1996 to January 1999) advocated a reform whereby the possibility of creating Universities of the Arts was recommended, but this initiative did not manage to achieve the necessary collaboration and impulse in the lower echelons of the Ministry, who were lacking decision and conviction: already, two years, before a representative of the administration had stated that the Act for this reform would not come about in the current legislature, which comes to an end in the spring of 2000. And that is how it has turned out, an attitude caused by the unawareness of how things are in Europe in this aspect of education. The great problem-excuse was given thus: 'there needs to be a comparative study of the legislation'.

This comparative study of legislation was not carried out before the work of the committees set up to study the question in March 1999, and when a working party was given responsibility for this question, the preliminary study included generalities and even errors of information: e.g. when explaining the situation in Germany, no mention was made of the *Musikhochschulen*, institutions specifically responsible for higher Music education (as well as Drama and Dance); the situation in eastern Europe was treated in general and without data, when everybody knows their legal and academic status; for example, it was stated without any further comment or precision that '*the case of Finland would need a separate analysis given the three-way Russian–German–Anglo-Saxon influence in the organisation of this type of education*'. Mrs Kootilainen, in her capacity as Vice-Chancellor of the Sibelius Akatemia in Helsinki, can testify to the fact that her institution enjoys the status of a university faculty.

However much the Administration promises, without imposing a deadline, a reform which is increasingly essential, this has been going on for years and the 'preliminary studies' by 'pre-consultation sub-committees' in the first half of 1999 did not bear fruit and were halted that July. In February 1999, '*the Congress of Deputies urges the Government to approve, with the agreement of the Autonomous Communities, within a maximum period of six months, a Bill to regulate the specific character of the higher level of arts education*'. The effect of this 'green paper' has been nil up to now. Parliament's deadline is long past.

By way of comparison, I have an item from an Italian newspaper talking about the approval '*by the VII Committee of the Chamber of the reform of Fine Arts Academies etc .... This measure has been achieved after three terms of government. This marks the end of the state of neglect in which academies and conservatoires have been maintained for decades*'. Sad to think that the only prospect we have in Spain is a journey through the wilderness as long as that of our Italian colleagues.

To complicate the problem even more, the government wants to integrate the reform of Higher Arts Education within the overall regulation of arts education at all levels, including the teaching of everything involved in being a professional artist, for which it would be very hard to attain the maximum level of higher study. The confusion thus generated will hold back reform at its draft stage (preparatory committees), white paper (government) and bill stages (Parliament) and its practical application after the Act has been passed.

The preparatory committees are made up mainly of politicians and civil servants from central administration and the autonomous community governments, some of whom are quite low down in the ranking, with no decision-making powers, and what is worse, without any professional background to qualify them as experts in the way higher arts education functions. Occasionally they are advised by arts education professionals (not always belonging to the world of higher education), among which are four music professors. Two of these were asked to attend just one meeting, the final one.

Also ignored as such is the Spanish Association of Higher Arts Education Centres (ACESEA), which, as I have said before, encompasses Conservatoires, Higher Drama Schools and other arts education establishments, which has been suffering this problem for years and studying solutions. This association has presented numerous objections to the working documents prior to the drawing up of a green paper. The repercussion of these objections on the administration has been nil. No acknowledgement of receipt and, of course, no discussion. The only response has been silence.

This impression of neglect by the educational authorities may be a personal opinion, subjective but real, formed by repeated contacts at all levels with the ministerial authorities, and experienced at first hand.

The *Defensor del Pueblo* (equivalent to the Ombudsman), a Parliamentary institution of great prestige, contacted the Ministry of Education and urged them to put this reform into motion. The reply was couched in rose-coloured terms, full of magnificent intentions, but even now, after a number of years, lacking in action. There is no sign in our Educational Administration of any political willingness to clear the path for putting us on the same level as Europe, and this is keeping us apart from her and makes it difficult for us to cooperate on level terms.

Even the Crown, through the offices of HM the Queen of Spain, has shown no interest in the problem of State music education, although her link with the private school that bears her name is well known (a worthy enterprise, but far removed from today's general education system). She was asked to be so kind as to receive the Association of Higher Arts Education Centres, so that it could explain to her the situation of this type of education, with such a big influence on a country's culture. The Palace gave a negative reply, claiming that Her Majesty had too many commitments.

On 1 October 1999, the Plenary Meeting of the State Educational Council approved the *Report on the state and situation of the educational system* for the academic year 1997–98, which stated:

> In addition, the Higher Grades of this type of education, equivalent to diploma or Degree courses, are subject to norms applicable to non-university education, and this causes major disruptions ... The State Educational Council therefore considers urgent the drawing up of a Legal Framework Planning Act for arts education with regard to the higher levels.

The problem is so great that the Council and Assembly of the *Association Européenne des Conservatoires* (made up of 130 higher music education institutions), aware of the situation in southern European countries and especially Spain, agreed to approach the Spanish Minister of Education with the following plea:

> The Council and the Assembly of the Association Européenne des Conservatoires resolved in its meeting of 8 November 1999 to request the Spanish Minister of Education to accelerate the urgent reforms in musical education in higher music conservatoires and enable them to be given the status of higher university level institutions with legal autonomy.

Three months after this request was submitted by the Chairman of the AEC, the Minister, through a very low-ranking official (as happened on the occasion mentioned above with regard to another personal letter from the Chairman of the AEC), replied by explaining, in highly complacent tones, the achievements of the Spanish system which had integrated music education into the general system. However, he did acknowledge that '*with regard to the centres that teach these subjects, equivalent to university centres, it is true that they have not yet had their legal framework adapted to this higher level*' (after 10 years! An eternity in the fast-moving evolution of our society).

Thus, the educational administration officially acknowledged in writing that the administrative and legal framework had not achieved parity with its academic level, but that it was being studied, since it was a difficult question '*which needs to be studied with care*'. For our consolation, it could possibly be deduced from these words that he is now convinced of the need for reform, even though it has been five years since the publication of what is known as the 'Embid Irujo Report'.

In her reasons for participating in the ELA Conference, the Deputy General Director for Arts Education (reporting to the Ministry of Education General Directorate of Schools) observed that '*it is this Ministry that has the authority and initiative in the basic regulations for this type of education*'. Professionals in higher music education are the first to ask the Ministry of Education to exercise this authority. Any solution that is adopted will be preferable to the current situation. At any rate, we hope so.

ANTONIO EMBID IRUJO

Higher Arts Education in Spain: Legal Aspects

(I) THE LEGAL FRAMEWORK OF HIGHER ARTS EDUCATION IN SPAIN

Higher arts education's current situation in Spain is the result of a complex historical evolution which has always been framed by the legal and, to all intents, precarious nature of this type of education, which, up to a relatively short time ago, was generally accepted to be due to its scant social importance. When I say precarious situation, I am referring to how it has been regulated, in that its situation, at a basic level, is not endowed with the force of law; it is merely regulatory, with very little input from public budgets and virtually overlooked by the Administration. Nevertheless there came the time when, as a result of the logical evolution of all branches of higher education in Spain, the overall legal system of education was to include clear mandates concerning the need for this branch of education to be given university or near-university status. However, paradoxically, in spite of these legal mandates, the Legislature has subsequently failed to establish a definitive framework on this matter, and successive Governments have failed to back this decision, when they had the obligation and opportunity to do so.

1. *Some brief legal data from the recent past*

Little is to be gained from devoting too much space to the historical-legal evolution mentioned above. Suffice it to say here that the General Education Act (hereinafter referred to as the LGE) of 4 August 1970[1] contained a mandate for higher arts courses given in Fine Arts Colleges, Music Conservatoires and Drama Colleges to be integrated into the status of University Education (temporary provision number

[1] This Act was a notable milestone in Spanish Educational Law, coming after what was known as the Ley Moyano of 9 September 1857 and before the third great step forward in the evolution of Spanish Educational Law, consisting of the LOGSE, the 1990 Organic Act on the General Organisation of the Education System.

Jan De Groof, Chantal De Smet and Hilde Penneman (eds.), Art meets Law in Education, 137–144.

two). The Act also stated that this integration was to take place 'in the three cycles' of university education, meaning, among other things, that it also contemplated the existence of a level in which a doctorate could be obtained, and this suggests the LGE's desire for a complete reconsideration of this type of education, something very positive from the point of view of their worth.

However, unlike what happened with the LGE's mandate for the integration of various types of Technical College, which was complied with shortly after the Act came into force, higher arts education was not so fortunate. Furthermore, higher arts education paradoxically was not specifically regulated for in the body of the LGE,[2] neither were other levels of arts education. Perhaps the author of the LGE thought that, in view of the fact that this integration with University status was to come about as a result of the Act's intention, there was no need to pay lip service to more regulations within the Act itself, since this was a task which would be undertaken by the subsequent regulatory norms regarding higher education, and I believe the author thought the same for the other levels of arts education – that they should be contemplated in subsequent regulations whose shaping would be in line with the higher level's integration into University status. The result, however, was to be 20 years of vague regulations, since arts education continued to be regulated by increasingly archaic norms, on a purely regulatory, never legal, basis, with no attempt to attain clear and coherent inclusion with the rest of the educational system.

2. *The significance of the LOGSE: A joint consideration of arts education within the terms of 'special system education'*

However, the situation was to change with the LOGSE, as the heading of this section shows. In fact, arts education was to find a defined position in this Act under the overall heading of 'special system education', and continuing in this comprehensive group under its traditional category of arts education. Thus, the LOGSE was to include a much more extensive regulation of this type of education than had ever been seen before in Spanish Law. It can easily be said that this Act was perfectly aware of its importance from the historical point of view, and it reasons thus in its stated purpose:

> This Act includes for the first time, within the context of educational reform, a far-reaching regulation of the teaching of music and dance, drama and fine and graphic arts, in view of the growing social interest for these subjects, specifically shown by the marked increase in demand. For various reasons, it is advisable that these subjects be connected to the general structure

[2] I have already stated that the regulation of arts education in the past was usually at an exclusively regulatory, never legal, level, and therefore it was no surprise – on the contrary, it was in line with its previous development – that the LGE did not contain much in the way of substance on this matter.

> of the system, and yet at the same time, be organised with the necessary flexibility and specific nature to cater for their own particular aspects and produce different professional grades, with qualifications equivalent to those of Universities, which in the case of Music and Stage Arts, comprising Dance and Drama, shall be equivalent to a Licentiate (*Bachelor's Degree*).

The structure of arts education in the LOGSE is unusual. As I said before, it is included within the framework of special system education which embraces both the arts and languages. Obviously, this relationship has no connection with reality, and in fact it seems that the legislator, seized by a sort of 'Cartesian' methodology, grouped together under 'special system education' all subjects that did not 'slot in' with 'the general education system' – Infant, Primary, Compulsory Secondary, Vocational Training and Baccalaureate (Sixth Form) Education – and therefore this group of subjects has a specific position within the LOGSE and the system, in the eyes of the legislator, enjoys a certain harmony. Of course, when one then goes on to think about the common legal system, now endowed with specific provisions, that arts and languages subjects should have in order to warrant a systematic placing side-by-side, the answer is – there isn't one.

But what must be understood is that the LOGSE regulates all levels of non-University education, and just that. University education, in fact, is governed by the 1983 University Reform Act (LORU), and the fact that arts education appears exclusively in the LOGSE means that the higher level still has not achieved the integration into the University system that the LGE talked about 20 years before, and which I referred to in an earlier section. This is a decisive fact which irrevocably reveals the current situation of arts education in Spain, although we may subsequently note how there is varied contradictory evidence to show that there is a far from perfect knitting in of higher arts education with non-University education.

I conclude by stating that in the LOGSE, in the section devoted to higher arts education, the subjects are divided systematically into: (a) Music and Dance, (b) Drama and (c) Fine Arts and Design.

3. *Characteristics of higher arts education in the LOGSE: What is common and what is specific to these subjects*

Having said all that, and without considering the regulation of arts subjects as a whole, since that would obviously be beyond the scope of this work, I shall now summarise under a few headings how the LOGSE views higher arts education. The overall objective of what follows is to demonstrate a certain uniformity that exists in this Act between its consideration of higher arts education and that of university education, although there are certain singular features of these higher arts subjects that should be noted at once in order to understand their relevant consequences.

(A) *Common ground between University education and Higher Arts education*
(a) With regard to *higher arts education entry requirements*, one has to pass the Baccalaureate exam to gain entry to the higher grades of Music and Dance (art. 40.3), Drama (art. 44.1) and Fine Arts and Design (art. 48.2), which is the same qualification stipulated by the LOGSE for access to Higher Grade Vocational Training and, what is particularly relevant to our case, to University Education (art. 29.2). This uniformity of entry requirements is obviously a significant piece of data for the considerations which, in a general form and as a conclusion, will be taken in section II of this chapter.

(b) *The qualification obtained at the end of the higher grade of arts studies is equivalent to a University Degree or University Diploma.* This is expressly stated in the LOGSE for the qualification of University Degree with regard to Music and Dance (art. 43.2) and Drama (art. 45.1). In the case of Fine Arts and Design, a major in Preservation and Restoration of Cultural Works brings a qualification equivalent to a University Diploma (art. 49.1), as does the successful completion of higher design studies.

(B) *Distinctive features of higher arts education*
But in spite of the above, there are several distinctive features in the regulation of higher arts education as opposed to characteristics of the general education system, and of course, as opposed to university education. The peculiarity, from many 'material' points of view – particular features of centres, provision of teaching staff, the necessarily diverse methods of entry for young people (sometimes children) to this type of education – of arts education is undoubtedly the 'cause' of these distinctive features which separate their make-up from that of university education, these can be summarised as follows:

(a) *Peculiarity in one particularly special method of student entry to higher grades of Arts education.* It is possible to gain entry to the higher grades without having passed the exam that is generally required (the Baccalaureate) provided that 'the applicant shows that (s)he has the knowledge and skills of the intermediate level as well as the specific attributes necessary for successfully following the corresponding courses' (arts. 40.4 for Music and Dance, 44 for Drama and 48.3 for Fine Arts).

(b) *The legal requirements for acceptance as a teacher in Arts Education Centres.* To gain a post as an arts education teacher, all that is required is a University degree, even when the regulations refer generically to the holding of a higher qualification (Doctorate) or equivalent (Engineer, Architect). (See supplementary provision 15 of the LOGSE). However, in University education, for a teaching post it is necessary, as a practically general rule, to hold a Doctorate (Art. 35 of the University Reform Act, the LORU, which only makes an exception in the case of Lecturers in University Schools).

(c) *Particularity in specific provisions for contracting teaching staff for stage arts, which appear to offer more options than in a University context.* In this context, I must add that there is provision for contracting foreign specialists for the teaching of music and stage arts, and the contract may be subject to Labour Law if it is a permanent contract, in which case the Government has to give that teacher the status of emeritus professor (supplementary provision 15.7 of the LOGSE[3]).

4. *Further development emphasising features of arts education that draw it closer to university status*

The LOGSE was submitted to various far-reaching reforms by an Act of great significance, Act 9/1995 of 20 November concerning the participation, evaluation and governing of educational establishments (the LOPEG). It must be pointed out that the few mentions contained in this Act regarding arts education heighten the significance of the similar aspects between the status of higher arts education and that of University education. Among these aspects, worthy of mention are:

- A reference to the increase in *research programmes in higher arts education centres* (supplementary provision 4, LOPEG).[4]
- Emphasis is given to *specific norms for the provision of teaching vacancies in higher arts educational centres* in connection with general norms governing the body of State education teachers in the non-University general education system (final provision 2).

Similarly, and in another regulation which was also subsequent to the LOGSE, when Higher Conservatoires were given the opportunity to teach higher music studies exclusively, the highly anachronistic reference to students' 'parents' in the corresponding participation body (the School Council) was done away with, in that this had no place in the higher level that we are talking about; just as parent participation has no place – nor does it exist – in any body of University administration.

(II) An Alternative: The Need for the Higher Grade of Arts Education to Have University Status or Similar, and to Be Taught in Appropriate Centres

The legal situation that I have described previously is literally indefensible. Without diminishing any of the merit due to the LOGSE for having regulated as a

[3] It seems obvious that this status is based on the corresponding status in University teachers, which is regulated by supplementary provision 7 of Act 30/1984 of 2 August concerning changes in public sector employment, and its ratification in art. 22 of Royal Decree 898/1985 of 30 April, concerning the system governing University teaching staff.

[4] Prior to the LOPEG, there had been a specific norm that had established clear lines in this direction. I am referring to Royal Decree 617/1995 of 21 April, whereby basic aspects of the syllabus for the higher grade of Music studies were established and the entry test for these studies was regulated.

whole entity, and introduced, all arts subjects into the educational system for the first time, it should be acknowledged that the specific aspects of the higher grade that the LOGSE recognises – with another set of regulations, from which I have quoted just a small part, emphasising its importance – reveal the unsatisfactory aspects and lack of practical effectiveness in the daily management of higher arts education produced by consideration of this situation.

In this respect, we should acknowledge the 'isolation' that higher arts education finds itself in with respect to other 'old' higher education studies called thus in the 1857 Ley Moyano, and which have in every case gone through the process of integration with the University system, mainly since the LGE but also, in some cases, prior to that. Arts education, then, is the only one called higher at one of its levels that remains anchored in a legal system that apparently, and from the viewpoint of integration into an educational level, does not make any distinction between higher and lower levels.

But apart from this purely comparative, and therefore initially only formal, aspect, there are deep-seated reasons for proposing a radical change of course in the consideration of higher arts education. Primary arguments to play with would be as follows:

(a) *Entry requirements and qualifications awarded*, as shown above, are similar to those in the University sector, because, among other things, they are referring to a student body which, for age and training reasons, is fully congruent with students who follow courses and gain qualifications in centres which are now integrated into the University system.
(b) The *demands made by culture*, and the role it plays in modern society, call for higher arts education to be afforded the highest recognition, from the point of view of its worth. It is clear that, more than any other type of education, higher arts education is linked to customs and a cultural 'state' of society as a whole, which I am convinced it is in everyone's interest to cultivate and promote.
(c) *The majority of European countries give University status, or similar, to higher arts education.* Standardisation procedures which are starting to be developed for higher arts education, and which are to be developed on a much larger scale in the future,[5] call for a similar consideration for this type of education in all countries, with a view to promoting international contacts between teachers and students, the potential equivalence of subjects, national recognition of specialist studies carried out in other countries, etc. Obviously, all this can be specifically applied when applying for employment in which certain qualifications are required which should be easily universally acceptable.
(d) The *prestige of the work carried out by teachers* in higher arts education centres will be much more elevated in a legal situation in which there is practical

5 I believe this will come about with ever-increasing intensity, based on the few provisions concerning education added to the Treaty of European Communities by the Maastricht Treaty (1992).

equivalence with University teaching staff, which would produce various consequences and not just at the salary level. Obviously, this would call for the corresponding legal fine-tuning to enable, for example, these teachers to obtain a Doctorate.

(e) Similarly, we would see the end of the problems regarding *recognition of students' qualifications*, since the 'equivalence' with the degree level which the LOGSE takes as its basis is often hindered by practical obstacles to prevent this equivalence under all imaginable circumstances.

(f) Finally, *the management of this type of centre calls for a certain autonomy* which is literally impossible to find within the current regulation of non-University levels. The management of a higher arts education centre has nothing to do with Infant or Primary education, or with any educational level in the general system, and yet the basic regulation applied is similar for all of them. Only a type of autonomy similar to that which currently governs University levels would permit an education fitting the requirements that the term 'higher grade' specifically expects of the management of these centres.

(III) Summary and final reflections

All of the arguments developed in this work, especially those in the previous section, support a legal reform in Spain to produce one of the following alternatives:

(a) either the full integration of higher arts education into the University system.

(b) or the shaping of a legal system for this type of education and its centres to give it similar status to University education and to centres integrated into the University system, without the need for arts education centres to be integrated into current University structures. Moreover, these structures in Spain are proving to be ever more inadequate for higher education and research of good quality, especially when taking into account the reduced staff working in these centres, and in any case these structures would be the responsibility of Higher Arts Education Centres once integration had taken place.[6]

To this effect, it should be stated that a profusion of arguments and data supporting both these alternatives has been proposed in Spain, and what is essential now is decisive action from the authorities for one alternative or the other. Some evidence that in the recent past has suggested that this might be coming about[7] has

6 Thus, it seems impossible for these centres, because of teacher and student numbers, to be able to 'compete' for the financial resources and other 'advantages' that are fought over in the daily flow of University life, by the traditional University centres, such as Medicine, Law, Science, Engineering etc. This should give food for thought before any headlong rush into integrating this type of education into the traditional University system.

7 All-party parliamentary agreements, the setting up of committees, the drawing up of reports, etc.

gradually melted away over the course of time without any specific decisions being reached. The situation of indecisiveness that we find ourselves in is the most reprehensible aspect of all this, since even though politicians have been stating recently that changes are necessary, they have not managed to propose anything specific, and they are not likely to in the near future.

I shall end by saying that the role of the State in this sense is fundamental. Although Spain is a State made up of Autonomous Communities, and responsibility for arts education, as with education as a whole, lies with the Autonomous Communities on an executive, and to a certain extent legislative, level, State action is necessary to modify the LOGSE or approve any type of legal norm necessary for either of the two alternatives mentioned above. The configuration of a level of education, as well as the qualifications that may be obtained upon successfully completing that level, is clearly and without any doubt among the competences reserved for the State, according to the Constitution (art. 149.1.30),[8] and it is the State, therefore, that must act. I hope that the celebration in our country of such an important event as this Conference will be the right occasion for finally encouraging those responsible for this situation to proceed with the necessary legal reform. It will be to everyone's advantage.

8 Let alone other additional considerations, such as the State's jurisdiction on the basic legal framework of the public sector, since any decisions adopted would have a profound effect on the teaching staff of higher arts education, or the necessary consideration of private initiative in this type of education (recognition of centres, etc.).

CHARLES J. RUSSO

Artistic Expression in American Public Schools

INTRODUCTION

In light of controversies over the rights of students and teachers to engage in artistic expression in school settings, this chapter briefly examines case law dealing with disputes over the place of various art forms such as speeches, books, films, videos, plays, and other types of expression in curricular and non-curricular settings in public American elementary and secondary[1] schools. More specifically, the chapter examines such important questions as who should control the content of the curriculum, the rights of students to free expression, and the academic freedom rights of teachers.

There are at least three significant preliminary legal issues that must be kept in mind when addressing the place of 'art' in the public school curriculum. First, and perhaps most important, is that neither the American courts, nor most schools systems, have provided a workable definition of the expansive concept of art in an educational context.[2] At the same time, while art, such as it is, is typically a required component in grades K-8 in American schools, it is frequently and elective in high school. Moreover, since art is often among the first subjects to be removed from a curriculum, or to have teaching staff reduced during times of budgetary shortfalls, it

1 This chapter is limited to K-12 public school settings for two reasons. First, nonpublic schools, which are governed more by the law of contracts, are generally not subject to the same principles dealing with freedom of expression that are applicable in public schools. *See Pierce v. Society of Sisters*, 268 U.S. 510 (1925). Second, in addition to the fact that there is virtually no litigation in the area, the rules governing higher education are significantly different from those that are employed in elementary and secondary schools.

2 Perhaps the closset definition can be found in 42 U.S.C.A. § 8143 (1), a part of the federal law covering the National Endowment for the Arts, which states:
For the purpose of this subchapter –
(1) the terms 'art' and 'arts' include, but are not limited to, architecture (including preservation, restoration, or adaptive use of existing structures),

Jan De Groof, Chantal De Smet and Hilde Penneman (eds.), Art meets Law in Education, 145–151.

is often perceived as a less significant topic of study; perhaps this is why there is no workable definition. Second, based on the lack of a common law or statutory definition of art and artistic expression, especially as it relates to schools, the courts, and educators, have tended to adopt an almost ad hoc, topical approach that ordinarily upholds the right of school officials, even over the protests of parents,[3] to permit, prevent, or limit, the use of certain films, books, and other forms of expressive content in American public schools. This lack of definition is exacerbated by the fact that the United States, unlike many other nations, especially those in Western Europe, lacks a National Curriculum to provide guidance for educators and policy-makers.[4] Consequently, the all too often determining factor in terms of whether an art form is acceptable in a school setting, judicial niceties aside, is that 'I know it when I see it.'[5] A third concern reflects the ongoing struggle to balance the rights of students to learn, teachers to teach, and school boards[6] to control/direct the content of the curriculum.

---

landscape architecture, urban design, interior design, graphic arts, fine arts (including painting and sculpture), performing arts (including music, drama, and dance), literature, crafts, photography, communications media and film, as well as other similar activities which reflect the cultural heritage of the Nation's communities and their citizens.

3 *See, e.g.*, *Brown v. Hot, Sexy, and Safer Productions*, 68 F.3d 525 (1st Cir. 1995), *cert. denied*, 516 U.S. 1159 (1996) (upholding the right of educational officials, in the face of a challenge from parents, to permit a sexually explicit AIDS awareness program involving suggestive skits at a school assembly).

4 Consistent with the Tenth Amendment to the United States Constitution, '[t]he powers not delegated to the United States by the Constitution, nor prohibited to it by the States, are reserved to the States respectively, or to the people,' education is ordinarily the responsibility of the states.

5 In *Jacobellis v. State of Ohio*, 378 U.S. 184, 197 (1964), a case dealing with whether a motion picture was hard-core pornography, Justice Stewart, in his concurring opinion, wrote that 'I shall not today attempt further to define the kinds of material I understand to be embraced within that shorthand description [of pornography]; and perhaps I could never succeed in intelligibly doing so. But I know it when I see it, and the motion picture involved in this case is not that.' (Stewart, J., concurring).
See also, *Cohen v. United States*, 403 U.S. 15, 25 (1971), where, in writing for the Court in holding that the mere wearing of a jacket bearing the words 'Fuck the draft' in a courthouse where women and children were present cannot be made into a criminal offense, Justice Harlan stated that 'it is nevertheless often true that one man's vulgarity is another's lyric.'

6 In *Board of Educ. of Island Trees Union Free Sch. Dist. v. Pico*, 457 U.S. 853 (1982) (a highly fractured Supreme Court acknowledged a school board's authority to remove books that it considered vulgar from a school library. *See also Virgil v. Sch. Bd. Of Columbia County, Fla.*, 862 F.2d 1517 (11th Cir. 1989) (affirming a school board's right to remove the works of Aristophanes and Chaucer from a school curriculum where members objected to their vulgarity and sexual explicitness).

Given the difficulties associated with trying to develop a 'one size fits all' standard for the arts, this brief chapter relies primarily on reasoning by analogy in exploring the nexus between artistic expression and the rights of school personnel, both students and teachers, to free expression. Moreover, in relying on an American approach as a departure point in the quest to determine whether, or what, limits may be placed on artistic expression in an educational setting, the author hopes that will stimulate discussion in those countries that are not as litiginous as the United States.

STUDENTS

Aware of the dearth of directly applicable precedent relating to student art work, the common thread in cases involving expressive activity is speech, regardless of whether it is spoken or written. As evidenced by its watershed ruling in *Tinker v. Des Moines Independent Community School District*,[7] the Supreme Court was unwilling to impose restrictions on student free speech, especially when it was political. In *Tinker* the Court upheld the rights of students in Iowa to wear armbands as a form of passive, non-disruptive protest against American involvement in Vietnam. In commenting that since school officials lack absolute power and that pupils do not 'shed their constitutional rights to freedom of speech or expression at the schoolhouse gate,'[8] the Court ruled that absent a reasonable 'forecast [of] substantial disruption of or material interference with school activities,'[9] school officials could not infringe upon students' constitutional right to freedom of expression. Even though *Tinker* dealt with political speech, it has been applied in a variety of settings.

Almost two decades after *Tinker*, and tacitly acknowledging the different political, and social climate in American schools, the Court modified its views, at least at it relates to non-political speech, in the two more recent cases which involved student expression, the first spoken, the second written. *Bethel School District No. 403* v. *Fraser*[10] examined a controversy where a high school student in Washington state was punished after he delivered a nominating speech at an assembly that violated the school's 'disruptive conduct rule' by intentionally including the use of sexual innuendo.[11] In upholding a three-day suspension and the student's being removed from the possible list of speakers at his graduation, the Court reasoned that school

7 393 U.S. 503 (1969).

8 *Ibid.*, at 506.

9 *Ibid.*, at 514.

10 478 U.S. 675 (1986).

11 The student's speech, which created a disruption at the assembly, read:

> I know a man who is firm – he's firm in his pants, he's firm in his shirt, his character is firm – but most… of all, his belief in you, the students of Bethel, is firm. … Jeff Kuhlman is a man who takes his point and pounds it in. If necessary, he'll take an

officials acted entirely within their permissible authority where a rule proscribing 'obscene' language and the prespeech admonition of teachers gave him adequate warning that his speech might have led to the sanctions that were, in fact, imposed. The Court concluded that the First Amendment did not prohibit school officials from punishing the student where his expressive activities undermined the school's basic educational mission.

Hazelwood School District v. Kuhlmeier,[12] reviewed a controversy over the rights of student-authors in Missouri who wrote articles about teenage pregnancy and the effects of divorce on students at their high school as part of an in-class, wholly school-sponsored newspaper, an activity for which they received academic credit. After a teacher and the school's principal reviewed the articles, the latter decided to remove them from the newspaper because it was being published too near to the end of the school year and there was insufficient time to make revisions. The principal was concerned not only about the inability to keep the identity of the pregnant students confidential, but also that the parents who were discussed in the article on divorce should have been afforded the opportunity to respond to remarks about them or give their permission for them to be printed. Aware of the need to permit educators to exercise discretion in light of local community standards, the Court declared that '[w]e hold that educators do not offend the First Amendment by exercising editorial control over the style and content of student speech in school sponsored expressive activities so long as their actions are reasonably related to legitimate pedagogical concerns.'[13]

Following *Hazelwood*, the few cases that have been litigated have led to mixed results where school officials have sought to limit student expression. For example, in a case from California, an appellate court affirmed that school officials could restrain student speech in a film arts class where the use of vulgarity in the production 'violate[d] the "professional standards of English and journalism."'[14] Similarly, members of a high school marching band in Missouri unsuccessfully sought to enjoin school officials from prohibiting them from playing the song *White Rabbit* at a preview show and at a football game. A federal trial court rejected the students' claim to free expression in the face of an argument by school officials that they had the authority and responsibility 'to refuse to sponsor student speech that might

---

issue and nail it to the wall. He doesn't attack things in spurts – he drives hard, pushing and pushing until finally – he succeeds ... Jeff is a man who will go to the very end – even the climax, for each and every one of you. So vote for Jeff for A.S.B. vice-president – he'll never come between you and the best our high school can be.

Ibid. at 687 (Brennan, J. concurring).

12 484 U.S. 260 (1988).

13 *Ibid.* at 273.

14 *Lopez v. Tulare Joint Union High Sch. Dist. Bd. of Trustees*, 40 Cal. Rptr2d 762 (Cal. Ct. App. 1995).

reasonably be perceived as advocating drug or alcohol use ... or conduct that was otherwise inconsistent with shared values of a civilized social order.'[15]

Conversely, the Supreme Court of New Jersey held that school officials violated the First Amendment rights of a junior high school student who wished to publish review of two R-rated movies, *Mississippi Burning* and *Rain Man*, in his school newspaper.[16] The court decided not only that the school lacked a policy prohibiting such articles, but also that the existing policy was vaguely defined and loosely defined. In another interesting case, the Supreme Judicial Court of Massachusetts maintained that students in public high schools have freedom of expression, in the form of wearing t-shirts, to engage in non-school sponsored expressive activity that may reasonably be considered vulgar as long as they do not cause disruptions or disorders.[17] Finally, in a case with an odd twist that may say more about American jurisprudence with regard to religion than art, a student successfully challenged a school district which permitted a portrait of Christ to hang in the hall of one of its buildings. The Sixth Circuit upheld an order requiring a school district in Michigan to remove the portrait, that was painted, and donated, by a former student-artist, who was not a party to the suit, more than thirty years earlier, from the school hallway on the ground that it violated the Establishment Clause.[18]

TEACHERS

Unlike the landmark rulings of *Hazelwood* and *Fraser*, which more directly implicated the free speech rights of students, the Supreme Court has yet to rule directly on the merits of a case implicating the free speech, *qua* artistic, rights of teachers. However, two recent federal appellate cases dealt with the rights, or more precisely, lack thereof, of teachers to artistic freedom to select a school play and/or to permit students greater freedom in expressing themselves in class. These cases reflect the post-*Hazelwood* and *Fraser* pendulum swing that has moved even further in judicial support of school board authority and the notion that teachers in public schools lack academic freedom when dealing with speech-related activities.[19]

15 *McCann v. Fort Zumwalt Sch. Dist.*, 50 F. Supp.2d 918, 924 (E.D. Mo. 1999) citing *Hazelwood*, *supra* note xii at 272.

16 *Desilets v. Clearview Reg. Bd. of Educ.*, 647 A.2d 150 (N.J. 1994).

17 *Pyle v. School Comm. of S. Hadley*, 667 N.E.2d 869 (Mass. 1996)

18 *Washegesic v. Bloomingdale Pub. Schs.,* 33 F.3d 679 (6th Cir. 1994), *cert. denied*, 514 U.S. 1095 (1995).

19 *Fowler v. Board of Educ. of Lincoln County, Ky.*, 819 F.2d 657 (6th Cir. 1987), *cert. denied*, 484 U.S. 986 (1987). In the interim between *Bethel* and *Hazelwood*, the Court refused to hear an appeal in a case where a board dismissed a tenured teacher for showing an R-rated video, *Pink Floyd – The Wall,* to her high school class on a non-instructional day. Relying in part on *Bethel*, the court was of the opinion that the vulgar content

In a case from North Carolina, the Fourth Circuit affirmed that a school board could transfer a high school drama teacher in North Carolina who selected a controversial play that administrators later decided was inappropriate for her students.[20] Even though the well-respected veteran teacher had won many awards for the school and assisted her students in receiving scholarship to study drama in college, the court relied on authorities from Plato to Edmund Burke to Justice Frankfurter that the board, rather than the teacher, has the right to set the curriculum and its content. Similarly, the Eighth Circuit upheld a school board in Missouri's firing of a tenured high school English teacher who allowed her students to use vulgar language in the context of creative, expressive assignments in her class.[21] Even though the court found that the punishment was excessive in light of the her otherwise good record and more than twenty years of service, the court reiterated that since the teacher failed to enforce its policy that prevented students from using profanity, even in a creative writing class, it had a legitimate interest in dismissing her.

IMPLICATIONS

When viewed together, the litigation involving the rights of teachers and students to artistic expression gives rise to four interesting questions. First, as the United States finds itself in the midst of a school reform movement that includes increased calls for the professionalization of education, it remains to be seen whether teachers will be granted a greater say in curricular matters that would afford both them and students greater freedom, including the arts, or whether the discourse remains at the level of rhetoric. Second, if teachers are granted greater latitude in curricular matters, it will be interesting to observe what self-checks might they impose, perhaps in the form of peer review or intervention, to demonstrate that they have earned the right to share this professional responsibility with school boards. Third, if teachers are provided with greater freedom in directing the content of the curriculum, it will be interesting to observe what, if any, limits they place on the artistic expression of students and themselves. Fourth, as public schools develop alternative approaches that afford teachers greater freedom to select course content, a rewards structure

---

of the movie shown to a captive audience justified the teacher's dismissal. Subsequently, a federal trial court, in *Krizek v. Board of Educ. of Cicero-Stickeny Township High Sch. Dist. 201*, 713 F. Supp. 1131 (N.D. Ill. 1989), refused to enjoin the dismissal of a nontenured teacher who showed an R-rated film, *About Last Night*, to her high school English class.

20 *Boring v. Buncombe County Bd. of Educ.*, 136 F.3d 364 (4th Cir. 1998), *cert. denied* 525 U.S. 813 (1998).

21 *Lacks v. Ferguson Reorganized Sch. Dist. R-2*, 147 F.3d 718 (8th Cir. 1998), *rehearing and rehearing en banc denied*, 154 F.3d 904 (8th Cir.1998), *cert. denied*, 526 U.S. 1012 (1999).

will have to be devised to determine whether success will be measured by accepted criteria or by some new means. Fourth, one can only wonder about the impact of what the widespread use of computers[22] and the Internet[23] will be, as both students and teachers seek greater access to artistic materials and seek to express themselves in new, and different, ways.

[22] *Board of Educ. of Monticello Cent. Sch. Dist. v. Commissioner of Educ.*, 667 N.Y.S.2d 671 (N.Y. 1997) (upholding the suspension of a high school student who used a home computer to prepare an underground newspaper that called for the destruction of school property and insubordination).

[23] *See Beussink v. Woodland R-IV Sch. Dist.*, 30 F. Supp. 1175 (E.D. Mo. 1998) (enjoining educators from suspending a high school student for including remarks on his personal homepage on his home computer that were critical of his school's administration).

IZAK OOSTHUIZEN

A Constitutionalised View on Freedom of Artistic Creativity in South Africa

1. Introduction

The urge to express oneself in various ways is a characteristic of the human being. The existence of freedom of expression is essential in order to create a democratic social and political society build on constitutianalism and human rights (Van der Westhuizen, 1994: 264). The various ways in which man expresses him/herself include verbal and non-verbal communication, as well as various forms of artistic creativity, etc. According to De Waal *et al.* (1999: 305) the need to protect the creation of art flows from the fact that artists are sometimes responsible for radical criticism.

2. The legal basis for freedom of expression

Freedom of expression is generally acknowledged to be an important fundamental right and protected in national and international human rights instruments.

National instruments

The final Constitution of South Africa came into effect in 1996. Section 1 should be deemed as one of the key sections in the founding provisions of the Constitution. It is phrased as follows:

> The Republic of South Africa is one, sovereign, democratic state founded on the following values:
> (a) Human dignity, the achievement of equality and the advancement of human rights and freedoms.
> (b) Non-racialism and non-sexism.

Jan De Groof, Chantal De Smet and Hilde Penneman (eds.), Art meets Law in Education, 153–160.

(c) Supremacy of the constitution and the rule of Law.
(d) Universal adult suffrage, a national common voters' role, regular elections and a multiparty system of democratic government, to ensure accountability, responsiveness and openness.

South African freedom of expression is strongly rooted in these founding values of *democracy* and *human freedom*. Freedom of expression as well as freedom of artistic creativity are specifically addressed in section 16 of the Constitution:

(1) Everyone has the right to *freedom of expression*, which includes –
  (a) freedom of the press and other media;
  (b) freedom to receive or impart information or ideas;
  (c) *freedom of artistic creativity*; and
  (d) academic freedom and freedom of scientific research.
(2) The right in subsection (1) does nor extend to –
  (a) propaganda for war;
  (b) incitement of imminent violence; or
  (c) advocacy of hatred that is based on race, ethnicity, gender or religion, and that constitutes incitement to cause harm.

International instruments

For the purposes of interpretation of the South African Bill of Rights it is mandatory to take into account the contents of applicable international law and foreign law. In this regard it is important to take note of sections 39(1) of the SA Constitution (SA, 1996(a)):

39(1) When interpreting the Bill of Rights, a court, tribunal or forum –
(a) must promote the values that underlie an open and democratic society based on human dignity, equality and freedom;
(b) must consider *international law*; and
(c) may consider *foreign law*.

As far as international law is concerned one need not go any further than article 19 of the Universal Declaration of Human Rights which determines as follow (UN, 1948):

(19) Everyone has the right to freedom of opinion and expression, including freedom to hold opinions without interference, and to seek, receive, and impart information and ideas through any media and regardless of frontiers.

Other international instruments such as The European Convention on Human Rights (1950), the American Declaration on the Rights and Duties of Man (1948) and the African Charter on Human and Peoples' Rights (1981) all confirmed freedom of expression.

3. Defining of concepts

In an effort to define the relevant concepts, an analysis of the concepts *freedom of expression* and *artistic creativity* amplifies the following:

- freedom of expression

The word *expression* in the first instance refers to verbalisation of thoughts. The Oxford Dictionary explains it as a process 'to put thought into words' (Sykes, 1976: 366). This obviously includes speech. Van der Westhuizen (1994: 264) says that it arguably includes 'utterances with some intelligible content intended to inform, ask, or persuade'. He contends that it also includes 'appeals to the emotions or the senses, through sound, colour, etc.' (Van der Westhuizen, 1994: 264). The latter opens the way for the inclusion of the concept of art.

- artistic creativity

It is almost impossible to give a satisfying definition of the concept *art.* It is even more difficult to define the concepts *artistic creativity* and *artistic expression.* One of the reasons for this lies in the fact that 'beauty lies in the eyes of the beholder'. In *Cohen v California* this age old truth was phrased as follow: one man's vulgarity may be another's lyric.

A very liberal and broad approach to the description of the concept *artistic expression* is to be found in the literature of Heins (as quoted by Chaskalson *et al.,* 1999: 20–3):

> [Artistic expression] should include books, movies, painting, posters, sexy dancing, street theatre, graffiti, comics, television, music videos – anything produced by creative imagination, from Shakespeare to sitcoms, from opera to rock. Freedom of expression may mean that we have to tolerate some art that is offensive, insulting, outrageous, or just plain bad. But it is a small price to pay for the liberty and diversity that form the foundation of a free society.

A local approach by De Waal *et al.* (1999: 305) to the concept *freedom of art* should be regarded as more moderate and narrower. They define it as to include activities such as the making of films and music. Their further amplification of the concept shows that it includes all the activities associated with the creation of art: both art as a *product*, as well as those activities or processes necessary for the *creation* of the art product (De Waal *et al.*, 1999: 305). Van der Westhuizen (1994: 286) takes it one step further when he suggests that unsuccessful and experimental *attempts* at producing art will also enjoy constitutional protection.

The advantages and dangers of a broad definition

Some of the *advantages* of a broad (and liberal) definition (e.g. as portrayed by Heins) are:

- The interpretation of the broad definition reduces the problem for the court to decide whether a specific activity can indeed be classified as art for the purposes of constitutional protection, or not.
- A wide definition of the concept acts as a safeguard against censorship.
- Artistic creativity should be limited as little as possible because of its function in the promotion of self-fulfilment, autonomy and dignity in the life of an individual.
- The supporters of the liberal approach regard it as their right – as citizens of an open and democratic society based on human dignity, freedom and equality – to enjoy unlimited freedom of artistic expression.

Some of the *dangers* of a broad (and almost unlimited) definition are:

- The wider the definition the more difficult it will become to determine the appropriate level of constitutional protection on a case-by-case basis.
- Artistic expression is quite often known to embody some of the most radical challenges to society, and also to have a severe impact on the values of a society. An unbridled and a too liberal approach might therefore have adverse effects on society values. It must be accepted that law cannot be separated entirely from morality. Although it is 'immoral' to force the religious and moral prejudices of one group upon others, legal mechanisms are often used to support and strengthen the moral values of a society (Van der Westhuizen, 1994: 272).
- Although difficult to prove a causal link between pornography and sexual crime, some people regard the unbridled viewing of artistic expression in the form of pornography as a reason for sexual crimes. Van der Westhuizen (1994: 283) for example makes the statement that a 'considerable body of material' of 'some identifiable harm' done by pornography has been produced over the years.
- Unbridled art which takes the form of pornography is regarded by some as a degradation and an insult to woman. Van der Westhuizen (1994: 283) wrote:

> Pornography is said to create or perpetuate a stereotypical view of women as not really meaning to say 'no', loving to be used and abused, and even raped. It creates a 'rape culture' and tends to degrade women in their own eyes as well as in the eyes of men. Furthermore, harm to women may include sex discrimination and the perpetuation of sexual inequality of women. The fact that pornography – for whatever social or economic reason – often portrays men in a dominant position over women and depicts violence against women constitutes discrimination against women.

4. The limitation of freedom of expression

It is trite that, like any other right, the right to freedom of expression is not absolute. Although this is the case in all legal systems it may vary and change with time and culture. It is also linked to the historical background as well as political and social environment of a specific group.

In the South African context freedom of expression is limited in terms of:

- the *internal limitations* regarding freedom of speech (as quoted in paragraph 2 of this chapter) listed in section 16(2) of the Constitution, and
- by law of *general application* as taken up in the limitation clause of the Constitution – section 36.

The general limitations of section 36(1) of the Constitution read as follow (SA, 1996(a)):

> (1) The rights in the Bill of rights may be limited only in terms of law of general application to the extent that the limitation is reasonable and justifiable in an open and democratic society based on human dignity, equality and freedom, taking into account all relevant factors, including –
> (a) the nature of the right;
> (b) the importance of the purpose of the limitation;
> (c) the nature and the extent of the limitation;
> (d) the relation between the limitation and its purpose; and
> (e) less restrictive means to achieve the purpose.

An analysis of section 36 shows the first question to be asked is: is the limitation of the artistic expression in question justifiable in an open and democratic society based on freedom and equality?

The second question to be asked is: does the limitation in question meet the requirements set out in the 5 factors listed in section 36(1)(a)–(e)? In other words, one has to balance the conflicting rights in question (e.g. the right to freedom of expression against the morality and values of a specific society).

Foreign law

Due to the lack of a long South African constitutional tradition, one should take counsel from foreign law as how to deal with the limitation of the right to artistic creativity.

As early as 1973 in *Miller v California,* which did involve minors but not in a school situation, the American judiciary has held that individuals cannot rightfully claim First Amendment rights for *obscene* or *vulgar* expression. In an attempt to distinguish obscene material from constitutionally protected material, the court used the following basic test: (a) whether the average person, applying contemporary community standards would find that the work, taken as a whole, appeals to the prurient interests; (b) whether the work depicts or describes, in a patently offensive way, sexual conduct specifically defined by the applicable state law; and (c) whether the work, taken as whole, lacks serious literary, artistic, political or scientific value.

Referring to *Miller*, Fischer *et al.* (1999: 186) concluded that although many parents and teachers equate obscene expression it cannot be unconditionally equated by American lawyers and judges. This brings us to the problem of defining the concept of *obscenity*. In an effort to find a satisfactory definition, the European Court of Human Rights in *Müller and others* referred to the following description:

> Any item is obscene which offends, in a manner that is difficult to accept, the sense of sexual propriety; the effect of the obscenity may be to arouse a normal person sexually or to disgust or repel him. The test of obscenity to be applied by the court is whether the overall impression of the item or work cause moral offence to a person of ordinary sensitivity.

The 1988 *Hazelwood School District v Kuhlmeier* established a basic approach with regard to the censorship of students' rights to freedom of expression. It confirmed that students do not enjoy an unlimited and unconditional right to freedom of speech at school and that these first amendment rights are not violated by: exercising editorial control over the style and content of student speech in school sponsored expressive activities so long as their actions are reasonably related to legitimate pedagogical concerns. Furthermore, it contended that schools may refuse to sponsor student expression in ways that advocate drug or alcohol use, irresponsible sex or a controversial political position.

In *Hazelwood* students filed suit against the principal who deleted two articles from a school news paper, *Spectrum,* one of which was based on the experiences of three pregnant students. The principal felt that the references to sex were not suitable for younger students to read. The court ruled that the principal acted reasonably in removing the article about pregnancy, since it would protect the younger students from 'frank talk about sex'.

In 1995 the limitation of students' rights to free speech was confirmed in *Lopez* v *Tulare Joint Union High School District Board of Trustees.* The students in question contended that the use of profane words in the script of an art film would enhance the level of realism in the film. The court upheld the censorship in order 'to maintain professional standards of English' required by Californian law.

5. Implications for SA schools

In terms of section 4 the National Policy Act (SA, 1996(b)) one of the directive principles for South African education is 'the advancement and protection of fundamental rights of every person'. Therefore, South African educators have a responsibility towards their pupils to educate them in accordance with a culture of fundamental rights (freedom of expression, including artistic creativity). On the other hand, the educator is under an obligation to protect the pupil against possible adverse effects of pornography. The right to freedom of expression should not, therefore, be regarded as an absolute right, but a right which is to be limited by general limitation, as defined by section 36 of the South African Constitution (SA, 1996(a)).

The concretisation and imbalance within the school realm of the two 'seemingly' opposing viewpoints should be a matter of local definition. In terms of the purposes of the South African Schools Act (SA, 1996(c)) – as stipulated in the preamble of the Act – devolution of power to the community of a local school is to be one of the priorities in the governance of South African schools.

Within this line of thought the refinement censorship powers should therefore evolve to the governance of local schools. In terms of section 20 of the SA Schools Act (1996(c)): the Governing body has to set the mission statement of a particular school. Religious and/or moral undertones are normally inherent to the mission statements of school. In arbitrary cases a work of art should first be evaluated against the norms and standards specified in the mission statement by the school. If this does not provide a satisfactory outcome, it should be evaluated by (a committee of) the governing body in the light of the schools mission statement.

References

Chaskalson, M, Kentridge, J, Klaaren, J, Marcus, G and Spitz, Woolman, S. *Constitutional Law of South Africa.* (Kenwyn: Juta & kie, 1999).

De Waal, J, Currie I and Erasmus, G. The Bill of Rights Handbook. (Kenwyn: Juta & kie, 1999).

Fischer, L and Schimmel, D and Kelly, C. Teachers and the Law. (New York: Longman, 1999).

Sykes, JB (The Concise Oxford Dictionary) (Oxford: Clarendon Press, 1976).

SA: see South Africa.

UN: see United Nations.

United Nations General Assembly, 1948. (Universal Declaration of Human Rights). (UN: New York).

Van der Westhuizen, J. 'Freedom of expression', *in* Van Wyk, D, Dugard, J and De Viliiers, B and Davis, D (Rights and Constitutionalism). (Kenwyn: Juta & kie. 1994).

Court cases:

Cohen v California 403 US 15 (1971).

Hazelwood School District v Kuhlmeier, 484 US 260 (1988).

Lopez v Tulare Joint Union High School District Board of Trustees, 40 Cal. Rptr.2d 762 (1995).

Miller v California 413 US 15, 24 (1973).

Müller and others 25/1986/123/174. European Court of Human Rights.

Bystrom v Fridley High School Independent School District, 822 F.2d 1149.

SA: see South Africa.

South Africa, 1996(a). Constitution of the Republic of South Africa. (Pretoria: Government Printers).

South Africa, 1996(b). National Education Policy Act. (Pretoria: Government Printers).

South Africa, 1996(c). South African Schools Act. (Pretoria: Government Printers).

Country Reports

HILDE PENNEMAN

Synoptic Review of the Country Reports

GROUP I: ORGANISATION OF EDUCATION

The following review is the result of a comparison of the most salient features of the various national reports from European countries taking part in the conference. The questionnaire which resulted in these reports was drafted in a professional way by Michael Scheck, Professor Emeritus and Chantal De Smet, President of ELIA. In most of the Member States we found experts who were prepared to write a state of the art paper. The full texts of the national reports can be found following this comparative study.

1. *What form of education does the designation 'Art Education' refer to?*

It seems to be difficult to define Art Education, but in a narrow sense it refers to architecture, music, theatre, visual arts, dance and design. The Austrian report tried to situate Art Education from a university perspective. From that point of view to the tasks of the universities regarding the Arts. Their tasks are: to cultivate the Arts, to educate through the Arts, to prepare students of the Arts for careers in the Arts as artists, educators or scholars and to provide continuing education for graduates of universities of the Arts.

2. *At what level of your national education system is Art Education assimilated in your country: university education – non-university higher education – other?*

In some countries like in Austria, Spain and England, Art education is assimilated to all levels. In Belgium, Sweden, Greece and Germany it is assimilated to secondary and higher education. Only Belgium mentions the opportunity of evening classes in art education. It would appear that this system of part-time artistic education through a broad network of Academies of the Arts is peculiar to Belgium. This

Jan De Groof, Chantal De Smet and Hilde Penneman (eds.), Art meets Law in Education, 163–169.

form of part-time education is considered to be 'adult education', even through most students are under eighteen years of age. This is because the programmes are offered on a part-time basis (i.e. in the evenings, on Wednesday afternoons, and at weekends). The education centres are known as academies, their programmes fall outside the scope of compulsory education, and therefore this is a fee-paying form of education.

3. *What are the entrance requirements for higher Art Education (age, certificates, skills)?*

Most countries require a secondary school degree for a student to be accepted in the higher art education institutions, but sometimes a student can be accepted without a degree if they have some special abilities. The latter does not apply to England, where acceptance is strictly conditional on a student's having obtained a secondary school degree. The normal age to enter higher Art Education is 17–18 years. In Austria some courses at the music universities accept young people of 15 years. In Denmark theatre branches require a minimum age of 21.

In Belgium an artistic examination is sometimes organised for candidates for the audio-visual and fine arts, music and theatre. In Austria, such entrance examinations are a requirement for all courses at Arts Universities. These entrance examinations are intended to test a student's artistic aptitude.

4. *Which degrees or certificates are awarded in Art Education?*

Universities can offer Bachelor's or Master's degrees. The exception is Denmark, where BA and MA equivalents are offered only in the fields of architecture and conservation. For other art disciplines there is no formal degree although music, design, visual arts, theatre and film schools do provide programmes of the highest level.

In England the almost universal title within British Universities for a Doctorate by research, whatever the subject area, is that of Doctor of Philosophy (Ph.D.) Higher Doctorates (e.g. Doctor of Music) are rarely awarded, and are generally based upon major published work.

5. *Are Art degrees linked to the general education system?*

Art degrees are indeed integrated within the general education system. In Denmark, the link exists only for architecture and conservation. In Greece and Germany there are exceptions too.

6. *What are the standards of flexibility of strictness in formal higher Art Education curricula? Is it mandatory for a student to sit examinations?*

In most countries students have to pass exams. Sometimes and for some disciplines there are exceptions.

In Belgium there is no flexibility. Every student must sit an exam every year. The detailed curricula vary from school to school, although the authorities do guarantee the scale of the programmes. The maximum study time is 1800 hours. The content of the curricula is decided at department level, with individual teachers deciding the detailed content of their courses. The authorities also define professional profiles, which contributes to the establishment of broadly similar curricula.

In Spain there is no flexibility: syllabuses are fixed by the Educational Authorities and not by the centres. Belgium and England mention the quality assessment and auditing of the teaching and learning process. In England this is the task of the Higher Education Funding Council.

In Sweden the Higher Education Ordinance establishes the basic minimum requirements for degrees and for what should be included in course curricula.

Denmark is remarkable for the extensive freedom it allows without examinations and grading. It would appear from the Danish report that, as far as artistic education is concerned, Denmark is the least regulated of all Member States.

7. *Is the avarage Art student aware of the usefulness of regular studies and securing a degree?*

The avarage Art student is indeed aware of the usefulness of regular studies and securing a degree; especially in England and Wales students are aware of the limited opportunities to resit failed examinations. However, certain countries also refer to the labour market, where talent and standing can be more important than a degree, particularly in the artistic field.

8. *What type of recognition is conferred to a degree in higher Art Education?*

In general, art degrees have the same recognition as other degrees in higher education. Some countries mention that recognition depends on the content of the programme.

In Germany the *Länder* have set standards by frame regulations; in Belgium these standards (*eindtermen*) are defined in the professional profiles.

9. *How would you describe the role played by private education institutes without formal accreditation?*

Private education institutes without formal accreditation do not have an important role in most countries. They are only supplementary. Exceptions are Portugal, where private schools are better than public schools. In Greece these schools cannot deliver a degree, despite the increasing number of students.

10. *Which qualifications are required to teach in recognised Art Education? Are teachers appointed as statutory teachers or as contract workers?*

Teachers are appointed as statutory *or* contract workers. In Denmark teachers work on a contractual basis and sometimes on a temporary basis if they are external.

Teachers must have a higher education degree, Some countries require a supplementary pedagogical certificate. In England this is known as a Postgraduate Certificate of Education. Sometimes a Bachelor of Education may qualify to teach. Teachers are required to be registered with the General Teaching Council established under the Teaching and Higher Education Act of 1998. In Germany art students who wish to become teachers have to finish the normal teacher examinations followed by a practical orientated training course and a second examination. In Portugal professionals can be engaged as guest teachers in the higher education system.

In Greece a higher education degree is, as a rule, required in order to be appointed as a teacher. There are, however, two exceptions to this rule. Certainly, for certain courses in theatre studies, no specific degree is required, and appointments are made on the basis of a person's recognised artistic standing. Secondly a doctorate or third-level degree may, under certain conditions, be replaced by a work of art, thus allowing its maker to be appointed as a teacher without formal qualifications.

11. *Under which Ministry's competence does Art Education fall? Ministry of Education or Ministry of Culture?*

As a rule, the department of education is responsible for art education. There are few exceptions: in Denmark and Bavaria, Art Education comes under the Ministry of Culture. In Greece most forms of art Education come under the Ministry of Education. The exceptions to this rule are higher Art Education institutes and private art schools, which are the responsibility of the Ministry of Culture.

Group II: Mobility

1. *Percentage of Art students participating in European exchange programmes compared to technical and scientific streams?*

In most countries only 4 to 5 per cent participate in European Exchange programmes. The only country where this percentage is significantly higher is Austria, where over 20 per cent of undergraduates participate in exchange programmes.

2. *Are there any apparent reasons for students to refrain from taking advantage of the opportunities offered by such programmes?*

The most commonly mentioned reasons for not taking advantage of the European exchange programmes are budgetary problems, accommodation, administrative problems, such as the organisation of the school and academic year, the difficulty of sitting exams before leaving the host country and the fact that certain programmes in the host country do not include training programmes.

Certain problems are peculiar to certain countries. In England the system of loans repayable after several years poses specific difficulties. In Greece there is a language problem.

Certain problems relate specifically to artistic education. The lack of suitably adopted studios in other countries, or too long a period abroad. Certain arts students also take private lessons which they cannot interrupt for any length of time. Other difficulties concern the fact that the differences between the programmes in the various European countries are too great.

3. *Percentage of Art teachers taking advantage of the opportunities offered by European exchange programmes?*

The rate of participation of teachers is extremely low. The highest figure in Sweden is only 4 per cent.

4. *Are there any apparent reasons for teachers to refrain from taking advantage of the opportunities offered by such exchange programmes?*

The most widespread problems for teachers are lack of information, language difficulties and budgetary constraints. Most teachers in art education have special talents, and they cannot find anyone to replace them. They have to prepare new courses and this means an extra burden for them. Lodging is difficult too: if they work for two or three months in the host country, they cannot leave their house in their home country and thus have to pay for two houses at the same time.

Sometimes they give individual courses and cannot be missed. There are no good and appropriate EU programmes for Art students.

5. *Should specific mobility conditions and procedures be set for student and teacher mobility in the Art Sector?*

It was suggested that programmes for arts students should be more intensive and more specialised than other programmes. The European Community can establish and give funds for such specialised centres in a few countries.

Perhaps more information and less administration would be beneficial to student and teacher mobility in the Art Sector. Especially for teachers and professors with a low income, a financial stimulus could be helpful. This also applies to students with limited opportunities. The European grants for the exchange programmes are no longer adopted to the real cost of living in the host country.

More quality control by the national authorities can be helpful for stimulating mobility. An independent European group of experts should have the power to monitor on the spot whether students are being guided correctly.

6. *Does the European Credit Transfer System (ECTS) apply in your country? Is the ECTS sufficiently harmonised in Europe?*

Within the framework of the Socrates/Erasmus programme the European Community Course Credit Transfer System (ECTS) was developed. This system is based on voluntary cooperation between universities in order to facilitate the academic recognition of study periods in an education institution in another Member State. The system is aimed at the transfer of so-called 'study points'.

The European Credit Transfer System applies in most countries, but a greater degree of harmonisation would be beneficial. The autonomy which most institutions have in determing their own programmes and curricula makes harmonisation very difficult. In many European countries the application of this system is just starting. Outside the Erasmus programme, academic recognition is practically unknown. The English report emphasised that there can only be mutual trust if other Member States operate a system of external monitoring of exams, strict rules on the resitting of exams and an external organ charged with rigidly supervising the quality of education.

7. *To what problems does the comparison of curricula give rise?*

The principal problem to which the comparison of curricula gives rise, is that of the recognition of degrees. A useful measure in this respect would be the elaboration of a descriptive overview at European level, based on formal quantifiable elements. His framework would relate elements such as study hours, lecture hours, the reading of literature, papers and exams, to a number of study points. These study points could form the basis for an objective comparison of degrees between member states. A specifically Danish problem is that higher education centres in the arts sector do not as a rule issue degrees. So the high level of Danish Art Education might in some cases be misjudged.

Group III: Equivalence of degrees

1. *What are the existing problems in connection with the equivalence of degrees?*

In Germany and Sweden it seems that the general recognition of a student's artistic competence is more important than formal examinations. In Sweden the personal merits of teachers are more important.

In England the strict system of external examiners and supervision by Higher Education Funding Council results in degrees being regarded as being of equal standard.

In Austria artists are not a regulated profession, unlike teachers, who are in principle subject to directive 89/48. This has to be the rule in all Members States.

Denmark does not make use of internationally recognised degrees like BA and MA. Qualifications at higher level should be considered as full university qualifications.

2. *In your opinion, is recognition of the equivalences of degrees the remit of national authorities (bilateral) or the European Union?*

The last question was if the recognition of the equivalences of degrees was the remit of national authorities or of the European Union. On this point, opinions are strongly divided. In Belgium it is generally accepted that the mutual recognition of degrees is a matter for the European Community. From this point of view, the Member States' responsibility is to guarantee the content and the quality of their education programmes. The Austrian report suggests the setting up of an elaborate information system on the content of higher art education throughout Europe. Spain, Denmark and Portugal are in favour of a regulatory framework based on the assumption that recognition should be based on comparable elements and that any system of mobility and recognition of degrees presupposes mutual trust in each other's education system.

In conclusion, I should like to emphasise that there are still major differences between the Member States as regards both the organisation and the content of art education. If the purpose is to make free movement of students and workers a reality, then this will require more investment in an instrument suitable both for defining the structure of the various education programmes, and for comparing the value of different degrees. Only when such an instrument is devised, can the goal of free movement become a reality.

Questionnaire – ELA Conference: 'Art Meets Law in Education', Granada, December 1999

Group I: Organisation of Art Education

1. What form of education does the designation 'Art Education' actually refer to?
2. Into what level of your national education system is art education assimilated in your country: university education – non-university higher education – other?
3. What are the entrance requirements for higher art education (age, certificates, skills)?
4. Which degrees or certificates are awarded in art education?
5. Are Art degrees linked to the general education system?
6. What are the standards of flexibility or strictness in formal higher art education curricula? Is it mandatory for a student to sit examinations?
7. Is the average art student aware of the usefulness of regular studies and of securing a degree?
8. What type of recognition is conferred to a degree in higher art education?
9. How would you describe the role played by private educational institutes without formal accreditation?
10. Which qualifications are required to teach in recognised art education? Are teachers appointed as statutory teachers or as contract workers?
11. Under which Ministry's competence does art education fall? Ministry of Education or Ministry of Culture?

Group II: Mobility

1. Percentage of art students participating in European exchange programmes compared to technical and scientific streams?
   - basic training
   - master's degree programmes
2. Are there any apparent reasons for students to refrain from taking advantage of the opportunities offered by such exchange programmes?
3. Percentage of art teachers taking advantage of the opportunities offered by European exchange programmes?

Jan De Groof, Chantal De Smet and Hilde Penneman (eds.), Art meets Law in Education, 171–172.

4. Are there any apparent reasons for teachers to refrain from taking advantage of the opportunities offered by such exchange programmes?
5. Should specific mobility conditions and procedures be set for student and teacher mobility in the art sector?
6. Does the European Credit Transfer System (ECTS) apply in your country? Is the ECTS sufficiently harmonised in Europe?
7. To what problems does the comparison of curricula give rise?

Group III: Equivalence of Degrees

1. What are the existing problems in connection with the equivalence of degrees?
   - when it comes to exercising an artistic profession
   - when it comes to being appointed as a teacher
2. In your opinion, is recognition of the equivalence of degrees the remit of:
   - national authorities (bilateral)?
   - the European Union?

FRIEDRICH FAULHAMMER

Austrian Report

Group I: Organisation of education

1. *What form of education does the designation, 'Art Education' refer to?*

Art Education in a university perspective refers to the tasks of the universities of the Arts. Their objectives are to cultivate the Arts, to educate through the Arts, to prepare students of the Arts for careers in the Arts as artists, educators or scholars and to provide continuing education for graduates of universities of the Arts, in particular in the form of courses and course programmes. Art Education in a less formal way means very intensive interactions between the teacher and her or his students.

2. *Into what level of your national education system is Art education assimilated in your country: university education – non-university higher education – other?*

Art Education is assimilated into all educational levels. It starts at the primary school level, leads to the secondary school level and finally to the non-university and university level. In all levels a specific and assimilated Art education is offered.

3. *What are the entrance requirements for higher Art education (age, certificates, skills)?*

First of all there is an age requirement of 17 years. This age can be reduced to 15 years in some courses at the universities of music. Certificates such as the secondary school leaving certificate are required only for some study programmes. For all courses at the universities of the Arts the applicants have to pass an entrance examination in order to prove their artistic aptitude.

Jan De Groof, Chantal De Smet and Hilde Penneman (eds.), Art meets Law in Education, 173–177.

4. *Which degrees or certificates are awarded in Art education?*

In university Art education academic degrees are awarded (Master of Art).

5. *Are Art degrees linked to the general education system?*

Yes.

6. *What are the standards of flexibility or strictness in formal higher Art education curricula? Is it mandatory for a student to sit examinations?*

The present curricula are drawn rather strictly. The new curricula will provide for more flexibility for the students. Examinations remain mandatory in all cases, however.

7. *Is the average Art student aware of the usefulness of regular studies and of securing a degree?*

Yes.

8. *What type of recognition is conferred to a degree in higher Art education?*

The degree has the recognition of an academic degree like other university academic degrees.

9. *How would you describe the role played by private educational institutes without formal accreditation?*

Those institutions play a very important role in basic Art education, but the higher non-university and university Art education takes place only at institutes with formal accreditation.

10. *Which qualifications are required to teach in recognised Art education? Are teachers appointed as statutory teachers or as contract workers?*

The teachers have to complete school teaching accreditation programmes at non-university higher education institutes or universities of the Arts. They are appointed as statutory teachers as well as contract workers.

11. *Under which Ministry's competence does Art education fall? Ministry of Education or Ministry of Culture?*

University Art education falls under the competence of the Federal Ministry of Science and Transport. In the non-university Art education the federal government has no competence, it is part of the competence of the regional and local governments.

Group II: Mobility

1. *Percentage of Art students participating in European exchange programmes compared to technical and scientific streams?*

Undergraduate (basic training): 21.84% (1997/98).
Postgraduate and Doctorate studies (masters degree and beyond): 12.24% (1997/98).
In Austria, there are no doctorate studies offered in the field of the Arts.

2. *Are there any apparent reasons for students to refrain from taking advantage of the opportunities offered by such programmes?*

Yes there are, but the problems are more general and do not exclusively refer to the field of the Arts. Some problems are: recognition of foreign courses at the particular university, entry requirements and residence permits, language issues, costs of living and labour market pressure. Further obstacles are costs and availability of lodging, and as Art students sometimes need a room of their own for lectures and practising, this can cause problems.

3. *Percentage of Art teachers taking advantage of the opportunities offered by European exchange programmes?*

In 1998/99 11 Art teachers took part in one of the European exchange programmes. This is a total of 0.46% of the teaching staff at the six Austrian Universities of the Arts.

4. *Are there any apparent reasons for teachers to refrain from taking advantage of the opportunities offered by such exchange programmes?*

The main obstacles are

- the paperwork the applicants have to go through (it takes up to one and a half years to complete the process);
- inner university problems (lack of interest, problems of scheduling, appointments, and possibly, lack of confidence in their supply teachers);
- lack of time, as the universities are being restructured and the admininstration work is more demanding than ever;
- the EU exchange programmes are not specifically designed for Art teachers;
- it is financially not attractive for teachers to take part in these programmes;
- no financial support for intensive programmes that have been particularly attractive to Art teachers.

3. *Should specific mobility conditions and procedures be set for student and teacher mobility in the Art sector?*

All in all, less paperwork and more money would be very helpful.

Concerning the Arts, intensive programmes should be granted more readily, as they fit into the general structure of Art studies better – thus complying with the original intentions of the exchange programmes more easily, paving the way to further, prospective exchange programmes without the backing of the EU. Introducing an office that is in charge of the exchange programmes exclusively for universities of the Arts could be a big advantage.

4. *Does the European Credit Transfer System (ECTS) apply in your country? Is the ECTS sufficiently harmonised in Europe?*

Since the Universities – Studies Act of 1997 (the basic law for all university studies including university studies in the field of the Arts) obliges all university bodies to instal ECTS, it applies in Austria. The university bodies therefore have to implement ECTS in the curricula for university studies. To enforce the introduction as soon as possible, the Ministry for Science and Transport launches an initiative to inform all university bodies involved about ECTS. The enforcement of ECTS will hopefully solve many of the problems of university recognition.

5. *To what problems does the comparison of curricula give rise?*

Difference in status of the respective universities can cause problems of recognition, labelling the same courses differently can irritate, and last but not least, the difference in the duration of the equivalent course/degree can cause problems.

Group III: Equivalence of Degrees

1. *What are the existing problems in connection with the equivalence of degrees? – When it comes to exercising an artistic profession?*

Artistic professions (teachers excepted) are in most cases non-regulated professions, for which formal criteria of education do not have much importance. Therefore, all kinds of autonomy in the recognition procedures, especially the application of the directive 89/48/EEC, apply only very rarely. So far, recognition is granted mostly on a case-by-case basis. This situation is worse the more the educational systems of the country in which somebody has finished her/his studies and the country in which she/he intends to exercise an artistic profession differ from each other. Such differences can be the length of study, its level (secondary versus higher level) and the kind of teaching and examination.

– When it comes to being appointed as a teacher?

Teachers in artistic subjects are in many cases regulated professions and are therefore covered by the directive 89/48/EEC. The kinds of teaching charges and contracts, however, can be very different. Moreover, there are a number of authorities running music schools and therefore deciding on the appointment of teachers. Not all of them apply professional recognition in the same way.

2. *In your opinion, is recognition of the equivalences of degrees the remit of national authorities (bilateral) or the European Union?*

As far as the question can be understood, there is one global regulation, i.e. the scheme of EU professional recognition, and many authorities operating under this global recognition in each member country. Reliable decisions need a good information mechanism on higher education systems abroad.

W. MICHAEL SCHECK AND CHANTAL DE SMET

Flemish Community of Belgium: Belgian Report

1. Organization of arts education

Introduction

Within the Dutch-speaking Flemish community of federal Belgium the official arts education is highly developed and also generously supported by the government.

As well as the other branches of public education, arts education is one of the responsibilities of the Education Department. In adequate applications it is spread over all the educational levels, from primary school to higher education.

There are few private arts education establishments, because of the availability of a dense network of arts schools of all types and levels.

Primary education (6 to 11 years)

As a complement to the traditional, rather rational-minded educational concept, there was recently introduced a new subject called 'general artistic education' (*Muzische vorming*), as an obligatory part of the teaching programme over all the six grades of primary school. It aims to stimulate the child's creativity in the fields of verbal, corporal, musical and plastic expression.

Secondary education (12 to 18 years)

In the average secondary school, arts education plays only a minor role. This is somewhat counterbalanced by the possibility of choosing one of the full-time secondary art schools offering one or more of the following disciplines: music, plastic arts, dance, verbal and dramatic arts.

Jan De Groof, Chantal De Smet and Hilde Penneman (eds.), Art meets Law in Education, 179–181.

Evening courses

A special way – either for children, adolescents or adults – to take a more specific, active part in artistic education is to subscribe to one of the public art schools which are to be found in most of the Flemish communities. The national government remunerates the teachers and supports part of the working costs. The pupil only has to pay a nominal fee. He can follow a ten-year education in music, dance, verbal expression and drama, as well as all kinds of plastic arts, including architecture and handcrafts. Yearly examinations and the supervision of the public art schools by the government assures the realization of the imposed pedagogical standards. The awarded degrees have no civil effect.

Higher arts education

The admission to a higher arts school requires a certificate of secondary education. Besides this the candidate has to sit an entrance examination proving his talent and the skills already acquired.

There are two types of higher arts education, both full-time:

1. one cycle (3 years); polytechnic level; diploma *graduaat* (graduate);
2. two cycles (4 or 5 years); university level; diploma *meester* (master) or *licentiaat* (licentiate), depending on the type of education. At the end of the first cycle the diploma of *kandidaat* (candidate) is awarded.

The full-time curricula are obligatory. Examinations are held at the end of every year. There is no flexibility for organizing the studies in a personal (modular) way by acquiring credits.

A teacher's licence can be acquired by taking a number of modular courses, during or after the regular studies.

The average arts student is eager to obtain a degree, in order to be admitted as a teacher.

There are only a few private schools of the arts, thanks to a dense network of institutions of all types and levels.

2. Student and teacher mobility

Students

Art student mobility within European exchange programmes is on a low level: 3 to 5 per cent at the basic level, 0 per cent at the masters degree level.

Reasons:

- an arts student normally chooses an individual teacher, not a school;
- for fine arts students the availability of a studio abroad is often a problem;

- in many cases art students are obliged to earn (a part of) their lives as working students;
- Erasmus scholarships are only granted for periods of 3 months or more. This is too long for the purposes of an arts student.

Special programmes should be conceived for arts students.

Teachers

Art teacher mobility levels are 1 per cent of them.

Reasons:

- artistic activities (performances, exhibitions, teaching), which must not be interrupted;
- the individual responsibility for their students at home;
- lack of facilities abroad, such as studios, etc.

3. Equivalence of Degrees

The mutual recognition of degrees undoubtedly comes within the ambit of the powers of the European Union. On the other hand, the arts schools themselves should be free to determine the conditions for accepting students as well as teachers, in order to protect their own views on the pedagogic project, methods and artistic standards.

HENRIK JACOBSEN

Danish Report

GROUP I: ORGANISATION OF ART EDUCATION

1. *What form of education does the designation 'Art Education' actually refer to?*

Primarily training in practical arts, that is visual arts, theatre, film, music, design, architecture, and conservation.

2. *Into what level of your national education system is art education assimilated in your country: university education – non-university higher education – other?*

In Denmark art education is placed at non-university state-operated establishments under the Danish Ministry of Culture. It should be noted that educational establishments within architecture, visual arts, conservation and music operate with a university type structure, with the possibility of performing research on an academic level.

3. *What are the entrance requirements for higher art education (ages, certificates, skills)?*

Usually skills on a certain level are required, and in those cases entrance examinations are held before admission. Education within architecture and conservation also requires a high school diploma, passed with a certain average level of grades. Education in Acting requires applicants to be between 18 and 25 years old, whereas education within other branches of theatre (Directing, Stage Design, and Technical Arts) requires a minimum age of 21.

Jan De Groof, Chantal De Smet and Hilde Penneman (eds.), Art meets Law in Education, 183–186.

4. Which degrees or certificates are awarded in art education?

Only architecture and conservation graduates are assigned actual 'degrees' corresponding to BA and MA degrees.

Graduates within music, design, visual arts, theatre and film obtain no formal degree, but the schools provide study programmes up to the highest level.

5. Are art degrees linked to general education system?

Not directly. Only education in architecture and conservation, as outlined above.

6. What are the standards of flexibility or strictness in formal higher art education curricula? Is it mandatory for a student to sit examinations?

No general rules. Depends on the particular education in question. As outlined above, many fields within art education operate in a manner without examinations and grading.

7. Is the average art student aware of the usefulness of regular studies and of securing a degree?

In general, yes.

8. What type of recognition is conferred to a degree in higher art education?

Domestically recognised as the highest possible level of education within the arts.

9. How would you describe the role played by private educational institutes without formal accreditation?

Virtually non-existent.

10. Which qualifications are required to teach in recognised art education? Are teachers appointed as statutory teachers or as contract workers?

Teachers are employed on a contractual basis. It is possible to take in external teaching staff on a casual basis.

11. Under which Ministry's competence does art education fall? Ministry of Education or Ministry of Culture?

Ministry of Culture.

Group II: Mobility

1. *Percentage of art student's participation in European exchange programmes compared to technical and scientific streams?*

- basic training
  Currently, no statistics available.
- master's degree programmes
  Currently, no statistics available.

2. *Are there any apparent reasons for students to refrain from taking advantage of the opportunities offered by such exchange programmes?*

Usually not. Occasionally, however, the financing of such programmes might be a problem for some students.

3. *Percentage of art teachers taking advantage of the opportunities offered by European exchange programmes?*

Currently, no statistics can be provided. Would depend highly on the specific education in question.

4. *Are there any apparent reasons for teachers to refrain from taking advantage of the opportunities offered by such programmes?*

Due to the limited requirements for the educational establishments to report information on these matters, the Ministry of Culture has no general impression whether there are problems in this area or not.

5. *Should specific mobility conditions and procedures be set for student and teacher mobility in the art sector?*

It is the general impression of the Ministry of Culture that for students, mobility conditions and programmes are functioning properly. As for teacher mobility we do not currently retain the information required to answer this question.

6. *Does the European Credit Transfer System (ECTS) apply in your country? Is the ECTS sufficiently harmonised in Europe?*

The ECTS does formally apply in Denmark, but the system is not currently in use within Danish art education. In our opinion there is less need for ECTS in the artistic field of education than in the academic field of education.

7. *To what problems does the comparison of curricula give rise?*

Especially recognition of Danish graduate diplomas abroad. The high level of Danish art education might in some cases be misjudged, especially regarding those Danish educational establishments within the arts which do not perform grading or issue transcripts.

GROUP III: EQUIVALENCE OF DEGREES

1. *What are the existing problems in connection with the equivalence of degrees?*

- when it comes to exercising an artistic profession
  Domestically, none. Internationally, it is sometimes a problem that we do not make use of internationally recognised degrees like BA and MA, and that professionals abroad are not always familiar with the Danish educational standards.
- when it comes to being appointed as a teacher
  Domestically, none. Abroad, Danish applicants for a post as teacher in art could be expected to face problems similar to those of performing artists as described above.

2. *In your opinion, is recognition of the equivalence of degrees the remit of*

- national authorities (bilateral)?
  Yes, in co-operation with educational establishments.
- the European Union?
  EU-based recognition of degree equivalence could probably be an advantage – i.e. within design.

PAUL MEREDITH

Education, Law and the Arts: England and Wales

I. THE ORGANISATION OF ART EDUCATION

1. 'Art education' could be interpreted either widely or narrowly: a wide interpretation would encompass education in the humanities generally, including classical studies, ancient and modern languages, linguistics, history, archaeology, philosophy, cultural studies, media studies, film studies, theatre studies, drama, music, fine arts, the history of art, painting, drawing, sculpture and architecture. In keeping with this broader definition, the traditional first degree in the humanities in British Universities is commonly entitled Bachelor of Arts, although in some subject areas more specific degree titles are used – for instance Bachelor of Music, Bachelor of Architecture.

A narrower interpretation of 'art education' would restrict the phrase to education in a more limited range of subjects, including fine arts, the history of art, painting, drawing, sculpture, music and musicology, drama and possibly architecture and aspects of archaeology (e.g. rock art). This narrower definition will now be adopted in this questionnaire.

2. Art education is assimilated within the education system in England and Wales at all levels – primary and secondary schools, further education and higher education. At the school level, art and music form part of the national curriculum under the Education Act 1996: by virtue of section 354(2)(b), art and music are 'foundation subjects' within the national curriculum in relation to the first, second and third key stages, thus making their study compulsory for all children (unless specially exempted) attending maintained schools from the age of five to the age of fourteen. Programmes of study, attainment targets and assessment arrangements are promulgated for each foundation subject by the Secretary of State by Order in Council under section 356(2), and the detail of the programmes of study is set out in official documents referred to in those Orders (s. 356(4)). The substance of the curriculum in these subjects in maintained schools is thus closely regulated by law and

Jan De Groof, Chantal De Smet and Hilde Penneman (eds.), Art meets Law in Education, 187–191.

essentially uniform across England and Wales. The national curriculum does not apply in independent schools, although in practice most independent schools do broadly follow the same curriculum. In addition to being foundation subjects within the national curriculum, art and music are also examinable subjects within the public school examination structure in England and Wales – in particular, the General Certificate of Secondary Education Examinations, and the General Certificate of Education Advanced Level Examinations.

Education in art and music is also widely assimilated within colleges of further and higher education and within the University system. The legal power to award diplomas and degrees is complex, but broadly colleges of further and higher education are accredited for the purpose of conferring awards by Universities, while Universities themselves have their own independent degree awarding powers by virtue either of Royal Charter (in the case of pre-1992 Universities) or by virtue of the Further and Higher Education Act 1992 (in the case of Universities founded after that Act came into force, most of which are former Polytechnics).

3. Universities and colleges of higher education normally require entrants to hold qualifications in relevant subjects at Advanced Level in the General Certificate of Education examinations. Normally passes in three such examinations are required. The standard of the pass attained will vary from one institution to another. In the case of some students (e.g. mature students), some modification of these requirements may be permitted.

4. The degrees or diplomas vary enormously from one institution to another. In Universities, the first degree (awarded normally after three years of study) is a Bachelor's degree, e.g. Bachelor of Arts, Bachelor of Music. A Master's degree may be awarded after a further year's study, often including the submission of a dissertation. The almost universal title within British Universities for a Doctorate by research (following normally three years of research) is that of Doctor of Philosophy (Ph.D.), whatever the subject area. Higher Doctorates (e.g. Doctor of Literature or Doctor of Music) are rarely awarded, and generally based upon major published work.

Colleges of Higher Education may award similar degrees, subject to accreditation by one of the Universities. Specialist Colleges of art, music and drama award a range of diplomas and certificates with different titles (e.g. Diploma in Art, Fellow of the Royal College of Music; Fellow of the Royal College of Organists; and many others). The legal authority for the conferment of such degrees, diplomas and certificates will vary, depending on the foundation of the institution concerned, in some cases based upon Royal Charter as in the case of the older Universities.

5. Yes – see answer to 2 above.

6. Curricula, syllabuses and the entire teaching and learning process within higher education are increasingly being scrutinised under the auspices of the Higher Education Funding Councils, statutory bodies which provide much of the funding

for Universities and other institutions of higher education. The Higher Education Funding Councils conduct periodical subject reviews of teaching and learning throughout the higher education sector, involving a detailed quality analysis and audit of the teaching and learning process in each institution. Increasingly, the funding of institutions will be dependent on obtaining high ratings in these subject reviews. There is thus increasingly close scrutiny of standards.

In terms of the actual formulation of curricula, individual institutions do, however, have a substantial amount of flexibility, particularly those with degree awarding powers of their own (in particular, the Universities). Colleges of higher education which do not enjoy independent degree awarding authority but which are accredited for the purposes of awarding degrees by a University will have less autonomy and flexibility in formulating curricula as they will be subject to periodical scrutiny by their accrediting institution and will have to submit draft course curricula for approval.

It is generally mandatory for students to sit and to pass examinations, although many degrees and diplomas are assessed in part by essays, dissertations and projects in addition to examinations, and some may be assessed entirely by these more flexible methods. In all cases within the higher education sector external examiners from other institutions are appointed to scrutinise the examining process and ensure the preservation of academic standards.

7. Yes, this would be very clear. Students in British Universities have only limited opportunities to resit failed examinations and may well have their courses terminated if they do not pass on resitting. The detailed regulations for resitting and course termination vary from one institution to another and one degree course to another. Invariably an element of discretion may be exercised by the examiners in cases where examinations are failed under extenuating circumstances.

8. A degree or diploma can only be awarded by a University or by a College which is accredited for this purpose by a University, or by certain other institutions whose foundations confer on them the power to award degrees. All degrees and diplomas are thus fully authorised and mutually recognised. A degree in art would be thus recognised in exactly the same way as in any other subject.

9. They would have no degree or diploma awarding capacity and thus would have no formal role within the system.

10. A degree or diploma in art would be required. To teach in a state school, the teacher would also be required to undertake a course of teacher training, generally known as a Postgraduate Certificate of Education. In some cases a Bachelor of Education degree may qualify to teach art. Teachers are required to be registered with the General Teaching Council for England or the General Teaching Council for Wales, both established under the Teaching and Higher Education Act 1998 (ss. 1–10). Teachers have contracts of employment with either the governing body

of the school in which they work or with their local education authority, but their conditions of employment are regulated by statute and statutory instrument.

11. Department for Education and Employment.

II. Mobility

1. No exact figures are available but the broad pattern is that the percentage of students in the humanities participating in European exchanges is somewhat higher than students in the sciences and applied sciences, and considerably higher than in Law and medicine where the uptake is low. The somewhat higher percentage uptake among humanities rather than science students is explained largely by the presence among the humanities students of students of modern languages and other European studies who are particularly inclined to participate in European exchange programmes. In Law the uptake is rather low by virtue in part of the very different nature of the Common Law jurisdiction in England and Wales. Participation among students of art and music narrowly defined is average for non-modern language students within the humanities as a whole. Participation is significantly greater among undergraduate than postgraduate students.

2. The two key disincentives are money and language. Higher education students in England and Wales now have to pay tuition fees (by virtue of the Teaching and Higher Education Act 1998) and the former system of student grants has been replaced by a system of student loans repayable over a number of years after the student concerned has reached a given income. These operate as very strong financial disincentives as students in higher education generally finish their degree courses with substantial debts: the prospect of extending their period of study by spending a further year of study in another European country, and thereby possibly incurring further debt, would not be viewed favourably by many students.

With the exception of modern languages students, many students in England and Wales would feel that their foreign language skills were insufficient to participate in a year of study abroad, and many would not feel that the acquisition of greater foreign language skills held significant longer term career benefits.

3. Figures are not available, but it is not thought that the percentage of art teachers would differ from teachers in the humanities as a whole.

4. Language may be one disincentive. The low level of school teachers' salaries in England and Wales may be another.

5. It is not thought that mobility conditions and procedures in the art sector should be different from those in other sectors.

6. In some Universities and Colleges of Higher Education, yes. The position is not uniform. A greater degree of harmonisation may be beneficial, although adherence to the principle of autonomy within individual institutions as to curricular

formulation may make harmonisation difficult. Modularisation of courses is not uniform in higher education in England and Wales, and in many cases it is strongly opposed on the basis that it leads to a diminution in academic standards.

7. Universities in England and Wales operate on the basis of stringent entry conditions, very limited numbers of students, small group teaching, highly intensive courses, strictly limited rights to resit examinations or re-submit assessments or dissertations, and strict quality assurance. It may be difficult to make valid curricular comparisons unless these features are also present in the comparator institution.

III. Equivalence of degrees

1. There are few problems in connection with the equivalence of degrees as between UK Universities, given the strict quality assurance mechanisms that exist in all Universities by virtue of the external examiner system and the Higher Education Funding Council quality assurance system. Stringent entry conditions and limited resit rights apply throughout the UK University sector. While it is certainly true that certain institutions and Universities have a greater level of prestige than others, a general consequence of the highly selective University system in the UK is that degrees from different Universities are in principle and, broadly, in practice, regarded as of equivalent standard.

2. National authorities should have this responsibility. There may be many important differences between Universities and Colleges of Higher Education (e.g. entry qualifications, small group teaching, intensity of courses, curricular autonomy, external assessment of the examinations process, quality assurance) which would make the process of recognition of equivalence at European Union level extremely difficult.

HANS-PETER FÜSSEL

German Report

Group 1: Organisation of art education

1

In general terms one could say that at least three different 'types' of students could be distinguished in the colleges of art in Germany

- 'free artists';
- 'free' musical educators; and
- future teaching staff for schools.

This includes all those persons who study performing arts such as music, fine arts, architecture, design, theatre, film and dance.

'Free' musical educators (mostly for piano and violin) will also study at the colleges of art; they may work later in special local music institutions (*Musikschulen*, but these are not schools in the normal sense because the participants attend them voluntarily and also pay for the lessons!) or they give lessons as self-employed.

Those who are becoming teachers normally have to study a second school subject (this second subject will normally be offered only by universities or teacher training colleges, so these students have to enrol in two institutions); in some of the *Länder* (Berlin, Bavaria) teachers only study one subject (music or fine arts).

2

Most of the 46 colleges of art in Germany are equivalent to the universities, but some courses – like design, architecture or training to become a goldsmith in some places – are on the level of *Fachhochschulen* (equivalent to *Hoogeschools*), i.e. non-university higher education.

Jan De Groof, Chantal De Smet and Hilde Penneman (eds.), Art meets Law in Education, 193–196.

3

The system of entrance requirements is quite different and complicated.

In most courses a practical-orientated examination will be held at the start – for example, a musical performance, or the submission of pieces of art or design. Access is also possible for students without a school degree if they show extraordinary abilities.

4

The normal degree is the diploma; the participation in 'master-classes' is equivalent to a doctorate at the universities.

Students with the aim of becoming teachers will have to finish their studies with the normal teacher examinations followed by a practical-orientated training course and a second examination.

Some of the colleges of art have now initiated the first steps towards B.A. and M.A. classes for design.

5

The diplomas are equivalent to those from the other institutions of higher education – except the system of 'master-classes'.

6 and 7

In music at least an examination is mandatory to become a musician in an orchestra, or a teacher. The position is the same for design and architecture.

In fine art, the studies often end without a formal examination; an exhibition may mark the end of the studies.

In general terms, the necessity of a formal examination at the end of the studies will be decided by the labour market; therefore an art student may decide under these conditions how relevant an examination may be.

8

The German *Länder* have set standards by framework regulations in the Conference of Ministers of Cultural Affairs in Germany (*Kultusministerkonferenz*); therefore, a mutual recognition of degrees in higher art education is fixed.

For example:

- Empfehlung zur Förderung der Musikpflege und der Musikausbildung vom 19/20 January 1967;
- Empfehlung für die Ausgestaltung von Studiengängen im Bereich der Freien Bildenden Kunst an Kunsthochschulen vom 9 November 1984;

– Empfehlung über Rahmenbestimmungen für die Ausbildung und Prüfung von Lehrern an Musikschulen und selbständigen Musiklehrern vom 9 November 1984.

9

The 'free' (and private) institutions of art education in Germany are more or less of a supplemementary character.

They are sometimes in a way 'ideologically' orientated (for example, Steiner/Waldorf-Institutions) or follow therapeutic ideas (music-therapy, art-therapy), but they are also important in some fields, such as play-acting and dance.

However, these are free institutions, often not comparable with other institutions of higher education.

10

The qualifications are set by the discipline: high-ranked, and they may use statutory as well as contract teachers.

Professors are normally civil servants with an unlimited 'contract'. But for projects and other functions more and more contract workers with a limited contract are employed.

The system at the colleges of art in taking this direction is not different from those at the other institutions of higher education in Germany.

11

Normally the Ministry of Science is responsible; only in Bavaria is the responsiblity with the Ministry of Culture.

Group II: Mobility

1–5

To obtain answers for this very specific topic seems to be very difficult. The reason is that (in 1997) we had 1,674,700 students in all institutions of higher education in Germany, but only 24,400 in the colleges of art in the whole country.

6 and 7

The introduction of ECTS has just begun in Germany, especially in courses with international relations (where, for example, studies abroad are compulsory).

Because of the fairly recent introduction of ECTS not many experiences can be referred to, but the more or less formal comparison of the curricula within the ECTS has produced some problems, including acceptance of this new system.

Group III: Equivalence of degrees

In general a discussion in Germany has only now started regarding how far all the higher education institutions should in the future incorporate the system of B.A. and M.A. courses. Because of the more and more relevant orientation of the higher education institutions in Germany in the direction of international standards, the institutions must decide how far they will follow international trends. A solution that B.A. courses will be offered by the *Fachhochschulen* and M.A. Courses by the universities will not be accepted – at least, not by both institutions in Germany.

So this change of the system in general may cause a situation of competition in Germany between *Fachhochschulen* and universities in the same fields and subjects of studies – although one solution may be that the *Fachhochschulen* offer more practical-orientated courses and the universities the more theoretical ones.

This development can already be observed now with the design courses. There, the higher education institutions start with the first steps towards the B.A./M.A. structure – also because of the international labour-market and the international competition in that field. Therefore a kind of 'market-orientated' steering has started, not forced by recognition of national or European authorities, but by (labour-) market forces.

This may have a particularly important part to play in the field of art-education: the acceptance of artists became more and more an international one, given by the audience and public acceptance. This seems to be of much more importance than formal degrees – more or less indifferent to kinds of procedures and recognition.

Also, inside Germany, the acceptance of the public seems to be more relevant than formal examinations.

THÉODORE FORTSAKIS

Greek Report[1]

Selon l'article 16 de la Constitution hellénique, l'art et la science, la recherche et l'enseignement sont libres; leur développement et leur promotion constituent une obligation de l'État. L'instruction constitue une mission fondamentale de l'État et a pour but l'éducation morale, culturelle, professionnelle et physique des Hellènes, le développement d'une conscience nationale et religieuse ainsi que la formation de citoyens libres et responsables. Selon la même disposition, tous les Hellènes ont droit à l'instruction gratuite à tous ses degrés dans les établissements d'enseignement de l'État. En outre, l'enseignement supérieur est assuré uniquement par des établissements qui constituent des personnes morales de droit public pleinement décentralisées. Les professeurs des établissements d'enseignement supérieur sont titulaires de la fonction publique. Le reste du personnel enseignant accomplit également une fonction publique dans les conditions fixées par la loi. Le statut de toutes les personnes susmentionnées est déterminé par les statuts d'organisation de leurs établissements. L'enseignement professionnel et tout autre enseignement spécial sont assurés par l'État et au moyen d'écoles et de degrés post-secondaires dans un cycle d'études ne dépassant pas trois ans, comme cela est prévu plus spécialement par la loi qui, en outre, fixe les droits à l'activité professionnelle des diplômes de ces écoles.

Il ressort de l'obligation de développement et de promotion de l'art consacrée par l'article constitutionnel susvisé que l'État doit veiller premièrement à organiser un enseignement approprié de l'art, tant dans le cadre de l'éducation générale que dans des établissements spécialisés, et d'autre part, à promouvoir l'art et ses créateurs.

Les dispositions constitutionnelles susvisées, dans la mesure où elles se réfèrent à l'enseignement, concernent également l'enseignement de l'art.

De ces dispositions il ressort en outre que l'État non seulement a le droit, mais est tenu d'avoir une politique culturelle, à condition que celle-ci développe et assure la promotion de l'art sans le mettre sous tutelle.

[1] Aucun exposé systématique des réglementations de l'éducation de l'art n'existe, à ma connaissance, en Grèce. Les recherches à ce propos ont été menées dans le but de cet exposé par Mademoiselle Kalliopi Stougiannou, jeune détentrice de la maîtrise en Droit de la Faculté de Droit d'Athènes, que l'auteur remercie chaleureusement.

Jan De Groof, Chantal De Smet and Hilde Penneman (eds.), Art meets Law in Education, 197–211.

Cependant, il résulte de ce qui est exposé ci-dessous que la situation actuelle de l'éducation de l'art en Grèce ne correspond pas exactement à celle qui est annoncée par les textes constitutionnels ci-dessus. Cette éducation d'une part demeure fragmentaire, puisque des domaines importants, tel celui des arts populaires (pourtant si importants en Grèce: poterie, musique dite démotique, danses populaires, art des ombres ou karaghiose, etc.) ne font pas l'objet d'un enseignement organisé; d'autre part elle n'est pas systématisée et souvent même, ses institutions sont réglementées de manière vague, voire inappropriée.

Plan de développement. Les questions posées par le questionnaire sont traitées, selon d'une part le niveau, d'autre part l'objet de l'enseignement de l'institution concernée, à l'intérieur des trois unités proposées: Organisation de l'éducation de l'art (1), la Mobilité (2), l'équivalence des degrés (3).

1 – Organisation de l'éducation de l'art

A. Enseignement supérieur (universitaire)

A-1. *Études pré-licence (4 premières années)*

I. *École Supérieure des Beaux-Arts*

La loi 4791/1930 'sur l'organisation de l'École Supérieure des Beaux-Arts' (JO A 225), a rebaptisé l'École des Beaux-Arts, qui fonctionnait jusqu'alors dans le cadre de l'École Polytechnique Metsovio, 'École Supérieure des Beaux-Arts' et l'a mise sur un pied d'égalité avec l'École Polytechnique Metsovio, dans le but: (a) d'assurer la formation d'artistes et la promotion de l'art grec moderne; (b) de développer le sentiment artistique du public, et (c) de former des maîtres pour l'enseignement technique dans les écoles du système éducatif. L'École Supérieure des Beaux-Arts devenait ainsi une personne morale de droit public, disposait de son propre patrimoine et de son propre personnel éducatif et administratif. Les professeurs étaient élus par le collège des professeurs en toute liberté de jugement, parmi les artistes distingués dans leur spécialité, et étaient nommés par le ministre compétent. Les salaires du personnel étaient payés par l'État. L'École se trouvait sous la tutelle de l'État, exercée par le ministère de l'Éducation par l'intermédiaire d'un commissaire gouvernemental. Actuellement, toutes ces questions, à savoir celles qui touchent à l'autoadministration de l'École et en général à son organisation, sont réglementées par les différentes dispositions portant sur les Établissements d'Enseignement Supérieur (initiales grecques: AEI), constitutionnelles ou autres.

Au départ, l'École comprenait deux classes de préparation, en peinture et sculpture, et divers ateliers (peinture, sculpture, xylographie, lithographie, chalcographie, travail du marbre), une bibliothèque, une pinacothèque et une glyptothèque, une collection de moulages de sculptures anciennes et modernes, des relais artistiques (à Delphes, Mykonos, Hydra). Y étaient enseignées la peinture, la sculpture et la gravure (xylographie, lithographie, chalcographie) en toute indépendance et sous la pleine responsabilité des professeurs des ateliers. Les cours étaient d'ordre pratique et théorique. Les candidats à une inscription devaient posséder au moins un certificat d'études primaires pour déposer une demande. Les étrangers étaient admis aux mêmes conditions. Tout ce qui concernait la formation spéciale des candidats à poste de professeur d'enseignement technique dans les écoles du système éducatif était défini spécialement. Les candidats à un poste d'enseignant dans les écoles d'enseignement secondaire devaient posséder un certificat de fin d'études secondaires et, après avoir suivi une classe préparatoire, concouraient pour leur intégration à l'École.

Entre 1930 et nos jours, de nombreux changements sont survenus, bien entendu, dans le programme d'études de l'école, sans que, toutefois, le caractère de celle-ci en soit essentiellement altéré. Selon le dernier Programme d'Études (JO B 362), sont dispensés les cours suivants: peinture, sculpture, gravure, matériaux et technologie des matériaux, histoire de l'art, théorie de l'espace, histoire de l'architecture, divers cours en atelier, langues étrangères, arts graphiques, philosophie et esthétique, fresque et technique des icônes portatives, mosaïque, scénographie, gravure (xylographie, chalcographie, lithographie), pédagogie, psychologie de l'éducation, techniques diverses, photographie. Ces cours sont dispensés dans le cadre de divers ateliers, sur cinq années au total. Les candidats intègrent l'École après des examens qui se déroulent au niveau national, auxquels ils peuvent participer s'ils possèdent le certificat de fin d'études secondaires, des réglementations spéciales étant prévues pour ceux qui ont une prédisposition particulière pour l'expression artistique (décret présidentiel 160/1990, JO A 58).

II. *L'École Supérieure des Beaux-Arts de l'Université Aristote de Thessalonique*

Il existe à Thessalonique également, dans le cadre de l'Université Aristote de Thessalonique, une École Supérieure des Beaux-Arts (décret présidentiel de fondation 169/1984, JO A 57). A côté du Département des arts figuratifs et des arts appliqués fonctionne aussi un Département d'études musicales et un Département de théâtre. Les arts appliqués comprennent aussi le verre, le dessin animé, la photographie – vidéo, l'illustration des imprimés.

A l'heure actuelle, comme pour l'École Supérieure des Beaux-Arts, les questions qui concernent l'autoadministration et plus généralement l'organisation de l'École Supérieure des Beaux-Arts de l'Université Aristote de Thessalonique sont réglementées par les différentes dispositions portant sur les Établissements d'Enseignement Supérieur (AEI), constitutionnelles ou autres.

III. *Université Nationale et Capodistrienne d'Athènes, Département des Études musicales et Département des Études théâtrales*

Le décret présidentiel 527/1989 (JO A 223) a fondé à l'Université Nationale et Capodistrienne d'Athènes les Départements d'Études musicales et d'Études théâtrales, dans le but de promouvoir la science de la musique et du théâtre, de cultiver les arts en Grèce en mettant l'accent sur le patrimoine culturel du pays, de soutenir la recherche dans les domaines de la musique et du théâtre, de former un personnel adapté pour répondre aux besoins de l'enseignement et des autres secteurs de la vie sociale, économique et culturelle. Ces Départements fonctionnent, à l'instar de tous les autres départements universitaires, sur la base de la législation universitaire, y compris pour les questions concernant les membres du personnel d'enseignement et de recherche, et délivrent une licence.

Tel qu'il est défini actuellement par l'Assemblée Générale du Département, le Programme d'Études comprend, entre autres, obligatoirement ou à titre optionnel, l'histoire du théâtre européen, la théorie du théâtre et de la tragédie, le théâtre grec des temps modernes, une introduction à l'art du théâtre, Cocteau et Giraudoux, la théorie et la philosophie de la tragédie, la scénographie et l'art su costume au XXe siècle, l'histoire de l'art, l'architecture du théâtre grec antique, les étapes de la critique théâtrale en Grèce, etc.

Le Programme d'Études du Département des Études musicales, tel qu'il est défini actuellement par l'Assemblée Générale du Département, comprend, entre autres, obligatoirement ou à titre optionnel, la musicologie historique, la musicologie byzantine, la musique populaire grecque, l'ethnomusicologie, l'histoire de la musique occidentale (européenne), l'acoustique physique et musicale, la musique grecque ancienne, l'histoire de l'art du psaume byzantin et postbyzantin, l'histoire de la musique grecque moderne, la pédagogie et la psychologie, l'informatique, l'anthropologie de la musique, les systèmes musico-pédagogiques, etc. Le programme comprend en outre de nombreux cours pratiques obligatoires, comme l'harmonie, le contrepoint, l'apprentissage élémentaire des instruments de musique, de chant choral et de direction d'orchestre, la notation musicale byzantine, la notation musicale sur la portée. A quoi viennent s'ajouter des séminaires et des options.

A-2. *Études universitaires de troisième cycle*

I. *Université Nationale et Capodistrienne d'Athènes, Département des Études théâtrales*

Le Département des Études théâtrales de l'Université Nationale et Capodistrienne d'Athènes dispensent des cours qui mènent à l'obtention d'un diplôme de troisième cycle d'un an, dans le cadre de la législation universitaire générale, 'Théâtre grec de l'Antiquité à nos jours, théorie et représentation'.

II. *École Supérieure des Beaux-Arts*

Le décret présidentiel 612/1981 (JO A 155) a créé un Département d'Études de troisième cycle à l'École Supérieure des Beaux-Arts, dont le siège se situe dans l'île de Chio. Le but est de former des scientifiques spécialisés dans les problèmes de la création artistique et de l'histoire et de la théorie de l'art. Le cursus est de deux ans.

B. ENSEIGNEMENT SUPÉRIEUR (POST-LYCÉE, NON UNIVERSITAIRE)

I. *Les Établissements d'Enseignement Technologique*

Par la loi 1404/1983 (JO A 173) a été créé au sein des Établissements d'Enseignement Technologique d'Athènes l'École des Arts Graphiques et des Études Artistiques. Un arrêté du ministre de l'Éducation nationale et des Cultes n°9/24-2-1984 (JO B 99) a créé, dans le cadre de cette École, les Départements suivants: (a) graphisme, (b) décoration, (c) conservation des antiquités et des oeuvres d'art, (d) technologie des arts graphiques. Les candidats peuvent s'inscrire après avoir réussi des examens organisés au niveau national, comme pour toutes les autres Écoles des Établissements d'Enseignement Technologique. Le cursus est de trois ans; il est suivi d'un stage pratique. Le diplôme qui est délivré n'est pas reconnu jusqu'à présent comme diplôme d'un Établissement d'Enseignement Supérieur, en dépit de la demande insistante des intéressés. Le personnel de l'École est organisé d'une manière semblable à celle qui vaut pour les autres Établissements d'Enseignement Technologique, dans le cadre législatif correspondant, qui est similaire à celui des Établissements d'Enseignement Supérieur.

II. *L'École Nationale d'Art du Ballet*

Cette école a été créée par la loi 342/1976 (JO A 138) en tant que personne morale de droit public, sous la tutelle et le contrôle du ministère de la Culture et dans le but de former des cadres professionnels dans le domaine de l'art du de la danse, c'est-à-dire des professeurs, des danseurs et des chorégraphes. Ses ressources lui viennent essentiellement des subventions étatiques. L'École dispose d'un personnel enseignant et administratif. Les élèves peuvent s'inscrire après avoir subi des examens et à condition de posséder un diplôme d'enseignement secondaire, sauf pour ceux qui font preuve d'un talent particulier pour l'art de la danse.

Le décret présidentiel 598/1985 (JO A 212) a intégré l'École au degré supérieur de l'enseignement artistique. La chose a son importance, étant donné que de nombreuses Écoles d'enseignement artistique restent non classées, ce qui fait que le diplôme qu'elles délivrent n'est pas reconnu.

Actuellement, le programme d'études (décret présidentiel 598/1985) fait l'objet d'un enseignement dans le cadre de deux Départements, celui des professeurs de danse et celui des danseurs; il comprend: ballet classique, danse moderne, rythmique, théorie et histoire de la musique, anatomie, histoire de l'art, art populaire, psychologie enfantine, analyse de la tragédie, langues étrangères, piano et flûte.

III. *Les Écoles de Danse amateurs*

Le décret présidentiel 457/1983 (JO A 174) prévoit des règles concernant la création et le fonctionnement d'Écoles de Danse amateurs, qui peuvent ouvrir après avoir obtenu l'autorisation du ministère de la Culture et qui sont placées sous sa tutelle. Sont dispensés dans ces Écoles une partie des cours qui sont prévus pour les écoles supérieures de danse par le décret présidentiel 372/1983 (cf. *supra*).

Ce Écoles peuvent être ouvertes par des particuliers ou des personnes morales de droit privé ou de droit public. Le décret présidentiel définit tout ce qui concerne l'organisation de leur personnel enseignant et administratif, ainsi que leurs installations et la répartition des élèves en fonction de leur âge. Ces Écoles ne peuvent délivrer que des attestations d'assiduité aux cours; il leur est interdit de délivrer quelque diplôme que ce soit.

IV. *Les Écoles Supérieures d'Enseignement Artistique*

La loi 1158/1981 (JO Á 127) prévoit 'l'organisation et l'administration d'Écoles Supérieures d'Enseignement Artistique'. Ces Écoles sont des écoles: (a) d'art dramatique, (b) de danse, et (c) de cinéma – télévision. Chacune peut comprendre plusieurs Départements. Elles sont créés sur autorisation du ministère de la Culture, soit par des particuliers soit par des personnes morales de droit privé ou public. Elles sont placées sous la tutelle du ministère de la Culture, qui contrôle l'entrée des étudiants ainsi que leur fin d'études. Ces contrôles sont exercés par diverses commissions (arreté interministériel des ministres de la Présidence du gouvernement, des Finances et de la Culture, numéro 44046/22/23-9-1992, JO B 577).

Sur la base de cette loi ont été pris des décrets présidentiels qui ont organisé des Écoles Supérieures de Danse (décret présidentiel 372/1983, JO A 131) et des Écoles Supérieures d'Art Dramatique (décret présidentiel 370/1983, JO A 130). Jusqu'à ce jour, les décrets présidentiels concernant les Écoles de cinéma et de télévision n'ont pas été publiés, si bien que toutes les Écoles de ce type qui fonctionnent restent non classées.

Cette loi définit les diplômes d'études qui sont délivrés par les Écoles d'Enseignement Supérieur Artistique: il est plus particulièrement prévu pour les diplômés des écoles d'art dramatique qu'ils peuvent intégrer les Départements ou les Écoles de Théâtrologie de la Faculté des Lettres, ainsi que la possibilité, pour les diplômés des Départements ou des Écoles de théatrologie, de dispenser des cours de leur spécialité dans les écoles de l'enseignement secondaire. La même loi définit les conditions de recrutement des professeurs des Écoles d'Enseignement Supérieur Artistique. Elle fixe aussi les conséquences d'une éventuelle violation de ses dispositions, les droits d'inscription que doivent verser les étudiants, les conditions des inspections effectuées par le ministère de la Culture, et tout ce qui touche aux prêts et subventions accordés aux Écoles.

Notons qu'en vertu d'une disposition de cette loi, ses dispositions ont été étendues aux écoles de danse amateurs (cf. *supra*).

La loi 1158/1981 (article 26) dispose que: (a) l'École Dramatique du Théâtre National, (b) l'École Dramatique du Théâtre de la Grèce du Nord, et (c) l'École Nationale d'Art du Ballet sont intégrées au niveau supérieur de l'enseignement.

V. *L'École Dramatique du Théâtre National et l'École Dramatique du Théâtre de la Grèce du Nord*

Le décret présidentiel 336/1989 (JO A 156) ont intégré au niveau supérieur de l'enseignement (troisième cycle) l'École Dramatique du Théâtre National et l'École

Dramatique du Théâtre de la Grèce du Nord, qui fonctionnaient jusqu'alors comme des services du Théâtre National et du Théâtre National de la Grèce du Nord. Le but de ces Écoles est de dispenser un enseignement supérieur dans le domaine de l'art dramatique et de donner une formation de qualité à des artistes et membres, d'une manière générale, de la Scène grecque. Chacune comprend les Départements de jeu d'acteur, mise en scène, théâtre, costumes – scénographie – masques. Les études durent trois ans dans tous les Départements et sont gratuites. Pour s'inscrire, les candidats doivent avoir réussi un examen d'entrée auquel ils ne peuvent participer que s'ils possèdent un diplôme d'enseignement secondaire et s'ils n'ont pas plus de 25 ans. Le programme des cours principaux comprend le jeu d'acteur – l'improvisation, la diction, la danse, l'expression corporelle. Pour être nommé comme personnel enseignant de ces Écoles, il faut posséder un diplôme ou un titre d'une école supérieure correspondant à l'objet de l'enseignement. Mais pour certains cours, la valeur reconnue du candidat dans la pratique théâtrale est suffisante. Le personnel enseignant est nommé avec contrat de travail de droit privé à durée déterminée. Les Écoles disposent également d'un personnel administratif.

VI. *Le Conservatoire National de Thessalonique (enseignement non universitaire, en partie de troisième degré)*

La loi 349/1914 (JO A 325) avait constitué le Conservatoire de Thessalonique. Par le décret législatif 1445 daté du 30-5-1942, le Conservatoire a été organisé en établissement public placé sous la tutelle du ministère de l'Éducation nationale et des Cultes, avec pour but le développement de l'art musical en général et la promotion de la musique grecque (en Grèce du Nord notamment). Le Conservatoire avait été organisé en Écoles et Départements. Fonctionnent en particulier: (a) l'École de composition (avec des Départements de morphologie, de sensibilité, de contrepoint, de fugue, de composition); (b) l'École des cours théoriques et historiques (avec des Départements de lecture musicale, théorie de la musique, harmonie, histoire de la musique, orchestration, instrumentation); (c) l'École de musique instrumentale (avec des Départements de piano, instruments à cordes, à vent et à percussion); (d) l'École d'orchestre et de choeur (avec des Départements de technique de la direction d'orchestre, choeur, lecture de la partition); (e) l'École de chant solo et d'art dramatique (avec des Départements de diction, chant, opéra, récitation, danse, théâtre, rythme); (f) l'École de musique religieuse (avec des Départements de musique byzantine, d'études musicales religieuses). Les classes supérieures des Écoles et Départements du Conservatoire de Thessalonique constituent l'École Supérieure d'Art Musical et d'Interprétation. Le Conservatoire avait un personnel ordinaire titulaire ou contractuel. Il était prévu à l'origine que soient nommés comme professeurs des artistes diplômés et distingués ou des professeurs de conservatoires ayant déjà fait leurs preuves au cours de leur carrière. La loi prévoit que le règlement intérieur est rédigé par le Conseil du Conservatoire de Thessalonique et est publié par un décret pris par le ministre de l'Éducation nationale et des Cultes. C'est sur la base de cette disposition qu'a été pris le décret royal du 11-11-1957 (JO A 229) qui a défini en détail le Programme des cours des

Écoles et Départements du Conservatoire de Thessalonique et l'inscription des élèves.

La loi 2557/1997 (JO A 271) a officiellement rebaptisé le Conservatoire de Thessalonique 'Conservatoire National de Thessalonique'; fonctionnent en son sein une 'École Supérieure d'Enseignement Musical' et une 'École d'Enseignement Musical Élémentaire'.

VII. *Les Établissements Musicaux Privés (non classés)*
Le décret royal 16/1966 (JO A 7) avait prévu la création d'établissements musicaux privés en en définissant les conditions et la procédure. Toujours selon ce décret, il avait été prévu que les établissements musicaux (privés ou non) se distinguaient en Écoles musicales, Orchestres symphoniques, Ensembles de musique de chambre et Choeurs. La loi 299/1976 (JO A 90) portant 'réglementation de questions concernant le règlement de fonctionnement des établissements musicaux privés' prévoit que la matière enseignée, le programme des examens et la durée des études dans les établissements musicaux privés sont régis par les dispositions qui sont valables pour le Conservatoire National de Thessalonique (cf. *supra*). Cela a eu pour effet d'élargir considérablement le domaine de développement des activités des établissements musicaux privés. Des examens de fin d'études sont organisés par une commission de ces établissements musicaux privés, et le ministère de la Culture agrée l'ensemble de la procédure (arrêté interministériel 44046/22/23-9-1992, JO B 577). Ces examens de fin d'études mènent à un titre qui permet d'enseigner la matière.

VIII. *Les Écoles d'art dramatique et d'opéra privées (non classées)*
Le décret législatif 1715/1942 avait réglementé ce qui concerne les Écoles d'art dramatique et d'opéra privées qui fonctionnaient sur autorisation du ministre de l'Éducation nationale et des Cultes. Les titres de fin d'études ou diplômes délivrés par ces Écoles accordaient le droit à un permis provisoire d'exercice de la profession d'acteur dramatique ou d'opéra. Ce décret législatif a été aboli par la loi 1158/1981, article 30 par. 3 (qui a également aboli, article 37, le permis d'exercice de la profession d'acteur). En vertu d'une délégation accordée par cette dernière loi a été publié, par le décret présidentiel 370/1983 (JO A 130), le règlement portant organisation et fonctionnement des Écoles Supérieures d'Art Dramatique. Pour s'inscrire à ces Écoles, il faut déposer une demande au ministère de la Culture et participer à des examens d'entrée organisés par une commission désignée par ce même ministère. La durée des études est de trois ans, l'assiduité est obligatoire et les droits d'inscription sont fixés par les écoles elles-mêmes. Y sont principalement enseignés: le jeu d'acteur-improvisation, l'expression corporelle et la danse, la musique et le chant, etc. A l'heure actuelle, 23 écoles ont obtenu l'autorisation requise et fonctionnent à Athènes, et 2 à Thessalonique.

IX. *Les Écoles Privées de Cinéma (non classées)*
Le décret législatif 4208/1961 portant 'sur les mesures en vue du développement du cinéma en Grèce' (JO A 176) a réglementé les questions touchant à

l'enseignement cinématographique. Plus particulièrement, il a prévu que ces écoles relèvent des dispositions du décret législatif 1715/1942 portant sur les Écoles d'Art dramatique et d'Opéra privées (cf. *supra*). Le fonctionnement de ces Écoles (qui fonctionnaient jusqu'alors sans réglementation spéciale, par décision du ministère de l'Éducation), a été soumis à l'obligation d'obtention du permis relatif de fonctionnement, délivré par le ministère de l'Éducation nationale et des Cultes, qui exerçait la tutelle.

Le décret royal 394/1963 (JO A 113) a posé une nouvelle réglementation pour les Écoles de cinéma, qui fonctionnent toujours sur autorisation du ministère de l'Éducation nationale et des Cultes. La tutelle a continué à être exercée par le même ministère, jusqu'à ce que la loi 1158/1981 la transfère au ministère de la Culture. Actuellement, il y a 4 écoles privées de ce genre, toutes installées à Athènes, avec des Départements de mise en scène, de prise d'images, de photographie, de scénographie, de costumes et de prise de son.

X. *L'Université Ouverte Hellénique*

La loi 2083/1992 (JO A 159) a fondé un Établissement d'Enseignement Supérieur autonome et entièrement autoadministré, sous forme d'une personne morale de droit public, qui est placée sous la tutelle du ministère de l'Éducation nationale et des Cultes. Elle a pour but de dispenser un enseignement et une formation pré- et post-licence. Ces buts comprennent la promotion de la recherche scientifique dans le domaine de la transmission des connaissances à distance. L'Université Ouverte dispose d'un personnel enseignant et de recherche qui correspond aux autres Établissements d'Enseignement Supérieur (les universités, par exemple). Pour s'inscrire au programme d'études pré-licence, il faut posséder un titre de l'enseignement secondaire, mais il n'y a pas d'examen d'entrée. Le cursus dure 4 ans et se termine par l'obtention d'un diplôme d'enseignement de troisième degré. Il convient de préciser que les matières enseignées sont peu nombreuses, d'étendue généralement limitée, et qu'elles ne comprennent pas celles qui sont enseignées dans les autres Établissements d'Enseignement Supérieur.

L'arrêté ministériel B1/685/8/21-10-1998 du ministre de l'Éducation nationale (JO B 1101) a créé des unités thématiques dans les Écoles de l'Université Ouverte; plus particulièrement :

- à l'École des Études Humanitaires, les unités suivantes (chacune comportant des matières différentes): (a) les arts figuratifs grecs; (b) revue de l'urbanisme architectural grec, de la musique et de la danse.
- à l'École des Arts appliqués, les unités suivantes (chacune comportant des matières différentes): (a) l'art et la communication dans les arts graphiques; (b) le graphisme; (c) la technologie des arts graphiques; (d) informatique, multimédias.

XI. *Les Ateliers d'Études Libres*

Le décret législatif du 9-10-1935 (JO A 451) permet à des particuliers de créer des écoles professionnelles spéciales. Depuis l'entrée en vigueur de cette loi, les écoles professionnelles privées qui ont été fondées ou les écoles, académies et en général établissements d'enseignement apparaissant sous quelque forme que ce soit, sont considérés comme des Ateliers d'Études Libres. Ces Ateliers fonctionnent sur autorisation du ministre de l'Économie nationale. Ils n'ont pas le droit de délivrer de titre d'études, hormis de simples attestations mentionnant la durée du cursus et les résultats de l'élève.

La loi 1966/1991 (JO A 147) a réitéré et élargi l'interdiction formulée par le décret législatif précédent d'utiliser, à côté du nom 'Atelier d'Études Libres', des appellations telles que 'université', 'centre', 'école', 'organisme', 'collège', 'institut', 'académie', etc. La loi ne réglemente ni la durée des études ni le programme d'enseignement. La forme juridique des Ateliers n'est pas déterminée par une disposition législative spéciale. Les raisons sociales de toutes celles qui fonctionnent comme sociétés de droit commercial ainsi que leurs signes distinctifs sont déposés au ministère du commerce.

De nombreux Ateliers d'Études Libres offrent un enseignement artistique de différentes sortes, comme la peinture, la sculpture, les arts appliqués, etc. Chaque institut dispose d'un règlement complet fixant ses règles de fonctionnement, qu'il doit déposer au ministère de l'Économie nationale pour obtenir le permis de fonctionner.

Dans la pratique, certains de ces Ateliers offrent jusqu'à trois ans d'études. Nombre d'entre eux ont passé des accords privés avec des écoles supérieures de l' étranger et, suite à l'agrément de leur programme d'études et au contrôle de leurs travaux par ces dernières, délivrent à leurs élèves un titre d'études étranger, éventuellement supérieur, reconnu en Europe. Toutefois, le problème de la reconnaissance de ces titres a été posé en Grèce (par l'organisme collégial compétent, le DIKATSA – Centre Interscientifique de Reconnaissance des Titres d'Études de l' Étranger), parce que les études ne se sont pas déroulées à l'étranger et que la Constitution hellénique interdit le fonctionnement d'universités privées en Grèce. Les lèves qui ont terminé leurs études dans ces Ateliers peuvent solliciter une inscription dans des Établissements Supérieurs de l'étranger, mais non pas en Grèce.

XII. *Les Instituts de Formation Professionnelle (initiales grecques: IEK)*

Dans le cadre du Système National d'Enseignement et de Formation Professionnelle créé par la loi 2009/1992 (JO A 18), a été prévue la création de l'Organisme d'Enseignement et de Formation Professionnels, en tant que personne morale de droit public ayant pour but l'organisation et le fonctionnement d'Instituts de Formation Professionnelle (IEK) et la surveillance des Instituts de Formation Professionnelle privés.

En effet, la même loi prévoyait la création d'Instituts de Formation Professionnelle, publics ou privés, non intégrés au système éducatif ni à un degré d'enseignement.

Le but des Instituts de Formation Professionnelle se situe dans la formation professionnelle de toute sorte, l'apport aux élèves des qualifications nécessaires par l'enseignement de connaissances scientifiques, techniques, professionnelles et pratiques, et le développement des talents correspondants, de sorte à faciliter leur insertion professionnelle et à garantir leur adaptation aux besoins fluctuants des processus de production.

Les Instituts de Formation Professionnelle sont fondés par un arrêté commun des ministres de l'Éducation nationale et des Finances, suite à un rapport de l'Organisme de l'Enseignement et de la Formation Professionnelle.

La définition du contenu des études des Instituts de Formation Professionnelle revient à l'Organisme de l'Enseignement et de la Formation Professionnelle, dont la Commission des Programmes d'Études a introduit les spécialisations suivantes pour la formation artistique: prise de vue, musique avec technologie, mise en scène, graphisme, décoration à la main, dessin de meubles, sculpture sur bois, mosaïque, peinture d'icônes byzantines, hotographie, iconographie – dessin, maquette informatique d'imprimé, costumologie, arts appliqués à la danse, conservation des bâtiments traditionnels, coiffure, décoration, etc.

Les Instituts de Formation Professionnelle disposent d'un personnel enseignant titulaire ou contractuel (contrats à durée indéterminée).

Ils offrent soit un 'Certificat de Formation Professionnelle' (niveau 1) à des étudiants adultes ayant terminé leurs études au collège, suite à un cursus allant jusqu'à 2 semestres, soit une 'Licence d'Enseignement et de Formation Professionnelles' (niveau 2), à des étudiants des écoles professionnelles techniques, soit une 'Licence d'Enseignement et de Formation Professionnelles' (niveau 3), à des élèves sortis des écoles professionnelles techniques, soit un 'diplôme de Formation Professionnelle' (niveau de formation professionnelle post-secondaire) à des élèves sortis de l'enseignement secondaire ou aux titulaires d'une 'Licence d'Enseignement et de Formation Professionnelles' de niveau 2.

C. L'enseignement secondaire

I. *Lycées et collèges musicaux*

Les écoles musicales ont été fondées par la loi 1824/1988 (JO A 296). L'inscription des élèves en première année du collège a lieu sélectivement, suite à une évaluation par des spécialistes. Dans ces établissements, outre les matières d'enseignement général, sont enseignées l'histoire de l'art et du théâtre, ainsi que divers cours de musique.

II. *Les Établissements Professionnels Techniques (initiales grecques: TEE)*

La loi 2640/1998 (JO A 206) a intégré l'enseignement secondaire technique et professionnel au système national d'enseignement et de formation professionnels, et l'a confié aux Établissements Professionnels Techniques (TEE). Ils sont publics ou privés. Les Établissements Professionnels Techniques appartiennent à l'enseignement secondaire post-collège; peuvent y accéder sans examen les détenteurs d'un brevet des collèges. Les études durent jusqu'à trois ans et sont organisées en deux cycles, qui comprennent des secteurs particuliers et des spécialités. Les matières enseignées sont fixées par un arrêté du ministre de l'Éducation nationale et des Cultes pour chaque classe. Elles englobent, entre autres, les secteurs des applications artistiques et des instruments de musique, avec des cours différents pour chacun.

III. *Le Lycée et le Collège Unique Général*
Dans le cadre du Lycée et Collège Unique Général, le programme horaire de chaque classe prévoit un cours d'éducation esthétique qui comprend des éléments de théâtrologie, de musique et artistiques (JO B 1645/1999).

Est également prévu un enseignement de danses traditionnelles, dans le cadre du cours d'éducation physique.

D. L'enseignement de premier degré (école primaire)

Le programme horaire de l'école primaire (décret présidentiel 132/1990, JO A 53 et décret présidentiel 538/1982, JO A 107) prévoit un cours d'éducation esthétique comprenant peinture, artisanat, collages, poupées et marionnettes de théâtre, plastique, sculpture, musique, etc.

Pour les écoles maternelles, il est prévu un cadre de programme détaillé d'études (décret présidentiel 486/1989, JO A 208), avec pour but le soutien au développement diversifié de la personnalité. Citons par exemple les activités de peinture et le développement psychomoteur par le biais d'activités telles que le théâtre de marionnettes.

E. Les Écoles d'Éducation Spécialisée (enseignement primaire et secondaire)

Le décret présidentiel 603/1982 (JO A 117) a prévu l'organisation et le fonctionnement d'Unités d'Éducation Spécialisée. Sont considérées comme telles les écoles spéciales autonomes de tous les degrés, les classes spéciales ou départements d'éducation spécialisée qui fonctionnent dans les écoles normales de l'enseignement général et professionnel. Les Unités s'adressent aux personnes souffrant d'un handicap. Elles ne sont pas soumises à un programme horaire spécial; dans le cadre général de leur fonctionnement sont enseignées la musique et, parfois la peinture et la sculpture.

F. Les Programmes 'Mélina'

Rappelons l'existence du programme expérimental 'Mélina', qui comprend différentes activités ayant pour but 'la rencontre de l'art et des écoliers'. Ce Programme se développe à tous les degrés de l'enseignement (du primaire aux Établissements d'Enseignement Supérieur, AEI) et comprend trois activités indépendantes su niveau de réseaux européens, en relation avec l'éducation artistique des élèves qui choisissent l'art comme domaine de leur future activité professionnelle, les écoles d'éducation spécialisée et les enfants grecs de l'étranger.

2 – La Mobilité

A. Les Organismes

I. *L'École Supérieure des Beaux-Arts*
Selon les informations fournies par le Bureau SOCRATE de l'École Supérieure des Beaux-Arts, sur 900 inscrits chaque année, entre 40 et 50 étudiants pré-licence partent à l'étranger, soit un pourcentage de 4.5 à 5.5%. Le principal motif qui décourage les étudiants à partir à l'étranger est d'ordre financier. Le Bureau considère cependant que les conditions de mobilité des étudiants dans le secteur de l'art sont en grande part favorables, à en croire l'expérience acquise par l'École en dix années de collaboration avec 45 Écoles des Beaux-Arts de l'étranger. Enfin, le Bureau observe que les divers programmes d'études qui existent dans les différents pays ne présentent pas de problèmes particuliers, simplement parce qu'ils concernent des cours d'art (peinture, sculpture, gravure, photographie, vidéo, graphisme) et non des enseignements théoriques.

II. *Département d'Études Musicales et Département des Études Théâtrales de l'Université Nationale et Capodistrienne d'Athènes*
D'après les informations fournies par le Secrétariat du Département des Relations Européennes et Internationales de l'Université Nationale Capodistrienne d'Athènes, les Départements d'Études Musicales et Théâtrales ne participent pas pour l'heure à des programmes européens d'échanges d'étudiants. Cependant, le Département d'Études Théâtrales a signé quelques accords avec des universités d'Europe similaires dans le cadre du programme SOCRATES/ERASMUS en vue de l'échange d'étudiants n'ayant pas encore obtenu leur licence. Ces échanges concernent l'année universitaire 2000–2001.

III. *Les Établissements d'Enseignement Technologique (initiales grecques: TEI)*
Les quatre Départements de l'École des Arts Graphiques et d'Études Artistiques de l'Établissement d'Enseignement Technologique d'Athènes appliquent avec succès des programmes d'échanges d'étudiants, et en particulier le programme SOCRATES/ERASMUS. Les Secrétariats concernés ne nous ont pas fourni de statistiques précises à ce sujet.

IV. *L'École Nationale d'Art de la Danse*
Selon les informations fournies par l'École Nationale d'Art de la Danse, des accords bilatéraux sont en phase préparatoire avec des écoles européennes de même niveau, dans le cadre du programme SOCRATES/ERASMUS, pour les années à venir.

V. *L'École d'Art Dramatique du Théâtre National et l'École d'Art Dramatique du Théâtre National de Grèce du Nord*
D'après les informations dont nous disposons de la part de l'École, il n'existe pas à l'heure actuelle d'échanges d'étudiants. Il semble bien régner dans l'Ecole la conviction que la langue grecque constitue un barrage qui rend impossible la mise en application de tout programme européen d'échanges dans l'avenir.

VI. *Les autres Établissements Supérieurs et Élémentaires*
Nous ne disposons pas d'informations concernant les échanges d'étudiants. Il semble qu'il n'en existe pas pour l'instant.

VII. *Éducation secondaire*
Il existe des programmes de mobilité, pour les individus et des groupes, destinés aux enseignants, parmi lesquels sont compris les responsables des cours artistiques, ainsi que des programmes de mobilité pour les étudiants et des coopérations scolaires inter-européennes et multilatérales. Ces programmes sont l'une des 'actions' du premier sous-programme du Programme Entrepreneurial pour l'Enseignement et la Formation Professionnelle Initiale (initiales grecques: EPEAEK).

B. Le Transfert des unités d'enseignement (European Credit Transfer System)

Notons à propos du European Credit Transfer System (ECTS) qu'en Grèce, les accords bilatéraux indispensables à sa mise en application n'ont pas encore été signés. Mais dans la pratique, les professeurs des établissements grecs d'enseignement délivrent des attestations à des étudiants étrangers qui participent à des programmes d'échanges et qui viennent d'universités qui reconnaissent l'ECTS.

3 – L'Équivalence des degrés

L'équivalence des diplômes est réglementée dans le cadre de la législation universitaire générale pour ce qui s'agit des titres de l'enseignement supérieur universitaire (comme décrit au paragraphe 1 ci-dessus).

Pour ce qui est de l'enseignement supérieur post-lycéen non universitaire (comme décrit au paragraphe 1 ci-dessus), est en vigueur la pratique, chaque fois qu'un poste est proclamé, de préciser spécialement les qualités requises. C'est également le cas dans l'enseignement non classé (comme décrit au paragraphe 1 ci-dessus). Pour ce dernier plus particulièrement, les questions d'équivalence des diplômes délivrés par les différents degrés de l'enseignement artistique sont considérés en Grèce de manière dispersée, étant donné qu'il n'y a pas d'organisme unique ayant compétence de les réglementer.

Il se pose deux problèmes essentiels:

(a) quand le détenteur du titre souhaite exercer une profession artistique: en ce cas, la sélection a lieu en fonction de critères posés par celui qui veut recruter un candidat sur un poste d'artiste.
(b) quand le détenteur du titre souhaite être nommé comme enseignant dans un organisme éducatif: hormis les réglementations habituelles de la législation universitaire générale, il faut mentionner plus spécialement la possibilité qui est accordée (arrêté E5/2448/23-12-1998/26-1-1999 du ministre de l'Éducation nationale et des Cultes, JO B 35) concernant le remplacement d'un diplôme de doctorat ou d'un titre de 3e cycle d'études par une oeuvre artistique. Notons que pour pourvoir les postes de personnel enseignant dans les écoles supérieures post-lycée non universitaire d'art dramatique (décret présidentiel 336/1989, JO A 156), pour un certain nombre de cours, le candidat n'est pas obligé de posséder un titre particulier: il suffit que sa valeur soit reconnue dans la pratique du théâtre.

DELFINA PORTO

Portuguese Report

Group I: Organization of Art Education

1. Music, Dance, Visual Arts (Painting and Sculpture), Design, Theatre Cinema and Video.
2. Each one of the above-mentioned art forms is represented in both branches of the Portuguese higher education system: the university and the polytechnic.
3. A secondary education diploma and specific examinations/auditions.
4. As in any other higher education disciplinary field, universities and polytechnic institutions can award the following degrees *bacharelato* (3 years) and *licenciado* (4 years). Postgraduate programmes (masters, PhDs) can be offered only by the universities.
5. Yes.
6. The design of art education curricula comprehend a core curriculum and a complementary group of disciplines, some of which the student can choose from among a more or less wide range available. Every subject in the curriculum is formally assessed, either by examinations, written tests or practical work.
7. Yes.
8. Degrees in higher art education are the same as those in any other field of the Portuguese higher education system.
9. Private art education institutes play a prominent role, some of them being very innovative and delivering better training than public ones.
10. The qualifications required to gain admission to a teaching career in higher art education are the same as for any other field, according to the type of education (a master's for the polytechnic and a PhD for university education). Professionals without the academic requirements can be engaged as guest teachers in both branches of the higher education system.
11. Under the Ministry of Education (hence the isomorphism with any other field of the higher education system).

Jan De Groof, Chantal De Smet and Hilde Penneman (eds.), Art meets Law in Education, 213–215.

Group II: Mobility

1. As for basic training, see Table. No data available about the master's degree programmes.
2. Lack of information about that opportunity; sense of 'property' of some teachers who neither encourage or prevent their students from going abroad and following other programmes, with other teachers; budgetary constraints.
3. No data available at central level (Socrates National Agency), staff exchange being done on bilateral level between institutions.
4. Lack of information about that opportunity and about the programmes abroad; in such a field as Art Education, highly individualized, the less-known teachers or institutions are invited 50 times less often as the most *renommées* ones; budgetary constraints.
5. In the arts sector the core curriculum is delivered to small groups, or even on a one-to-one basis. The 'ratio' of teacher/students is therefore very different from any other field of higher education and its consequences on the organization of the activities, both at the sending and the receiving institutions must be highlighted by this and taken into consideration by the European authorities.
6. ECTS applies in Portugal. In the arts, there are two institutions which have already implemented it: the University of Coimbra and the Polytechnic Institute of Oporto.

PROGRAMMA SOCRATES! ERASMUS
Acção 2 – Mobilidade de Estudantes 1998/1999

Speciality of Students	*%age studying at foreign institutions*
Ciëncias agrãrias	3.1
Arquitectura, planeamento urbanistico e regional	6.0
Arte e Design	5.1
Estudos comerciais, ciëncias de gestão	9.5
Educaçao, formaçao de professores	5.6
Engenharta, technologia	10.6
Geografia, geologia	2.3
Humanistica	1.7
Linguas e filogias	12.8
Direite	4.9
Matemática, infomatica	2.4
Ciéneias médicas	10.5
Ciéncias naturis	5.8
Ciéncias soeiais	13.3
Comunicaçáo e ciéncias da informaçao	3.9
Outras áreas de estudo	2.5

Some art institutions (mainly in the music sector) find it difficult to adopt ECTS (How do you quantify the workload on such individual training? is the question most often heard).

7. It is sometimes difficult to compare curricula because of (a) substantial differences on the European countries on the artistic education and level obtained by the students previous to their application to higher education; (b) lack of clearly established programmatic contents; (c) differences on the cycles, degrees and diplomas in higher education.

GROUP III: EQUIVALENCE OF DEGREES

1. Problems arise when higher art education in a country is not formally integrated in the higher education system of that country: it is not legally possible, in such cases, to recognize, in Portugal, the degrees or diplomas awarded by such institutions. This is a matter of little or no importance when it comes to exercising an artistic profession, but of great importance in gaining access to a teaching career.
2. Mainly bilateral, but in the framework of general rules defined at the European Union level.

ANTONIO EMBID IRUJO, ALVARO ZALDIVAR GRACIA,
JAIME ANGEL AND ISABEL BISCARRI

Spanish Report

GROUP I: ORGANISATION OF ART EDUCATION

1. The term 'Art Education' embraces a group of studies included in the Spanish educational system under the category of 'special status education'. Included in this category are music and dance, theatre, the plastic arts and design.
2. Artistic education is normally made up of three levels (elementary, intermediate and higher) although theatre is only at the higher level. The first two levels should be considered as being included in non-university education. The higher level is in the same category as university education in that the qualifications awarded are equivalent to university qualifications, although the centres are not included in the university system and are run according to non-university procedures.
3. There is no fixed age for access to the higher level. The requirement for music and dance are: to have passed the Baccalaureate, passed the intermediate level and also a special entry test. However, there is room for considerable flexibility, in that even without these requirements, one can still be accepted for the higher grade if one shows that one has the knowledge and skills of the intermediate level as well as the specific attributes necessary for successfully following the corresponding courses. This happens with Theatre where there is only the higher level. In the Plastic Arts and Design one must have passed the Baccalaureate and an entrance test to gain admission to what are called the III and IV Training Cycles. Preference is given to students who have studied the Artistic Baccalaureate.
4. In Music and Dance, at the end of the elementary level, a certificate is issued. At the end of the intermediate level, the corresponding professional title is issued. Those who pass the higher grade receive a qualification equivalent to a University Bachelor's Degree. The same applies for Theatre which only has a higher level. In the Plastic Arts and Design, where there are two specialities, the qualification awarded at the end is equivalent to a University Diploma.

Jan De Groof, Chantal De Smet and Hilde Penneman (eds.), Art meets Law in Education, 217–219.

5. Yes.
6. The fixing of the syllabus depends on the Educational Authorities and not on the Centres. There is not much flexibility. In the Plastic Arts' Training Cycles there is no flexibility or options for the student.
7. There is not a high proportion of students entering the higher level. Nor are Plastic Arts and Design students particularly concerned about doing so, as they basically want to acquire the resulting skills to practise their art. In fact, some Professional Institutions place obstacles in the way of newly-qualified people.
8. The Higher Grade qualifications in theory receive the maximum recognition possible in that they are equivalent to a University Diploma and Degree.
9. The number of private institutions in this area is growing all the time, but their role is not very significant. For the Plastic Arts and Design, some specialise in preparing students for the entrance tests for higher arts education.
10. In State Centres, the status of the teachers is that of civil servants, although there is a significant number of teachers with administrative contracts. Usually it is necessary to hold a University Degree or University Diploma (or equivalent). In the Training Cycles of the Plastic Arts and Design, we have the paradoxical situation that students passing them cannot go on to teach.
11. Artistic education is the responsibility of the Autonomous Communities, and in all cases run by the Department of Education, not Culture.

Group II: mobility

1. Although there are no official reliable statistics, the percentage of higher students in music and the scenic arts participating in exchange schemes is relatively low and difficult to quantify in comparison with students of other artistic specialities (fine arts – painting, sculpture, restoration, etc.) as well as with the other courses, both arts and sciences which are within the University system, and therefore these students have access to official University exchange schemes.

   Students who do participate usually do so in postgraduate programmes.
2. The problems have their basis in the fact that this educational sector is run as if it were intermediate, not higher, education. In addition, the large variety of courses and the difficulty in obtaining standardisation of qualifications awarded in Europe is another of the reasons for this low participation.
3. and 4. The fact that artistic education is run as intermediate education also explains the low participation by teachers. There are no reliable statistics available.
5. In Spain, this is dependent on higher education being considered as university education.
6. Yes. We believe that this has not been sufficiently harmonised yet.
7. Basically, problems of standardisation and subsequent validation.

Group III: Equivalence of degrees

1. For qualifications awarded at the higher level to be fully effective, this level should be considered as fully university level, either within the traditional university framework or via the setting up of a new genre of Art Universities. This would avoid the 'similarity' or 'equivalence' of degrees, which often brings problems. They would be full university degrees.
2. There should be a EU regulatory framework which could then be applied by the competent institutions in each country.

FRANK NORDBERG

Swedish Report

Group I

1. Opera, music, dance, visual arts, theatre.
2. University education. These programmes are provided at some of the universities and also at specially designated schools (college of opera, dance, Royal University College of Art, etc.). There is also pre-university education, which is either at secondary school level, or special art schools.
3. Completed secondary schools (or equivalent formal schooling). The college usually sets up other requirements, such as tests, samples of production, etc.
4. There is a two-year programme which leads to a University diploma, a three-year Bachelor's degree (BFA) programme and a four-year Master's degree (MFA) programme.
5. Yes.
6. The Colleges are free to establish their own organisation of the programmes. The Higher Education Ordinance provides a framework for all undergraduate education which establishes that it should be organised as courses which can be linked together as programmes. According to the Ordinance, the scope of a course should be defined in a credit system, in which one credit corresponds to one week's full-time studies. Further, the Ordinance establishes the basic minimum requirements for degrees and for what should be included in course curricula (name, length, aims, main contents, admission requirements, examinations, etc.). The institution then makes decisions on curricula and their contents and examination models.
7. Yes, probably.
8. It depends on the programme.
9. They supplement public higher education and sometimes compete with it. In the case of art education, some of the private institutes organise training and education, which is regarded as an informal prerequisite for admission to a college.

Jan De Groof, Chantal De Smet and Hilde Penneman (eds.), Art meets Law in Education, 221–222.

10. For professors and assistant professors no formal requirements are set. They must, however, be extremely proficient in their field and in teaching.
11. Ministry of Education.

Group II: Mobility

1. The percentage of art students in basic training participating in European exchange programmes is 13 per cent.
2. This is an unusually high number!
3. The percentage of 4 per cent of teachers participating is a high number.
4. Reasons for teachers to refrain from participating are lack of time, money and someone to replace them.
5. We give priority to art students already.
6. ECTS is used at most institutions in Sweden. Whether it is sufficiently harmonised varies.
7. ?

Group III

1. a: depends more on the individual 'competence' than on formal recognition. b: depends on personal merits.
2. national authorities: Yes, to a certain extent, but also to employers, higher education institutes, etc.
   The EU: as far as directives are concerned – yes. Otherwise not.

List of Authors

GORDON H. BELL is Professor of Education and the Principal and Chief Executive of Bretton Hall, a College of the University of Leeds (U.K.) specialising in the Arts and Education. He has directed a number of research and development projects on the European dimension in education, and worked extensively in a consultancy role in member states of the E.U. since 1976. He is currently Consultant Evaluator to the Ministry of Education, Hesse, Germany in developing newly introduced 'Europeschools'.

ISABEL BISCARRI is 'Profesor de Técnicas de Diseno Gràfico, Escuela de Artes de Zaragoza', (Spain).

JERRY BOOTH is Professor at the School of Media and Communication of the University of Lincolnshire and Humberside (U.K.).

JAIME ANGEL CANELLAS is 'Profesor de Historia del Arte, Escuela de Arte de Zaragoza', (Spain).

MANUEL PEZZI CERETTO is Minister of Education and Science of the Community of Andalucia (Spain).

PIET CONVENTS is senior staff member at CANON, the Cultural Unit of the Education Department. He co-ordinates Masterpieces and the CANON culture days. He is a drama teacher. As a teacher and social-cultural worker, he has quite some experience in working with creative expression, art training and art education and integrating artistic means into education, mainly through teacher training.

FRIEDRICH FAULHAMMER is Head of the Department of Study Regulations in the Federal Ministry of Science and Transport in Vienna (Austria).

THEODORE FORTSAKIS is Professor at the National and Capodistrian University of Athens (Greece).

HANS-PETER FÜSSEL is Professor of Administrative Law at the Hochschule für öffentliche Verwaltung in Bremen (Germany). He has been active co-editor and author of a number of books and articles in the field of Educational Law.

CHARLES L. GLENN is Professor of Educational Policy at Boston University (USA), where he is Chairman of the Department of Administration, Training and Policy Studies. He is author of several books and articles on educational policy and

Jan De Groof, Chantal De Smet and Hilde Penneman (eds.), Art meets Law in Education, 223–225.

practice. He has worked recently with Russian and Chinese education officials on comprehensive legislation.

JAN DE GROOF is commissioner for universities in Belgium (Flemish Community) and Professor at the University of Ghent. He is head of the European Association for Education Law and Policy (ELA). He has published several books and articles in the sphere of public law. He was head of the cabinet of the Minister of Education and Vocational Training.

GAVIN HENDERSON is principal of the Trinity College of Music in London (U.K.).

ANTONIO EMBID IRUJO is Professor of Administrative Law at the University of Zaragoza (Spain) and Chair of the Spanish Association for the Study of Education Law and Policy.

HENRIK JACOBSEN is jurist at the Ministry of Culture in Copenhagen (Denmark).

PIERRE KUENTZ is President art-Accord (France) and ELIA project-coordinator on Higher Arts Education in Europe.

PAUL MEREDITH is senior lecturer at the University of Southampton (U.K.). He is joint editor of *Education and the Law* (Longman). He has been visiting professor at the Universities of Hamburg, South Carolina, Hannover and Groningen. He has published extensively in the field of Educational Law.

FRANK NORDBERG is Chief Legal Service at the National Agency for Higher Education in Stockholm (Sweden).

IZAK OOSTHUIZEN is Professor of Education Law at the Potchefstroom University for Christian and Higher Education in Potchefstroom (South Africa).

HILDE PENNEMAN is scientific researcher at the 'Interuniversitair Centrum voor Onderwijsrecht' (ICOR) in Belgium.

DELFINA PORTO is Professor at the 'Faculdade de Direito, Universidade de Lisboa' (Portugal).

INGO RICHTER is Director of the 'Deutsches Jugendinstitut e.v.' in München and Honorary Professor at the University of Tübingen (Germany).

MARIA LUISA ALEJOS-PITA RIO, Ministy of Education and Science of the Community of Aragon (Spain).

FRANS DE RUITER is Director of the Royal Conservatory in The Hague (The Netherlands).

CHARLES J. RUSSO is Professor at the Department of Educational Administration and Fellow, Center for International Programs, University of Dayton, School of Education (USA).

W. MICHAEL SCHECK is Professor Emeritus at the 'Hogeschool Antwerpen' (Belgium).

ANNICK SCHRAMME graduated at the University of Louvain (1985) and received her philosophy degree at the University of Antwerp (UFSIA 1999). Her main field of interest covers the cultural policies of Flanders and the European Union. She held positions as a teacher in history and fine arts, and as a research assistant at the University of Louvain and at the Kadoc centre (Catholic Documentation and Research Centre) in Louvain. Her doctoral dissertation was a treatise on 'Flanders and its big abroad. The building of a Flemish international cultural policy' (Vlaanderen en zijn grote buitenland. De opbouw van het internationaal cultureel beleid van Vlaanderen, 1965–1988), published in 1999. At present, she is a Professor at the University of Antwerp, lecturing on 'cultural policy' and 'Belgian foreign affairs policy'.

CHANTAL DE SMET is Professor at the Hogeschool Gent (Belgium) and President of the European League of Institutes of the Arts (ELIA).

DANIEL VEGA is Professor of Music and Art Education at the 'Real Conservatorio Superior de Musica' of Madrid (Spain).

MICHAEL WIMMER, Österreichischer Kultur-Service, Cultural Management (Austria).

CHRISTOPH WULF is Professor at the Faculty of Education of the 'Freie Universität Berlin' (Germany).

ÁLVARO ZALDÍVAR is Professor at the Higher Conservatory of Music, Zaragoza (Spain).

Yearbook of the European Association for Education Law and Policy

1. J. De Groof and H. Penneman (eds.): *The Legal Status of Pupils in Europe*. (1996). 1998 ISBN 90-411-0521-2
2. P. Akkermans, J. De Groof and H. Penneman (eds.): *Education Law and Policy in an Urban Society*. (1997). 1999 ISBN 90-411-1146-8
3. W. Berka, J. De Groof and H. Penneman (eds.): *Autonomy in Education*. 2000 ISBN 90-411-1311-8
4. J. De Groof, C. De Smet and H. Penneman (eds.): *Art Meets Law in Education*. 2001 ISBN 90-411-1537-4

KLUWER LAW INTERNATIONAL – THE HAGUE / LONDON / BOSTON